true stories of
Survival!

First Baptist Church
12037 Conley Road
Herald, California 95638
(209) 748-2242

A Word from
L. Joe Bass . . .

**President/Founder,
Underground
Evangelism
International**

I'm glad we can share these three "best-seller" books with you.

By special arrangement, we have been able to bring together, under one cover, the testimonies of three outstanding people, who, in widely-varying experiences, shared a common bond. Each had his own difficult set of circumstances; each suffered brutal, inhuman treatment and imprisonment: one in Nazi Germany; a second, in Communist North Korea; and the third, in Communist Viet Nam. Yet each, in a memorable way, found God's grace sufficient.

Share with them their remarkable stories, their desperate experiences, the darkness of their loneliest hours, the faith that sustained them through each new day. Be inspired by their unflinching commitment to Jesus Christ in the face of certain death, and thrill to the eventual victory that was theirs through their unwavering trust in Him.

These three warm-hearted, challenging testimonies can show us how we, too, can be joyful overcomers in our own, often limiting and difficult circumstances, through our wonderful Lord Who gives us the victory.

Though Nazi or Communist prison bars are not our lot, still we, too, sometimes face trying and disheartening experiences. From the testimonies and example of these three tried-and-tested Christians, survivors of indescribable ordeals of suffering and brutality, may we draw spiritual enlightenment, courage and strength.

Underground Evangelism provides you this book, with the prayer that it will greatly strengthen your own spiritual commitment to our Savior Jesus Christ. We pray that it may be a blessing and inspiration in your life.

As you read, and as you think of these, whose voices have been permitted to be heard, will you remember the tens of thousands of our fellow Christians, with similarly brave testimonies, who still — today — languish in Communist prisons? I pray that you will.

true stories of Survival!

PRISON LETTERS
by Corrie ten Boom

IN THE PRESENCE OF MINE ENEMIES
by Howard and Phyllis Rutledge

MY ANCHOR HELD
by Stephen R. Harris

Special edition for
Underground Evangelism
in association with
The Fleming H. Revell Company
Old Tappan, New Jersey

PRISON LETTERS

Library of Congress Cataloging in Publication Data

Ten Boom, Corrie.
    Corrie ten Boom's Prison letters.

    1. World War, 1939-1945 — Personal narratives, Dutch.   2. Ten Boom,
Corrie.   3. World War, 1939-1945 — Prisoners and prisons, German.
I. Title.   II. Title: Prison letters.
D811.5.T425   1975   940.54'72'4920924   75-15935
ISBN 0-8007-0739-7

IN THE PRESENCE OF MINE ENEMIES

Library of Congress Cataloging in Publication Data

Rutledge, Howard.
    In the presence of mine enemies, 1965-1973.

    1. Vietnamese Conflict, 1961-   — Prisoners and prisons, North Vietnamese.
2. Vietnamese Conflict, 1961-   — Personal narratives, American.   3. Rutledge,
Howard.   4. Prisoners of war — Religious life.   I. Rutledge, Phyllis.   II. White,
Mel.   III. White, Lyla.   IV. Title.
DS557.A675R87   959.704'37   73-7986
ISBN 0-8007-0624-2

MY ANCHOR HELD

Library of Congress Catalog Card Number: 75-123058
SBN — 8007-0402-9

PRISON LETTERS

BY *Corrie ten Boom*
The Hiding Place
Tramp for the Lord
Prison Letters

Corrie ten Boom's

PRISON LETTERS

FLEMING H. REVELL COMPANY
Old Tappan, New Jersey

Scripture quotations not otherwise identified are from the King James Version of the Bible.

Scripture quotation identified PHILLIPS is from THE NEW TESTAMENT IN MODERN ENGLISH, translated by J. B. Phillips. © J. B. Phillips 1958, 1960, 1972. Used by permission of Macmillan Publishing Co., Inc.

Edited selections from A PRISONER AND YET . . . by Corrie ten Boom are Copyright 1954 by Christian Literature Crusade, London. Christian Literature Crusade, Fort Washington, 1975. Used by permission.

These letters, sketches, and diary entries have been shared generously by Corrie ten Boom over the years. This material has been translated by different people at different times and in different places, and comparisons may sometimes suggest discrepancies in the presentations. All are agreed that the courage, the stamina, and the faith are undiminished—no matter the cell number, the date, or the interpretation.

Library of Congress Cataloging in Publication Data

Ten Boom, Corrie.
    Corrie ten Boom's Prison letters.

    1. World War, 1939–1945—Personal narratives, Dutch. 2. Ten Boom, Corrie. 3. World War, 1939–1945—Prisoners and prisons, German. I. Title.
II. Title: Prison letters.
D811.5.T425   1975   940.54′72′4920924   75-15935
ISBN 0-8007-0739-7

TO my family on earth
and in Heaven
whose testimony lives on through these letters
and through my life

Contents

Introduction

During the last world war as the German armies rolled over most of Europe, crushing countries in their path, Adolf Hitler set into operation a plan to exterminate all Jews. Many of the people of Holland responded by doing their utmost to help Dutch Jews to escape this peril. My own family and my friends and I did all that we could do to save Jewish lives until we were betrayed and arrested.

At that time, my father was eighty-four years of age and friends had often warned him that if he persisted in hiding Jews in his home under the very eye of the occupying armies, he could surely face imprisonment.

"I am too old for prison life," my father replied, "but if that should happen, then it would be, for me, an honor to give my life for God's ancient people, the Jews."

I recall with great clarity the day that we went down the winding staircase with our whole family and our friends. For some of them, it was the last time they would ever feel the worn staircase railing of the beloved Beje—name for our home, located in the Barteljorisstraat—in their hands.

Father leaned heavily on my arm and, passing the large Frisian clock in the hall, he suggested that I pull up the weights to wind it. He could not realize that the next day when the clock unwound, there would be no one, only silence, in that so recently crowded, lively and joyful house, and that never again, as a family, would we enter Father's beloved house with its many clocks.

Thirty-five of our family and friends were led through

9

the Smedestraat towards the police station that day. We
then entered a large gymnastics room and sat down together as a family on one of the gymnasium mats which
were spread out on the floor.

That night, God used Father to prepare each of us in a
special way for the unknown times that lay ahead. Father
asked my brother Willem to read Psalm 91 and then
Father prayed.

"He that dwelleth in the secret place of the most High
shall abide under the shadow of the Almighty.

"I will say of the Lord, He is my refuge and my fortress:
my God; in him will I trust.

"Surely he shall deliver thee from the snare of the
fowler, and from the noisome pestilence.

"He shall cover thee with his feathers, and under his
wings shalt thou trust: his truth shall be thy shield and
buckler."

That night in the police station was long and full of tension, but we were able to discuss the most important matters facing us. As we were loaded into the police van the
next morning, on our way to the Scheveningen prison,
people of our town of Haarlem were standing quietly in the
street with tears in their eyes. It was the last time they
would see Father, the "grand old man of Haarlem."

After an hour's ride, the van door opened and the gates
of the prison closed behind us. We were ordered to stand
with our faces pressed against the red brick wall. When
our names were called, I passed by Father who was sitting
on a chair. He looked up and we heard him softly saying,
"The Lord be with you, my daughters."

From that moment forward, everything in our lives was
changed. We did not know what was ahead of us, but I was

certain of one thing—that Jesus would never leave us nor forsake us and that, for a child of God, no pit could be so deep that Jesus was not deeper still.

During my months of solitary confinement, I often felt lonely and afraid. In such moments I recalled that last night with my elderly father, sharing Psalm 91 and praying. I could remember some of those verses, especially that, "He shall cover thee with his feathers, and under his wings shalt thou trust: his truth shall be thy shield and buckler." I would close my eyes and visualize that kind of protection. "He shall cover thee with his feathers," and with that thought in mind, I would fall asleep.

The letters in the first half of this book were written from the Scheveningen prison where my sister Betsie was confined in a cell with other prisoners, while I was kept in solitary confinement. There are also letters that were sent to us by my sister Nollie and her husband, Flip, and their children; some written by my brother, Willem, and his wife, Tine, and their family; and others written by various relatives and friends. We were detained in Scheveningen from February 29, 1944 to June 5, 1944.

Prisoners were permitted to receive very few letters in both the Scheveningen prison and later in the Vught prison. Thus, sometimes many people might share in the writing of one letter, just as Betsie and I would write *one* letter to many people. The brief sketches in smaller type are added feelings of my own on life in the prisons. I was able to include them in letters smuggled out.

When, on June 6, Betsie and I were suddenly transported together to Vught, a German concentration camp in Holland, we were much happier in the sense that we were once again together after a long and difficult separation. I was in my early fifties then and Betsie was seven years older. Betsie was chronically ill from pernicious anemia and the prison diet adversely affected this disease, so that she was occasionally treated by a prison doctor. However, one only requested to see a doctor when very ill, for even the sickest patients were discouraged by such cruelties as having to stand at attention throughout their wait for medical help. Betsie and I had been very close over many years and had learned to depend on each other for many little things. It was a great comfort and blessing to be together at Vught and to no longer be confined to cells. Still, barracks life, with its long work hours under the pressures of both mental and physical cruelties, was not easy and our lives were in constant danger, for we were in the grip of an enemy who could, at the slightest whim, do whatever he wished with us. It was typical of the sadistic mind to provide, for show, the niceties of massage and other sophisticated medical care while, for the prisoner, punishment and relentless hunger and neglect were the routine practice.

Several letters were written from Vught. We were, technically, permitted to write one letter every two weeks. This letter was, of course, censored by prison authorities and, if individuals or groups were receiving special punishment, we could often neither send nor receive mail. Recognizing this censorship and also the great concern of our family for our well-being, we did not feel free to express in letters the harder side of prison life. However, in both the letters from Scheveningen and from Vught, we worked out a simple code for terms we felt would be censored or do us harm. I have explained some of this in brackets in the letters.

Most of the letters in this book were smuggled out of

Vught by a German soldier who hid them in clean laundry that we prisoners washed for the Germans. This young man also took the enclosed sketches for me. Some of these I had written on toilet paper in my cell at Scheveningen and hidden under my clothing all that time while in camp at Vught. I had the opportunity, through this sympathetic soldier, to send them to my sister. It was a dangerous procedure. If one letter were intercepted, the penalty would be at least prolonged imprisonment. But we took the risk to send the letters and sketches out. Nollie saved every note, including bits and pieces of a kind of diary Betsie kept, and gave them to me after the war.

It was only a year ago that, after many years, I read through all these letters and notes and saw what a precious remembrance they are.

In September, 1944, the allied forces liberated part of Holland. When they attacked the Germans in Holland, countless numbers of Dutch prisoners were hastily sent to Germany. Thousands were killed and no one knows how many were transported in boxcars to concentration camps deep in Germany. Many women were shipped to Ravensbruck, north of Berlin. Prisoners there were forbidden contact with the outside world, and thus we have no letters from that time.

I feel fortunate though, that the letters presented here have been preserved. Many letters sent to Betsie and me, and letters we wrote while in prison, of course never did reach their destination. Other letters were so thoroughly censored that little was left of them.

But God, I know, helped to keep the ones in this book safe, surely for the purpose of my one day presenting them to others as a reminder of the great love He gave us and the comfort of His presence wherever we were.

PRISON LETTERS

1

Scheveningen

*"How greatly a prison
deprives people . . . ."*

From time to time I wrote short sketches on scraps of paper. These were smuggled out and escaped censorship. The sketches are set in smaller print to separate them from the letters.

The Prison.

A cell consists of 4 stone walls and a closed door. There are 3 little holes through which we secretly talk and exchange little bits of prison news. It does not really bring us news, but it gives us the feeling that we are not sitting there completely separated. (In my previous cell I was with 3 other prisoners.) Then the guard entered with a prisoner, a real gentleman—cultured, silent. A container of cement was also brought in and there was a search for holes. They were found and closed with a dab of the concrete. On the way out, our little pencil was snatched away. The door closed again and we were locked in even more than before. How greatly a prison deprives people of the most elementary conditions of life! If God still grants me chances, I hope to work in the area of rehabilitation. I will now also dare to visit a prison cell, which I did not do before.

Here is the first of my letters to be received. The top of all our letters bore this warning:

Every three weeks both sides may send a letter. Cards are prohibited and will not get through. Letters without stamps are not accepted. (Write name and address of sender clearly.) Only toothpaste, toothbrush, and soap can be sent BY LETTER. Visits are not allowed. Clean laundry will be issued by the prison.

C. ten Boom, cell 384

April 11, 1944

Dear Nollie and all friends,

Thanks so much for Atie's parcel. It was perfect. All those colors! I am using the threads of the bath towel to embroider everything. I am fine. Have severe pleurisy but have improved much, except I am still coughing. I have miraculously adjusted to this lonely life, but I am in communion with God. I speak often with the Saviour. I am obtaining a deeper insight into time and eternity and am being prepared for both life and death. To depart and be with Christ is far better. But life with Him here on earth is also attractive. However I am longing to be more active.

The most difficult thing for me has been my worries about Betsie and especially Father. But then the Lord said, "Sheltered in my immeasurable love." Since then, I have no longer worried about them. I do worry about our customers' watches left in the empty house [Jews hidden in our secret room], but the Saviour is all the time averting all worry and fear and homesickness so that the doctor said to me, "You are always cheerful." I sing inside nearly all day long and we do have so much to be thankful for—an airy cell through which the sea wind blows, no more poverty since Atie's parcel arrived with its good food, three Red Cross sandwiches, half a pan of porridge extra, and then that continuous communion with the Saviour. I am grateful that I am alone, me who loves company and people so much! I see my sins more clearly, my own SELF in capitals, and much more superficiality in me. Once I asked to be freed but the Lord said, "My grace is sufficient for you." I am continuously looking at Him and trying not to be impatient. I won't be here one minute longer than God deems necessary. Pray for me that I can wait for His timing.

At Easter we received a royal parcel from the Red Cross with, among other things, smoked eel. If another parcel should still be necessary [if I am still in prison], please repeat all the food items, especially the Sanovite and Davitamon. The brown cake was a bit too hard. Send especially a dress with short sleeves, pajamas, colored bath towel, white thread, needle, thimble, vest and girdle and if possible, apples and soap from my black traveling case. [I had to leave my preplanned and prepacked emergency suitcase at home as it was setting directly in front of the entrance to the secret room and I dared not draw attention to it. That was one of the greatest sacrifices I have ever had to make!]

Are Elske and Lenie still doing homework together? Are Toetie and Mary still alive? Who is now taking care of these animals? Are you allowed to visit Father in the hospital? [My code for prison.] How are Hennie and Ineke? Write soon.

I am writing with a pen with only one point. I had to go to a short hearing on March 8 and 28. Don't know anything about the result yet. They were very kind and asked little. Please write all you know about Father and Bep. Life's dimensions here are very strange. Time is something to be waded through. I am surprised that I can adjust so well. To some things I shall never get accustomed, but on the whole I am really happy. Please never worry about me. Sometimes it may be dark, but the Saviour provides His light and how wonderful that is. Bye now, dear, dear people. Give my regards to all friends. Hope to see you soon again, in God's time.   YOUR CORRIE

Receiving a Parcel.

The Red Cross parcel is outside, near my door. It is a contact by friendly people who are thinking of us and maybe later will free us. Everybody has more courage on the Wednesdays every two weeks when the Red Cross parcels arrive.

The door opens. I get up and am standing on wobbly legs. "Take it yourself! You are up anyway. I am not going to hand it to you."

How depressing unkindness is!

I unpack it. The items are nice and tasty. They are chosen by understanding people who knew what would be good for us. Will this be the last parcel? In another two weeks will we be . . . ?

Look out, thoughts! Better concentrate and contemplate on the Saviour. With Him there is certainty. With the other only uncertainty and delayed hope which hurts the heart.

. . . biscuits, a croquette, licorice. But why is there no happiness in my heart? Alone.

To eat this or that candy alone. How depressing it is. I am planning to offer the *Wachtmeisterin* something but decide against it.

I think that later (will there be a later?) I won't ever like to eat candies alone by myself. Somebody will have to share and then I will think of cell 384.

Betsie was writing to our niece that very same day . . . .

E. ten Boom, cell 314

                                        April 11, 1944

Dear Cocky   (Continue to pray fervently for me.)

So our dear father has now been promoted to Glory. And how? The Lord Himself crowned his head with the martyr's crown. Many years ago I had a premonition of this, but I steadfastly put it out of my mind. I often thought that a person in whom Christ was shown to such full advantage, who lived so close to the Saviour, to whom the eternal things were so real, and who had the gift of prayer in such a wonderful way—such a person has all the conditions for becoming a martyr. And then I thought, "He is not going to die in his bed." All this only came back to mind after he had died. The Lord gave him a happy life, such as not one in 10,000 has. Just before his death the Lord took him away from his dear ones in order to be able to give him the crown of honor. God did not let His Sovereignty slip from His fingers. No, this all had to be this way, even my being here in prison. I can also see this from the few preparations which I unconsciously made—among other things the many clothes I had on that I never ordinarily wore, also the fact that I was not allowed to take my glasses along. For now I have so much more opportunity to pray for all the family and friends than I ever had before in my busy life. Yes, I received the glasses on Easter Sunday morning. I cannot read with these. However, I can sew with them and enjoy doing that immensely. There is a kind teacher with me who daily reads to me from my old friend, *David Copperfield*, and I enjoy it. She also combed my hair with a fine comb, with results, and she is now writing for me.

Cocky, tell everybody who is praying for me that they should especially thank God because miracles are happening here every day. The rush of great waters came at me, but I did not despair for one moment. The Lord is close to me as never before in my life. Even in those first terrible days I felt His nearness and knew that this was not punishment for He suffered completely for me at Golgotha. But that this horror had come to us from His loving hand to purify me. From the first moment on, I have been able to adjust to my cell and to prison life. I sleep well, and do not suffer from cold, except that my feet were cold at first. Due to nervousness, my stomach could not tolerate the prison food. I hardly ate anything and was suffering from hunger. After 4 weeks of that I asked to see the doctor and now I am getting delicious porridge and things are going better.

We struggle daily in the cell to keep the cell, body, and clothes clean. The days fly. As time passes everything improves. Also the parcel helped, Cocky. Give my regards to your mother. [Nollie is still in prison.] I am longing so much for you and for news from Willem, Peter, Corrie [all in prison]. Now I can peacefully look forward to the future and the interrogation (on April 19th). May the Lord soon give deliverance.

BETSIE

Betsie hears from home . . . .

April 21, 1944

Dear Bep,

Your letter gave me so much consolation. I was worrying so much about your sorrow. We are now writing it to Corrie. She still does not know anything. She also wrote in good spirits. She is feeling much better but still has been coughing. She is talking much with the Saviour and is getting a deeper insight into time and eternity.

Where are your good glasses? Tine received notice that Willem will be home soon. We got a wonderful letter from Peter (from prison). The shop and the repair shop are open. Much has been stolen from the house and they broke into the shop. Henri is managing the shop. The house is still sealed up. Flip is apparently coming May 1st and will go to school. We pray much for you both. Please also pray for me, for it is much more difficult for me now than when I was in Scheveningen. I was in a cell there with Aukje. We had a good time. Aukje· is still there. Mary was taken care of in her home. Yesterday I was in Scheveningen, where I had to go to get Father's belongings. I am so grateful that you are doing well. Come immediately to us when you are free. How good we will be to you! God bless you darling!

YOUR NOLLIE

Best regards and lots of strength.
FLIP

Many regards.
PIET

Dear Aunt Bep,
    What a wonderful letter. And everybody in such good spirits. Aukje just got out. She is fine. Best wishes from Frits and Dora. They are fine. We hope and pray for a speedy homecoming. How wonderful that will be. It was such a consolation for us the way you accepted Grandfather's passing away. Mother only heard it after she came home. It was such a great sorrow for her. Now she is doing a bit better. Well, dear Aunt, strength and God's 'blessing. Love from,

ATY

Dear Aunt Bep,

How happy we are with your letter. Now we hope that
you may return soon. An elderly lady is taking care of
Toetie. Bye for now, dear Aunt. All the best. Kind regards
and a kiss.

ELSKE

Best regards and strength.
UNCLE JOOP

Dear Aunt Bep,

What a surprise! Three letters at the same time—from
Peter, Aunt Kees, and from you. How wonderful that you
are feeling so well! Everything is going well here. The
shop is open again. Father [Flip] is coming home the 1st of
May. He has recovered so much already. Isn't that wonderful? Toetie (the cat) is with the neighbors, but Mary
[a Jewish woman] cannot be found anywhere. She must
have missed her little women so much that she ran away,
but don't worry. You will get another one. Be brave, and
we'll meet you again. We wish you lots of strength.

RONNY and COCKY

Dear Aunt Bep,

I am so happy that you can be at rest through all this,
especially with the most difficult of all—Grandfather's
passing away. We will be missing him very much and I
have been very sad about it. But now I feel again the
gratefulness for all he has been for us through all these

years. His passing has been a motive for me to be baptized and make a profession of faith in the Reformed Church. I knew that he would have been very happy about this. The Bible text I used was: "What time I am afraid, I will trust in thee." It was very appropriate. Dear Aunt, be courageous. I am thinking often of you. Your nephew,

CASPER

Where Have the Children Gone?

A child was brought into the cell with her aunt. For half an hour her sad little voice sounded, "Daddy! I want to go to Daddy!" The next day that same little voice was singing, "The bells are ringing, the birds are singing." The lovely child's voice rose out above all misery and brought contact with the glory and praise of the Lord. Even that is possible!

Previously the same cell housed two even smaller children. Their voices sounded all day long, "Yes Mommy?" Normal children's sounds and expressions are so out of place here. It makes your heart shrink. But the little ones did not suffer from the cold cell. They stayed happy until in the night the guard came and took them away. Where to? After that it was even more quiet in that corridor.

. . . and so do I!

April 21st 1944

My Dear Kees [Corrie's nickname],

How happy we were with your letter and that the Lord has heard our prayers and you are at peace and happy. When I heard you were alone, I was so upset. Darling, now I have to tell you something very sad. Be strong. On the 10th of March, our dear father went to Heaven. He survived only 9 days. He passed away in Loosduinen. Yesterday I fetched his belongings from Scheveningen. I know the Lord will help you bear this. It was pneumonia. Bep knows it already, and wrote us about it. She had already had premonitions about this, years ago. She writes, "A person in whom Christ showed so completely to such full advantage, who lived so close to the Saviour, for whom the eternal things were so real, and who has all the conditions to become a martyr—and then I would think, 'He is not going to die in his bed.' God did not let His sovereignty slip from His fingers."

On Kierkegaard's tomb is written:

Only a little time and then everything is conquered.
Then the whole battle will all of a sudden be over.

Then he may drink from the water of life
And in all eternity speak with Jesus.

The Saviour will comfort you. We pray continually for you. Received a wonderful letter from Peter. Tine received notice that Willem will definitely come home [from prison] this week. The shop and repair shop are open. We are putting in a request [with prison authorities] for a family business appointment [with me and Bep].

Much has been stolen from the house and shop. Henri is in charge of the business. Flip will probably come home May 1st to go to school. Things are not so well with Mary. The others are fine. Come straight to us when you are free. How we will take care of you! Ask for permission to send us a request card for receiving parcel post. Otherwise parcels will not get through to you. May God bless you, my darling.

YOUR NOLLIE

P.S. Pray for me, too. It is more difficult for me now than when I was in Scheveningen.

Dear Aunt Kees,
   How wonderful to hear from you! We got three letters at the same time, your letter, one from Peter, and Aunt Bep. Everybody is in good spirits. The watch shop is open again. A neighbor is taking care of Toetie but Mary seems to have run away. We cannot find her anywhere. That's a pity, but maybe Toetie will have kittens soon again. We wish you lots of strength. With lots of love from both of us.

RONNY and COCKY

Dear Aunt Kees,
   How wonderful that you are so courageous, or better that God gives you so much strength, that you *can* be courageous. I have been baptized and have made a profession of faith. It was wonderful. The reason I did it was that I knew this had always been one of Grandfather's dearest wishes. Of course, it was sad that he could not be with us. The text [from the Bible] was, "What time I am afraid, I will trust in thee." It was a beautiful service. I am now a member of the Una Sancta to which my family in and outside prison, on earth and in heaven, also belong. That communion remains.

YOUR NEPHEW, CASPER

The Gift of Imagination.

A bird is softly singing a spring song. I can see the golden
evening clouds through the 28 little panes of my window. And
now my fantasy takes a flight: I see the sea, the white-capped
waves. I really hear the murmur of the sea. The wind is from the
West.

Betsie's at peace . . . .

E. ten Boom, cell 314

May 8, 1944

Dear Nollie,

Everything is well with me. Since I wrote on April 11
everything has improved. Physically as well as spiritually
I feel well. The atmosphere in the cell is fine. My soul is
very peaceful. Fortunately, I have overcome the shock of
the last months. I have trained myself to concentrate my
thoughts almost totally on my cell and cell mates and to
intensely share in their ups and downs. In the beginning, I
prayed for everything—everybody. I have learned not to
do that anymore. I had to concentrate on Bible verses and
meditations, psalms and hymns which I remember. I only
knew parts of some but I still enjoyed them. I became at
peace in the long weeks of waiting till April 28 when Mrs.
Pigge [a friend from Haarlem] was put in our cell. Last
Tuesday I got into a conversation with her about Haarlem
and because of this my whole life came clearly into mind
again. Then Wednesday your letter arrived. What a happiness and miracles. Casper's profession of faith. The shop
open again. Flip home. My good glasses were on the coun-
ter.

Thursday, Friday, Saturday, and Monday I had to go to a hearing. I signed the official report on Monday. The interrogation is one miracle! Your prayers were then, like always, around me. Every previous night the Lord revealed to me what to say. It was not an interrogation but a wonderful witnessing, telling the motives for our acts. Because of this, I could constantly witness of the love and the redemption of the Saviour, which I also always do in the cell.

I heard that Peter and Willem are free and that Father was liberated on March the 10th. What a liberation! The Lord leads me every minute and second. That gives me courage now that I have to wait and wait. I am longing so much for you, for freedom, and for work.

I sleep as I have never slept in all my life. Aunt Jane says, "Aunt Bep is the favorite in sleeping." Corrie does not have to go to interrogations any more. I am so very grateful that I could take that for her but the dear child herself does not know this.

The friendship in the cell is such that one by one I have invited my cell mates to come to our house. Nollie, do you remember that in the corridor of the prison I said to you, "It looks like Möttlingen here"? Well, I have learned here at least as much as we did at Möttlingen. [Möttlingen is a little village in Germany where plain farmers taught the Bible. The counseling ability was known all over Germany and Holland.]

Fortunately I am still getting porridge and have had liver injections. Long live the Red Cross!

Don't forget: "Pray and give thanks."

YOUR BETSIE

"I am not afraid."

May 8, 1944

Dear Nollie and all other loved ones,

On May 3rd I received your letter. First I was sad, but now I am comforted completely. Father can now sing:

> I cannot do without You,
> You Jesus, my Lord,
> Thank, praise, adoration,
> Never will I be without You any more.

How beautiful his voice will sound. I am so happy for him. When I think of those 9 days I quickly switch to the present and concentrate on how happy he is now for he sees the answer to everything. On the wall of my cell is written in English, "Not lost, but gone before." He will leave a great emptiness in my life. For the love and help I gave him, the Lord will surely provide many others. But what I received *from* him can never be replaced. What a privilege though that we could for so long so *intensely* enjoy him. For a few days I was upset. Now that has passed. During the last few days there was such a tension within me. I did not dare to think things through and when you are so alone it is difficult to get away from your thoughts. Now that is gone and I am thinking much about the future. I make plans and am experiencing much peace. How good the Saviour is to me! He not only bears my burdens, He carries me, too!

I have signed my official reports but must still appear before the judge. I must also ask him for permission to either interrupt or terminate my punishment so that I can be treated in a sanatorium. I hope to come home this month or in any case in God's good time. Write and tell me how Lenie is, the girl who helped Elske with her homework. Give Hennie and Marie my regards.

How is Dirk from North Haarlem? [A man who helped to provide us with illegal ration cards.]

What a pleasure all the notes are. Every day I reread the letter at least once. I so hope you will succeed in obtaining the business interview. There is so much to be discussed. How wonderful, Casper, that you made a profession of faith. I know that you did it with all your heart. May God bless this step. Don't be concerned anymore about my being alone, Nollie. The Saviour is everything to me. Everything I lack He supplies.

My caseworker will see if I can have somebody to take care of me. That would be nice. Good that Willem is home again. Please write me as to how he and his children are doing. How wonderful the letter was that Bep wrote about Father. During our last few nights in our home, Father rang the bell to call me in the middle of the night for no reason except to talk for a moment. It was like a farewell and that is what I sensed it to be.

How is Mendlik's portrait of Father? Not damaged? Nice that Henri is managing the shop. Give him my regards, and Ineke and Hennie, too. Hennie, I know that you will give of the best you have to give and I thank you for this.

Wednesday I will receive a parcel postcard. Yes, Nollie, how difficult your path is, but the Saviour will give you a strong heart to go on at this time. I pray much for you. Please pray much for me. Bye, dear children and friends. God bless you all.

Would you please ask in the repair shop how the clocks of Eringa, Siertsema, Vermeer, Bulthuis, Smit, and Minnema are? [Names of underground people.]

When you bring a parcel to the Binnenhof, doesn't it get through? Please don't worry about it. I feel rather well. The hearing was not upsetting at all, for the Lord gave me such peace of heart.

Pray for guidance for me when I have to appear before the judge. I am not afraid. The Saviour never leaves me alone and He will not here either. Much love,

CORRIE

My Saviour Calms Me.

There is now no longer such a strong expectation in looking toward England—only when I look at the Saviour, does it become peaceful. Often I can give thanks that I may experience this but mostly there is a strong wish that it may be over. Now I really know what it means to cast my anxieties on the Lord when I think of Father. Is there still a future for the Beje here on earth or are we now going straight towards the return of Christ? Or are we going to die? How wonderful to know that the future is secure, to know that Heaven is awaiting us. Sometimes I have self-pity, especially at night, then my arm hurts very badly. This has to do with the pleurisy, but then I think of how much Jesus suffered for me and then I feel ashamed.

They worry about me . . . .

May 21, 1944

Dear Aunt Bep,

We all pray for you and for Aunt Corrie.

ELSKE

Dear Bep,

Received your letter of May 8. We are so grateful that you are so well, but long very much for your homecoming. Corrie writes, "I hope to come home this month." She writes again very cheerfully although she was very sad about Father's passing away. She writes that Father can now sing,

> I cannot be without You,
> You, Jesus my Lord,
> Thank, praise and adoration,
> Never will I be without You again.

"I am so happy for him," she writes. "If I think of those 9 days, I quickly switch to the present and concentrate on how happy he is now."

She was upset for a few days but now it has passed. She still had to appear before the judge to ask permission to be treated in a sanatorium. She did not write it openly, but we deducted that she has tuberculosis. Elly [doctor friend from Haarlem] said that the last time after she had pleurisy this also happened, but it got better soon and that usually, at her age, this is not something serious.

The shop was closed again after a few days and now Hennie and Ineke are in the shop of the optometrist next door. The portrait by Mendlik is on the mantelpiece in our front room. First I could not look at it—now I love to do so, but will be happy when it is hanging in the Beje again. Father's clothes and other belongings he had with him are also here. Never would I have thought that we would have to bear Father's passing away without helping each other, but now you have had only the Lord to turn to and you have experienced His help and support richly.

For what reason did you get those shots?

How wonderful that you sleep so well! And on such a hard mattress. Did you receive our parcel? You are getting another one with your glasses. I am hoping that these will be the right ones.

We can only ask for the business interview when we know who your new caseworker is. We will probably hear that this week.

YOUR NOLLIE

Dear Aunt Bep,

How wonderful that you are so well. Aunt Kees also writes so cheerfully and is very interested in the shop. Asked about all the clocks of Bulthuis, Minnema, Smit, and so forth, and I was happy that I could write her that they remained undamaged.

LOVE FROM ATY

Everything fine. All the others, except Henk are free. Best regards.

PIET

We pray for God's strength and blessing for you in these so difficult days. From Father, Mother, and Andy, also best regards.

MARIAN [a friend]

We are so happy that the letters which we receive are so cheerful and because we may trust that this cheerfulness is an answer to your and our prayers.

LENIE

Unsaved.

I am no longer alone but am with someone who is sentenced to death. A Jewish woman was pushed into my cell yesterday. I have told her in detail about the redeeming death of the Saviour. She does not accept it. Although she does pray, it is without life. She has no awareness of sin and spends her time reminiscing about all the wealth she had accrued and reproaching herself for not having managed things differently. She is bitter and dwells upon every unkindness of the guards.

6:00 P.M. We just had our inspection by the new *oberwacht-meisterin*, the head guard. Had to stand at attention . . . I had too much food in my cell. In the adjacent cell, the prisoners remained seated. The *oberwachtmeisterin* snarled, "You are prisoners," and a moment later, "Do you think we are here for the fun of it?" A prisoner answered, "We sure aren't here for the fun of it either!" Prisoner was immediately taken to the "dark" cell. The other guards were shaken and inspected everything more thoroughly in order to curry favor. My plate and all the little tin cans and pots from my parcel were taken away. I don't know what to do with the apple butter (that was dumped out on my table). I was blessed that although the parcel was inspected in my presence, it was not taken away until later, for a little letter was in it.

Hate is such a bitter emotion, but I know that the Saviour with His cleansing blood is near me. The evil spirits cannot win.

At 9 P.M. my cell mate, Helen, was taken away. There was a heavy spiritual battle. She sat slumped over the table with her head in her hands. There was no ray of light anywhere in her. She seemed completely dark.

This morning I felt sick with misery but now I am quiet. Oh, how I enjoy the Psalms. I must once again adapt to being alone, but then, it is better than being with such a person I could not help.

"The clocks are undamaged. . . ."

May 21, 1944

Dear Aunt Corrie,

How are you? We all pray much for you and Aunt Bep.

ELSKE

Dear Kees,

Received your letter on May 17. We are so grateful that you both are well, but long for your return home. Mr. Kuhne was here. I am a little worried about your health. Write me, please. Tell me the exact details about it. Are you taking your temperature? Is the doctor visiting you? Are you in bed?

Yes, Father's passing away will leave a great emptiness. He has been for us everything a father here on earth could be. We don't have a single bad memory of him.

His clothes are with us, as is the painting by Mendlik, which I love although I will be happy when it is hanging again in the Beje. Never had I thought that we would have to bear his passing away without being able to support each other, but your only resource was the Lord and you experienced His help and support richly. I had the same difficulty as you did at first. I was forced to continually think of those 9 days but then I concentrated on the glory which he is presently enjoying. Now it is no longer difficult for me and I can peacefully look at his portrait. Did the doctor tell you that you have TB? Bep is feeling very well. She has completely overcome the shocks of the last couple months. She was interrogated 4 days in a row. Each prior night the Lord gave her what she was to say and it became not a hearing, but a conversation to the glory of Christ as she testified to her love of the Saviour. She sleeps at night like she never slept before in her whole life. She is still getting porridge and received 3 shots—for what, I don't know.

She also writes that she is wonderfully at peace.

The parcel postcard has not yet arrived but this week another parcel is being mailed to you. Wasn't it nice last week?

The business interview can only take place when we know who your caseworker is. That we shall hear this week, I hope.

Willem and family are fine. The shop is closed again after a few days of being open.

Ineke and Hennie are working in the shop of the optometrist next door. Those people are very nice to us. God grant that you come home soon.

YOUR NOLLIE

Be of good courage, Jesus lives.

COR and ELLY

Your bed is already spread in a sanatorium. You can come right away. Everything is fine with Hendrik and Marie and also with Dick. All the people who were taken prisoner have already been freed. I asked Hennie about all those clocks about which you wrote. They are all undamaged.

A kiss from ATY

Everything well. Am very busy finishing the repair work that was still pending. Keep courage, Aunt.

PIET

Dear Aunt, be of good courage. Peter is very busy in the work for the retarded. All the best.

COCKY

P.S. Stien is in Arnhem.

Airing in Scheveningen.

I entered the garden gate. Don't think that it was like Florence Barclay's garden gate! This gate was a bolted door and when I had gone through it, I was once *again alone*. After 9 weeks, this was my first time outside. Red flowering shrubs, colorful little primroses, grass, yellow dunes, and a wide blue sky. My legs were stinging from their unfamiliar movement, but I walked and walked, on and on, on the rectangular path around the center lawn, and I drank in the colors and the air. Tremendous emotion made my heart beat faster, and then an unspeakable melancholy descended within me. I saw the colors through my tears. In me and around me was more loneliness than in the cell, and all of a sudden I did not see any beauty in the bare yard, but an atmosphere of death and cruelty. At the end, they had dug a long, narrow pit. It looked like a freshly dug grave. Half the shrubs were without leaves and were dead, like shrubs in Holland when they are planted in sandy soil. Around the yard was a high, hard wall with pieces of broken glass in sharp points lavishly cemented in its top, and in the north the tall prison, bare and cold with rows of barred windows. Near the south wall was the gruesome stench of burned bones and I could hear Christiaan telling me, "There are already three crematories in Scheveningen." Behind the south wall the rattle of a machine gun broke the silence. Then everything was, again, terrifyingly quiet. It was 2 o'clock and it was as if everything around me were a ghost city and I the only one alive. I walked on and an uncontrollable homesickness surged up in my heart. Even in the garden there was only loneliness for the solitary ones [those of us sentenced to solitary confinement].

Suddenly I remembered Enoch. He was not filled with

homesickness when he walked with God and so I was no longer alone either. God was with me. Hand in hand, we walked on and saw the blue sky and the flowers and the flowering shrubs and I could see the yard as a part of a beautiful free world where I would be allowed to walk once again. In the same way, earth is a lonely garden and Heaven the Liberty where great joy awaits us children of the Light.

2

Vught

*"We don't know what
the future will bring,
but we are together."*

Transportation to Vught.

In the men's corridor I could hear them call, "All men, put on your own clothes." A moment later we hear in our department, "Be ready to take everything along." We don't understand anything that is happening. Hurriedly we gather all our belongings together, but it turns out that we have to wait for hours. At last we find ourselves in the corridor, two by two. A long row, the *Einzelhaften* [solitary prisoners], and the others, all alike. By bus to a small station. There we stand hour after hour. Behind us and in front of us, soldiers with their guns aimed and ready. *Wachterinnen* [female guards], are running up and down in front of us. What is in store for us? Are we going to Germany? There are rumors about an invasion.

A train arrives and this causes confusion, which I use to edge over to the side. There I see Bep! When at last we are being loaded into the train, I hang back toward the side till I am next to Bep. We arrive together in a small compartment and sit next to each other. Night is falling and the train slowly moves on. Everywhere we have to wait. We are not allowed to have the windows open. Even so, two women and later, close to Den Bosch, a few men escape and they are searching with floodlights all around the train. We don't know where we are going or what the future will bring—but we are *together, together!* And we talk.

We have been separated for 3½ months and now the journey does not seem long, even though the trip actually lasts from 4 P.M. till 4 A.M. next morning. We tell each other everything. We talk and are together, *together!*

The train brings us very close to the concentration camp of Vught. There we climb down from the very high step of the train.

Ahead of us is a forest with many, many soldiers with helmets and machine guns all aimed at us prisoners, for there are hundreds of us, all occupants of Scheveningen, and the guards fear more escape efforts. Many floodlights are aimed at us and shine on the trees, the helmets, and guns—it seems like a gruesome movie. After waiting a long time, we are ordered to start walking in rows of five. We carry our belongings in pillowcases. One rips open and I hold my arm around it. We are being hurried on through the darkness. Swearing, raging, and yelling is all we hear. One soldier kicks several women in their backs because they try to avoid a big puddle. Oh, night of terror—but we are *together*.

Somehow this fearful march ends and we arrive in a large hall with straight benches without support, and there they leave us from 4 A.M. in the night till 4 P.M. the next afternoon—without supervision and—without food! But this last does not matter, for now there is a feeling of freedom and then, too, we are *together*. The moments are progressively worse. We have to shower and undress along with about 20 under one shower and, after this, we have to put on a prison dress and wooden shoes. Soldiers are walking around and the women have to wait a long time, naked. Bep and I put our arms around each other and we implore, "O Lord, not that, not that!" Then they call, "Stop bathing. There is not enough clothing." We shed tears of gratitude. Bep and I had not yet had our turn. Ten days later, when we are being supplied with these dresses, we are alone with friendly girls in the dressing room and then there is nothing menacing or ugly anymore. God answers prayers.

I am no longer *Einzelhaft*, but am together with 150 other women, but there is also multiplied suffering and fear in our barracks. A dear young Jewess approaches us and says, "Can you comfort me? I am so terribly scared."

The next ten days in Barrack #4 are difficult, but we are able to share and pass on the light of the Saviour. [We were next shifted into the official camp.]

Betsie's diary begins:

Tuesday, June 6

Unexpectedly brought to Vught in the night, to Barrack 4. Corrie and I were together in the train compartment. We immensely enjoyed it. Everything terribly strict here but still so grateful not to be in a cell any longer.

Thursday, June 15

Transferred into the camp here. We sleep, eat and sew side-by-side, and are now so happy! Both had physicals and are fine. Corrie's lungs fully recovered. Must get up at five each morning. Wear overalls and wooden shoes. Have fun walking on wooden shoes. We enjoy Lenie and Mien [Hennie's sister]. Each day and by night we are experiencing thousands of miracles.

Tuesday, June 20

Saw doctor. Had blood test. Spoke with Corrie. Got up half an hour earlier for long roll call. Shoes so quickly worn. Had Phillips-mash [camp food for people who work in the Phillips factory] and porridge.

Meanwhile, we hear from "home" at last:

June 20, 1944

My Dear, Dear Kees,

How happy we were this morning when we received the card with your number. Oh, my dear child, how I am

longing for you. Every day we are waiting for you to come
home. As yet, we have heard nothing from Bep. Oh, child,
how I long to hear something from you personally. While
you were still in Scheveningen, I knew exactly where your
cell was and even all the guards. Now we don't know anything and all contact has been suddenly interrupted because of your departure for Vught. The only thing we
know, and it is our great consolation, is that the same Lord,
who looked after you in Scheveningen, is also with you
now and will make everything right.

After we were together in Scheveningen, the notary and
a few others went to see the gentlemen who are now in
charge of your case, and the result was that the house and
the shop were released. We went there immediately and
cleaned the whole house. The shop is open and everything is waiting for you both. We have been absolutely assured that the letter for your release was sent some time
ago.

Friday morning, June 9, we heard that you had left for
Vught and in the afternoon Mr. Rahms phoned again to say
that the letter, which will set you free, has been sent. We
understand that because of all the bustle of transporting
the whole prison, your case has been delayed, but you can
also understand that we are constantly in suspense to
know if you are coming home. You wrote once, "I won't
stay here one moment longer than God wants me to." I
think that maybe, you may still be a blessing to others or,
perhaps you still have to learn something yourself. But I
really would like to know how your health is and if you are
still being medically treated and if you get extra food. I
hope to send you a parcel soon. And Bep. We have not
heard anything from her, but today we received notice to
hand in your ration cards in the Zijlstreet. All we could

find were the potato cards. We found more of the belongings remaining in the house than we had anticipated. Lenie is sleeping there every night. Mr. Rahms phoned to tell us that he is unable to find out where your caseworker is located. He knew only that the letter in question had been mailed, so now it is just a matter of patience.

Now, my dear child, God bless you and bring you back to us very, very, soon.

YOUR NOLLIE

Dear Aunt Kees,

We here at home are all happy that you send such good news and are so well. Keep courage, Aunt. The last part is the hardest. Many regards from Mother.

AUNT JANNY and DICK

Dear Aunt Kees,

Also a little note from your caretaker of the retarded. I can tell you that they are doing well. Tomorrow, Stien and I will give them their first Bible lessons in the institute at the Zijlweg. It is a difficult time, but on the other hand also a wonderful time in which we learn so much about experiencing the power and love of our Saviour! I must also send you greetings from our church which shares in your suffering and prays much for you. It is really fantastic how people share with you in all this. Do you still remember how you told me, long ago, that it would perhaps become necessary for everybody to become evangelists? Well, maybe your wish has already partially come true now, although in a different way from what you had thought. Aunt, I wish you much strength and hope to see you again very soon.

YOUR PETER

Dear Aunt Kees,

Nice that we heard something again. Everything is fine here. All of us "turned the house with the broomsticks." It was quite a mess, but now everything looks spic and span again. Kindest regards and hope to see you soon.

YOUR COCKY

Dear Aunt Kees,

It is a fortunate coincidence that I can also write you, for I am home from Slootdorp just for a day. Although I am far removed from the busy city life and even though it is unbelievably peaceful there, I often think of you and pray constantly for your speedy return home. We are all with you in our thoughts. I very much like living in the *polder*. The work is wonderful. I am working under a very pleasant pastor and learn much. I am also eating so well that I have gained 4 pounds already. However, it is very difficult for Kathy and me to be so far away from each other —especially for Kathy. She is still very weak and listless, and her nerves, which already were not very strong, have to endure a lot. The doctor diagnosed a general nerve weakness. Still, we will also come through this. Aunt, keep well. We keep trusting in our Saviour.

YOUR FRED

Dear Aunt Kees,

Nice that I may write a little note. I am staying at Aunt

Nollie's for I have returned to Haarlem to stay. Tomorrow
I am going evangelizing with Peter, which I like to do
very much. The Damstreet inhabitants [my club girls]
send their best regards. Annie is also fine. Well, Auntie, be
strong. The Lord give you strength. Lots of love.

YOUR STIEN

Dear Aunt Kees,
   Isn't it nice that the house has been released? We have
already cleaned it for Aunt Bep, so that you will come home
to a clean house. We have not yet heard from Aunt Bep, so
we cannot write her. How do you like it there? We hope
it's better than Scheveningen. Our family is doing a little
bit of everything. It's so nice that Stien is here with us.
Lenie is staying in a nice boardinghouse but she sleeps in
her own bed in the Beje and can, at the same time, be the
caretaker. Bye now, dear Aunt. Kindest regards from Piet.
He is fine, works hard and is a bit tired.

A kiss from ATY

Betsie's Diary:

Saturday, June 24
   Braiding terrible today. (Braiding of heavy
rope is painful to the hands.) A nice walk with
Corrie in the evening. Doctor took another
blood sample.

Sunday, June 25

We had to report to sewing room. Fortunately I am being removed from the "braiding house of bondage." The morning flew by. In the afternoon, 50 of us gathered together outside. Wonderful! Then slept and did laundry. In evening, a discussion circle. Nice. Had a wonderful Sunday. Beautiful weather.

Monday, June 26

Sewing room. Saw doctor. Red blood cells and leukocytes good. Shots twice a week. Doctor gave me a whole bottle of glucose. Atmosphere in doctor's office very kind. Sister Hardenbrock [a nurse-baroness who was also a prisoner] was very kind. [She didn't survive.]

Barley not adequate so I got bread, *nutrogen,* and melba.

Tuesday, June 27

Yesterday someone gave a thimble to me. Today a Belgian lady gave me a piece of cake. Sewed socks. Yesterday the news was very good. Some have returned from 's Hertogenbosch (a nearby concentration camp) and there were embraces and greetings when the Phillips work crew passed by. Two especially were so happy to be back here. Last night Corrie led the evening devotions. Again have hardly eaten a thing—sauerkraut without potatoes, just in water. A kind lady gave me a slice of bread with a lot of butter. Tonight I had a slice of bread with *nutrogen* and melba.

Wednesday, June 28

Glasses fallen apart again.

Friday, June 30

Yesterday, many blessings. Had a good talk with Smid. Went to doctor and dentist. Jan gave me butter and cheese. Red Cross sandwich with bacon. Washed a blanket. Cabbage soup. Evening devotions. Got my glasses back from Kuipers. They are glued. The sewing is nice. Am sleeping one bed back from window now since it is so cold in front of the open windows. Now more towards rear of barracks. Corrie is doing well at Phillips. Together we enjoy the beauties of nature, the skies, very much. The weather is cold. Just right. Every day some sunshine. We receive amazing strength for this harsh life. I am often suffering very much from hunger. Corrie brings a warm meal of Phillips' mash for me and I eat it while we stand at roll call.

"Hoed 10 hours."

July 2, 1944

Dear Everybody

[The "Everybody" here and in following letters means Nollie
and anyone else at home who wishes news of us. The letter was
to be shared.]

Bep and I are well. We are now working together and
even sleep next to each other. We have gone through very
much, but life, side-by-side, is now very bearable.

Each week you may send a parcel. Send pencil, toilet
paper, vaseline, sugar, Bep's shoes.

Bep is not healthy. Weighs 96 pounds.

Monday, June 12—worked in the fields. Hoed 10 hours.

Tuesday, June 20—in the morning we went to the sewing room. In the afternoon to the rope factory with ten
others for a braiding detail. I got very hungry.

Wednesday—June 21—Again worked on braiding detail.
Got a sandwich with bologna.

YOUR CORRIE

The Lord's Day.

It's Sunday evening in the barracks. Races are being held. The
road has been lined off with strips of silvery paper for the event.
A little child of about 3½ years is crying sadly. Her mother is
Christian Reformed and considers it worldly to watch this on
Sunday. I explain to her that, by this approach, she is sowing
seeds of aversion where love should be sown. Fortunately, she is
convinced and the little child radiantly watches the girls who are
pushing each other in a wheelbarrow along the road, racing each
other in sack-hopping, and other funny games. There is laughter,

screaming, and applause. Suddenly, the gate opens and the guard dashes in. She is ranting and raving and immediately everybody gets *blocksperre,* which means that nobody may leave the block for the rest of the day and she promises us, "letter, package, and *blocksperre* ban" for at least a whole month. All of a sudden the grounds are empty and dead. I enter the dining room and expect grouching and complaining but that's not the case. Everybody is eating or talking and in a happy mood. The expressions of the faces seem to say, "We have already suffered so much, we can take this in stride, too. We don't lose our courage. We keep our heads high."

Betsie's Diary:

Monday, July 3

Yesterday a wonderful Sunday. Sang in the sewing room. Spent afternoon with our friends. Then, we both wrote a letter, slept, and washed a blanket. Again, a gathering with our friends, and in Barrack 23, a concert of French, German, and Dutch songs. Such quality! Almost too beautiful! I had to cry when "Ach Wie So Bald" was sung. In between, we spent the time walking outside enjoying the nice, cool weather. We noticed that we are not as easily fatigued now as when we were first permitted to take walks.

This morning to the doctor. Got a shot and had a urine test made as I am abnormally thirsty and thin. My glasses broke again.

Tuesday, July 4

Yesterday evening both a letter and a parcel

from Nollie. How good! Corrie had to read the
letter to me. Her voice wavered and she had to
stop several times. The letter for our release was
sent quite some time ago now. The house and
business have been released and the condition
of the house isn't too bad . . . just as I expected from the Lord! Aty, Cocky, and Mien
cleaned the house. Stien is also with them again
and Lenie is there, too. Everything is
wonderful! . . . sausage, cakes, fudge, sugar,
cheese, etc. . . . What an abundance! We almost had to let the seams out on our nighties!
[Of course, we had no nighties!]

5 P.M. Thursday, July 6
Last night another parcel from Nollie. How
rich we are now that we have some things to
share with others! Yesterday, the entire sewing
room had a physical exam for going to
's Hertogenbosch. Now, this morning, I had to
go to the braiding detail again. It was not too
bad today although my thumbs are burned raw
from it. This afternoon I went to the doctor.
Urine check good.

Yesterday we washed a blanket together again.
Those dear girls from Groningen are now in
's Hertogenbosch. Such a pity! Yesterday the
children stood in a row in the open field. They
are darlings, all these beautiful little children.

The Little *Doras.*

In the field in front of the hospital are lying in nice little cradles, the little *Doras,* fine healthy babies. The mothers work in the hospital. One of these, a sickly woman, had always had miscarriages and she had expected everything to go completely wrong here. But the finest gynecologist in the country, Dr. Heins, also a prisoner, was in charge of the hospital and everything went so well that mother and child turned out to be the happiest prisoners that you could imagine.

In the morning, the camp commander's car stops near the hospital and he gets out and plays with the children. He takes the little ones from their cradles and then he is just an ordinary human being, and one is not often allowed to be just that under the Hitler regime. When we march back to our barracks in the evenings, we pass the hospital and there they are standing, the three of them, each with a suntanned baby in her arms in that little field. This is maybe the most beautiful and also the most difficult moment of the day for all the mothers among us.

"We are aware that many are praying for us."

July 12, 1944

Dear Everybody,

Bep and I are well. Life is heavy, but healthy. I got vitamin B injections for my elbow. How beautiful are the Brabant skies. Please don't find it terrible that we are here. We can accept it ourselves. We are in God's training school and learn much. It is ten times better than being in a prison cell. Bep is aging fast, but fights her way courageously. She is brave. Letters and packages are high points. We are so happy to be together, especially when we grieve over Father. My lungs are healed. Write us how the children are going on. Bep is writing Nollie. Exchange these letters. Confer with Nollie how to send us woollen sweaters, also shoelaces, pillowcase, and strong towel.

We long much for freedom, but are unusually strengthened. Bep has gained 8 pounds! At the roll call often a skylark comes and sings in the sky above our heads, so we try to lift up our hearts. There is much fellowship of the saints here. Life is very simple. Everything is arranged for us, we never have to make a decision. We have nothing else to do but follow and obey. We enjoy little joys intensely. Great sadness we bear with God. We are aware that many are praying for us.

YOUR LOVING CORRIE

Flip.

Ours is a model medical facility and, thus, the most beautiful hospital of any located in the concentration camps. Ultraviolet lamps, massage, diathermy, X ray, etc.—all are available. Our masseur is named Flip. Flip has a funny, round head. He, like all the other male prisoners, has been shaved bald. When we pass the hospital, he is always hanging out the window with his silly, bronze-colored head, calling merry greetings. I just now asked him if he could give pedicures. "For you I have everything! I can give you a pedicure, a manicure, or I can give you a spanking! I'll give you anything, only just don't ask me for cigarettes!"

"You cannot imagine what letters mean . . . ."

July 16, 1944

My Dear, Dear Nollie,
    Yesterday we received your parcel and second letter

written July 6, The first letter arrived July 4 and the first parcel July 5. Oh, how delicious everything is! You cannot imagine what parcels and letters mean to us. Everything you sent is useful, as was all you sent to us in Scheveningen . . . every bit of everything! I won't go into detail.

Nollie, we are completely at ease here. The Sundays are wonderful, for then we gather together with our friends. Often we exclaim, "Our family should see us now!"

I am sitting outside on a bench as I write. The men are playing soccer. We can hear them yelling on the other side of the fence. If there is any food left in the house, Nollie, please use it. Do please send us some condensed milk if there is any left . . . and cake, tomatoes, and more hairpins. Can you still buy everything?

Thea is here and she is well. Things are really quite good here. Life is hard but we receive needed strength. Miracles are happening. I don't feel myself to be a prisoner here as I did when I was confined to a cell. They treat you more like human beings.

Why did Stien leave so late and return so early? What is the matter with her? I knew the day of your silver wedding anniversary was approaching but couldn't remember the date. I can understand that you don't feel like celebrating it now. How sweet that you cleaned the house for us. I didn't know what to do about it, so that is a load off my mind. Are little clocks still there? [Meaning the Jews left hidden in the secret room.]

Corrie and I work in a factory, but then women all over the world work in factories! We are always full of courage except when, from time to time, I have trouble with my stomach and intestinal tract, but that seldom happens and it passes quickly.

We welcome butter. If you send bread, please don't pre-slice it and do please send something to put on it, also bouillon cubes, jam in unbreakable containers, loose sugar, preferably no lumps. We no longer receive Red Cross parcels but are permitted a parcel every 14 days. From your parcel I could tell that you received my letter.

Good that Elske is being allowed to take her exam. No letter from Willem yet. You received, in our letter of July 6, the answer to your letter of July 2.

Nollie, please write every week—one week to Corrie, the next to me. Thea sends her best regards. She is fine. I am homesick for Father.

BETSIE

Dreaming of Home.

It's hot and the blankets are terribly itchy. I close my eyes and dream of a bed with sheets. I am walking in our house in the Beje. I stroke the railing post at the foot of the stairs. I walk through the Liberty room and throw some wood on the fire. Then I look at Father's portrait and my closed eyes fill with tears. I think again of the 9 days which Father had to spend in that cell, but quickly I switch over and lose myself in thoughts of the glory of Heaven, which he is now enjoying. I am saturated with joy. We will meet again in God's time.

"Lots of strength . . . ."

July 23, 1944

My Dear Kees,

Received your letter of July 2. How wonderful that you both are so well. You have received our parcels in the meantime, I hope? We have sent them every week and this week Tine sent it. But now we have heard again that no parcels may be sent and that a letter may contain only 15 lines.

Bep's weight was a shock to me. Wonderful that you both feel so healthy. The Lord performed miracles on you that you recovered without being treated. I am longing so much for news from you and to know if the contents of the parcels are right. Oh, how we will spoil you both when you are home again!

Hennie and Ineke are going on vacation for a week. Lenie, who up to now slept in the house, has gone home. Now Peter is sleeping there. *Everything is all right there. Here too.*

Fred is preaching today in Oosterwietwert in N.O. Groningen, where they want to call him after he has passed his final exam in September. Bob took an exam in German. It was very difficult. Aty celebrated her birthday Friday. That's the reason I am late in writing. Peter is fine, studies hard, works much with the retarded. Cocky is working hard and Els is going to high school.

You received a long letter from Mr. Vos [a soldier who before the war found the Lord Jesus through Aunt Jans] which I answered. He had heard everything over there.

The butter you receive is always from Piet. I even got a box of chocolates from the lady in the Carel's shop and a sausage from the butcher across from you in the Beje. If only the mail ban will be lifted now!

I am copying the letters which were scribbled too closely. [Those written by me and sent on toilet tissue.]

Bye, my dear child. We pray much for you. Lots of love from your,

NOLLIE

Dear Aunties,

How wonderful that you are together. On July 26 I am going out with the retarded girls. I'm also going to Möttlingen Conference with Peter and Cocky, too. The girls in the Bible circle are going to Friesland. In the Beje everything is fine. Regards from Hennie, Ineke, and all the others. Lots of strength.

YOUR STIEN

Dear Aunt K.

Very happy I am to hear that you are doing well. Still happier we will be when you are first safe and sound in our midst again. In my thoughts, I give you a strong handshake. Hope to see you soon and best regards.

YOUR JANNY

Slave market.

We are still newcomers. Little things upset us. We do not yet understand that this concentration camp, in spite of all the cruelty, is not nearly as bad as a prison.

We do enjoy the fresh air, being able to walk outside, and having many people around us.

We are ordered to appear before the personnel in charge of the Phillips factory prison squad. In Barrack #2 we are waiting in the hallway to learn what kind of work we will be selected to do. The younger women have already been called up. The rest are over 40 and some are even 50 or older. The Germans despise the elderly.

We are sitting at the side and waiting. A group of men enter and keep standing in the center. One of them is the *Oberkapo,* or boss. He has thick lips and the lower lip protrudes, giving his face a cruel expression. He has beaten many Jews to death. Before the war, he was a professional killer and was himself sentenced to sixteen years. He got a lot of experience in brutality as a prisoner in the German concentration camps and he is now in charge of the Phillips prisoners. The other ones are nice, friendly people, but that we don't know yet, and while they are talking among themselves, looking at us and evaluating what kind of work we will be able to do, I feel suddenly like a slave on the slave market. They point at me and I am commanded to come to the front. A light shiver goes down my spine and, still, I experience this as something totally unreal. A young prisoner leads the way to Barrack #35 and he is teasingly telling me that I will have to do the most difficult work they can think of. This man [Jo Kruizer, later a good friend of mine—not the least for taking care of my shoes] is in charge of the sanitation unit here. He was a leader in the A.J.C. [Socialist youth movement] before his arrest. [I don't know if he came out alive.]

This moment on the slave market I will remember for a long time.

"We pray that the shoes will get through . . . ."

July 24, 1944

Dear Hennie,

How wonderful it will be to work together in the shop again. Oh, my child, that you now have to solve everything alone. I am so grateful to you and Ineke that you are doing this. I do not know any details, but I know that both of you are doing everything you can. Write please a card, or write to Mien [Hennie's sister] something about your experiences in the shop. She is just as much interested. Mien is brave and very good to us. During lunchtime she and I are always together, we work in different barracks but both for Phillips. She is healthy but skinny and most of the time she is brave. It is a hard life also for her, but it is much better than in the cell. There, she often had sick people to take care of. Here she is helping the nurse in the First Aid in the evenings and helps with dispensing medicines. She does all this voluntarily. She often knows a way to obtain something when others don't know how to go about it.

Has business fallen off much because of the robberies? Or was it not too bad? Did we lose many customers or can you keep it going? Is ten Hove helping well? Do you get enough supplies? Where do you put the watches during the night? Are there still some supplies upstairs or is everything gone? Nice that you had a vacation. Did you still visit your family, Ineke? Oh, how I hope to see you soon. God bless you!

Nollie, you omitted the number. Bep is 01130 and I am 01131. Write every week even if Willem writes. It may pass through and you don't know how we enjoy it. The worst may be that the letter would not get through, then we would have bad luck. But still, then it's only the postage and the trouble of writing, that's wasted. And, if we are lucky we get it and the letter will be spelled out from A to Z, 10 times over. I am not sorry at all, Stien, that you returned to Haarlem again.

Bob, congratulations on your preliminary success, and Elske now to high school. Aty, where did you stay in Holten? Did you have a nice time? Oh, Cocky, how nice about that conference. Nollie, how wonderful that you also are going to a conference. I am more worried about you than about ourselves, but that's not right. The Lord will give you strength, but oh, darling, what will it be when I can put my arms around you again!

I think now also that it will be September, then it will be 6 months. Because of the parcel blockade, we did not receive the fruit and shoes. We pray that the shoes and the sweaters may still get through. God does work miracles.

Enclosed is a diary by Bep and an embroidered cloth made by me in prison. We cannot take it along if we would be called from here. Oh, yes, also the letters to us are treasures.

YOUR CORRIE

Mrs. Hendriks.

In the washroom of Barrack 42 lies a bag with sandwiches. Mrs. Hendriks prepared them this morning to give to her husband who works in the same barrack as she does. She is a delicate woman with an unusual, fine, intellectual face. She also carries a baby under her heart, her first one. Last night Mr. Hendriks was shot to death.

Betsie's Diary:

Saturday, July 28

Wednesday was an inspection of the braiding detail for going to 's Hertogenbosch. I got a scare! Thursday, another inspection and a group let out Friday. During the morning, about 35 were called out to go to the Phillips factory but not me. In the late afternoon they called for volunteers for the dressing room. I applied for that. This morning I had to stand and wait in the cold

for a long time and was then sent to the barrack
to wait. When I got "home" to the barrack, all
the beds were stripped and Barrack 24B was
empty. We had to move to Barrack 23B. Here we
sleep with 160 women in one room. The noise
and the activity don't bother me at all. The dining room is also very crowded. There are many
acquaintances and friends here. On Wednesday,
Corrie was caught talking to a laborer and a note
was made on her record. Let's hope this will not
cause trouble!

This evening Corrie had to report to the office.
Got a warning, nothing else. Everybody had
said she would be put in the "bunker" [the
worst building for punishment]. We had prayed
until our fears left us and now we have been res-
cued from those fears.

In 23B, we have two nice beds on top with a
beautiful view. We are continually protected by
the most extraordinary Providence so that we
can hold out in spite of the hard life. Last Sunday, a good conversation with Lenie. We have
received no letters or parcels yet this week. The
news we get continues to be good.

Wednesday, August 3
Sunday everybody was frightened. Friday a
letter from Nollie. Everything is going well.
Peter is sleeping in the house. Fred will probably be called to a pastorate in Oosterwietwert.
On Monday and Tuesday the prisoners' boxes
were inspected and much was taken from us.

Last night, after 4 weeks, a parcel arrived. Corrie brought Phillips-mash, too. There was nice porridge and an abundance of buttered sandwiches from the parcel. I am writing from the waiting room of the hospital now, waiting for a *lauferin* or guard [one whose duty is to escort prisoners]. I have seen lots of people . . . the optician Zijlstra, Jo who works in the kitchen, etc.

Friday they asked for volunteers to do sewing in the storage room where possessions of prisoners are kept. There is such a kind, considerate atmosphere there. We are treated like elderly women. We sit in a small room and sew on beautiful pedal machines. Each of us has a hundred shirts and undershirts for mending and I greatly prefer this to cutting paper. There is also a cozy kitchenette and we have 2 breaks for coffee, tea, and sandwiches. We climb in and out of a window to go to the bathroom, for the door is kept locked.

I should like to stay in the property room. Corrie and I always enjoy the wonderful air and clouds. The weather is excellent . . . fortunately, not too warm. Mostly cloudy skies and cool, especially cool at roll calls. We have only 2 blankets. Still, we don't catch colds.

It is August now and it smells so wonderful here. In the evenings, we have only a little while to enjoy ourselves. First, we eat together. Then there is the closing of the day with devotions, and finally, we wash and get quickly into bed. In the evenings, when we go to bed, it is still light and in the mornings when we get up it is still pitch-dark outside. We have a terrible lack of sleep and are tired but not overly tired.

Saturday I wandered around, first standing outside, then back to the barracks, and to the sewing room. In the sewing room Sunday morning, too. Wonderful morning! On the whole, a real Sunday!

". . . a time of bliss."

August 9, 1944

Dear Beppie,

Thanks very much for your letter which gives us at last the opportunity to write to you. One card, which we sent you previously, was returned to me undelivered. Nice that the communication has been reestablished and also, that the parcels are getting through again. This week, Nollie was going to send a parcel. Next week, we hope to take care of it. I know what that means. Also what the world outside and the fresh air means. The lack of these last things is, in my opinion, harder to take than the lack of sufficient food.

How wonderful that you bring your problems to Christ and how invaluably wonderful it is to be in contact with Him! What a blessing when you may witness about Him by word and deed in surroundings where sorrow and privation open hearts so easily. As far as that is concerned, I can be jealous of you both when I think of the deeper comradeship which a camp like Vught produces. It seems as if His grace is working more instantly there, and as if God wants to fulfill His work there at an accelerated pace. Of course, we think daily of you. Tine and I always walk together in the forest from 7 to 8 every morning. We enjoy nature and this is a wonderful opportunity to bring our daily happenings to the Lord. We experience the result of this all during the day.

Last night (it was the evening before Casper's birthday, which we celebrated today) many young people in our home gathered together in our salon, most of them from non-Christian backgrounds, and all kinds of questions were asked. One of them, a medical student, reflected his final impression after the closing prayer, in the following purified language: "The pastor was darn good tonight."

As far as your prolonged stay is concerned, probably God still wants to teach you something. He wants to give you a new basis for work, in which you can utilize all the old knowledge again, and in which the same Christ is manifest but now in a quieter and broader way. Christ molds and models our work after the work of His Kingdom, which He is going to carry out on earth, and which none of us can yet sufficiently grasp.

When I was in prison in Scheveningen I composed a youth hymn, which I wanted to be completely free of politics. The third verse went like this:

Young people, we were born for a future,
In which again, we can spread our wings.
For Satan long ago the battle was lost
When he went bankrupt at the Cross.

Quietly our King's business continues to win
He wants us to take part and today to begin!

A terrible time? No, a time of bliss
Since Christ for His young ones the Victor is!

Regards, dear Beppie. Love to Corrie.

WILLEM

Dear Betsie,

How happy we are with your letters. We will take care
of the parcels. We are grateful that you both are so well.
Today we celebrate C's birthday and the day ended with
an evening prayer, for you both of course. We are very
busy but are enjoying God's rich consolation. How wonderful it will be when we all can be together again.
But . . . we know so very little.

I hope that you will soon gain a few kilos and your
blood count will increase, for that is necessary. It is fortunate that Corrie's lungs are healthy. Good-bye for now.
From day-to-day we are with you in our thoughts. Kindest
greetings,

YOUR TINE

A Day's Work.

In the Phillips factory most of us sit bent forward with heads
on our arms. Outside the air is vibrating over the hot earth. I
wear nothing but my overalls and the legs of those are rolled
high. The door is flung open. Jan is trying to catch Janneke. They
are holding large mugs of water in their hands which they throw
across the work benches onto each other. Our tools and parts are
totally disregarded. It becomes a wild romp!

Janneke is a big, dark, Belgian girl with laughing eyes and
Jan is our foreman and a communist. The floor is soaking wet.
Amidst much cheering, Jan and Janneke are both carried into the

washroom by several of the others. Janneke is thrown into the sink and the faucets are turned on.

"Thick air!" [Danger!] someone shouts. Immediately everyone resumes working quietly and, seemingly, diligently. The smiles are hidden. Janneke hurries to the bathroom and the cleaning girl mops the floor. Muller, the German officer, enters. Everything is so in order that he can find no reason for shouting or giving warnings. Muller's eyes are more piercing than ever.

"Send sweaters or something."

August 13, 1944

Dear Everybody,

Parcel and letter ban, but keep on writing. It may be lifted August 15 or September 1. Try immediately to send a parcel then. If you do receive this letter, write, "I received a letter from Kees."

Do you know how long our sentence will be? When we signed our statements, we saw that we had only been accused of helping Jews. They give you half a year for that. Does that start from March 1 or June 18?

We are fine, in good health, and like our work. I am working at the Phillips factory and Bep does sewing. We experience so many longings! When you find out how long [our sentence is] please write "I saw a little child of . . . months," and start counting from March 1.

Does it look like the war will be over soon?

When it's cold we don't have enough clothing. Send sweaters or something. We are only allowed to wear it under our overalls and most importantly send new shoes. Mine are completely worn out.

Jap and Stien take turns writing each week to Bep and

me. We are able to witness here and there, but not nearly as much as we had expected. There is so much bitterness and communism, cynicism, and deep sorrow. The worst for us is not that which we suffer ourselves, but the suffering which we see around us. We also are learning to put the worst in the hands of the Saviour. We are very tranquil, in rather good spirits, but not cheerful. Our health is fine. I gained 10 kilos. My hair has turned gray. Life is hard. It's as if I've been drafted into the army but in the harsh German way. But don't worry too much about that. In many aspects it's not too bad. Nollie, write much. Your letters help so much. More letters can get through now. Thank all those nice people. Don't ever make the parcels too heavy. Is Hans having financial problems? Congratulate her for me. God bless them. Send a picture of Father as a postcard. On the whole, I can accept quite well being here, but I have too many thoughts of home. I think often of Father. Yes, Jap, how wonderful that he is in Heaven. Nollie, how difficult things must often be for you, but you will receive amazing grace for this time. I pray for that continually.

In the morning we walk outside and pray aloud together. Everybody thinks that we are just talking, but then, we *are* just talking—talking with the Saviour, and that is such a joy. Bye darlings.

Keep courage! Cocky and Nol, my special regards.

                                                  CORRIE

The Prostitutes.

Pretty but nondescript faces, loud voices, saucy mannerisms. One always knows when the prostitutes are around. They never seem afraid. When everyone is standing in utter silence, listening

to the threats and raging of our superiors, they call out daring replies. They know they are safe if the guards are men. They are the
last to report for roll call. Some of them are always near the barbed-
wire fence which separates us from the men's section. They sometimes climb up on the windowsills and we are warned at roll call
to report anyone we see there. "Not all of you can be whores!"
the guard yells. Late in the evening the little bell that hangs on
the barbed wire tinkles innocently. A girl is climbing over the
fence. "Mother," a fat woman and the eldest in the block, who is
here for an abortion and is now in charge of 140 women, goes
with the girl.

"He that is without sin among you, let him first cast a stone at
her."

In the sewing room Bep sees that a lady is sewing a large
round red piece of material on to a white square and this in turn
is sewn on the back of a blue overall. It is for Mrs. Boosmans,
who tried to escape and was caught with 2 others. As long as she
will be wearing her overall, she will wear the red round cloth, the
token of honor. She climbed over a few roofs, ran far away, was
then caught and brought back; had to stand for hours and was not
allowed to go to bed at night. She looks very tired, but seems not
to worry. How brave she is! She just heard that her husband, Dr.
Boosmans, was wounded in the train by shell splinters. He will
have to lose a few fingers, but for the rest he is well. I have to say
I am proud of our Dutch women.

Bep's birthday

August 19, 1944

Dear Everybody,
    You must be asking what we did to deserve the parcel
ban. It's a collective punishment. In our barrack the beds
were not made neatly enough and much was hidden under

the mattresses. Besides, some of the prostitutes had been talking with the guards through the window across the barbed-wired fence. Punishments are taken collectively. This will last till September 5. If by then we still are not home, send on that date a few parcels and before that time every week a good-sized parcel to Mien. She is sleeping in another barrack and therefore does not have the punishment. Keep on writing to us, and now and then also to her. Sometimes letters will slip through. On September 5, especially send heavy sweaters. When the mornings are getting colder we are not dressed warm enough. We have to be at roll call before sunrise. Oh, how beautiful the skies are then, but sometimes we are shivering with cold, if the weather is like autumn, chilly and foggy. At the moment we have a heat wave here. How I long for cool sheets and for much more. Will the end of the war be near? The world outside is at the moment not so attractive either. But even if it would be 10 times worse, we still long to go home.

Jap, will you maybe from my previous letters type the parts which are important for everybody? Pencil writing fades so easily. We are fine. It's Bep's birthday and what a much better day it is than mine was. Then [April 15] I was lying alone and was on cold food, no warm food and for the rest—no airing, no books. Everybody snarled and I felt so sick and miserable. A doctor gave me a shot and I told him that it was my birthday and then he gave me a firm handshake. He himself was a prisoner. Never did I appreciate a handshake so much as this one! The next day a corridor-girl came in front of my door and gave me congratulations from Aukje. Then, from her, I heard for the first time where Bep was. That was my first contact with Bep.

We sleep together now, Bep and I, and last night we

woke up from the terrible flying over Vught. It sounded like thousands of airplanes. In the afternoon, I sleep for nearly an hour in the sunshine. One can admire here the most beautiful skies, heavenly beauty. We have enough to eat, are healthy, do like our work, many friends and acquaintances, and are healthy. I am very tanned and even Bep's face has a tan. She looks much better than some time ago and looks 10 years younger. My hand, in which I suffer from neuritis, is nearly better. I gained much weight. Just got a wasp sting on my leg, but I got a walking permit to go to the first aid a few barracks away. There I received a piece of cottonwool with some eau de cologne, but the nicest was the walk. Without a walking permit you are never allowed to leave your barrack.

Don't worry about us, that we would not have enough. Every time the Lord cares for us in a miraculous way, so that if we don't have anything, somebody gives us something. For instance, I went to the hospital for vitamin B and the cleaning girl gave me half a cake.

Did you know that Lenie den Engelsen is a cleaning girl in Barrack 42? Her husband is in 43. She works, mops, and is taking it beautifully. She is a heroine. How is it with Pickwick and Hans, Cocky and Henk, Jan, Ineke, and all the others? I pray much for all of them. Also for Bob Weener. There is "summary justice" here. If anybody passes on news or a notice, he gets the bullet. Do you know if our prison time ends September 1 or December 9? Everybody here says that 6 months at Vught is too short. If they also include the time at Scheveningen, then it would be September 1.

God knows the way. We are at peace with everything. Write for sender, on the parcel to Mien, the name and address of Jap or Fie.

Now that I read my letter again, it looks a little too optimistic. It is very difficult for us but God's grace is endless. Bep is often hungry, and is at the moment not gaining any weight. Therefore, please send parcels soon with the sweaters and shoes.

YOUR CORRIE

At Twilight.

It is evening. About 30 of God's children are standing or sitting between the barracks. Two very old little women with wooden shoes on their feet are sitting against a tree. Bep is reading Psalm 91, "He that dwelleth in the secret place of the most High shall abide under the shadow of the Almighty." The light of the setting sun is shining on her. She looks so pretty and even healthy [though very chronically ill from pernicious anemia]. She is standing there, bent over her little Bible. It's such a quiet evening. In a laundry room, two beautiful voices are singing a duet from Mendelssohn. *"Denn in Seiner Hand ist, was die Erde bringt."* ["For it is in His Hand, what happens on earth."] The barracks are so ugly and the barbed wire so horribly visible everywhere, but wagtails and skylarks are sitting in the birch trees and over all this is spread God's beautiful firmament with its magnificent colors which proclaim His handiwork.

"How long still?"

August 22, 1944

Dear Nollie,

I have written some sketches. Keep them for me. Will you send these letters on quickly? We hear some hopeful rumors. Could liberty be near? Oh, if it should be near, I hope we will be here [Vught] till the end, but also if they call me Monday the 28 or Thursday, I'll be tremendously happy, too. Oh, we are longing so much. Do you know yet when our time will be done? We have much peace about it. We miss our parcels very much and are hoping that you can send Mien van Dantzig our parcel. I once wrote you, "Don't send bread." But that was not good advice. If you don't slice it, then it stays delicious. Also, rolls are good. The crust prevents spoilage. Send *Haagsche Hopjes* [special Dutch candies] and write little notes on the thin paper inside the wrappers, but only in the ones in the bottom of the bag, for the guards steal them right in our presence. If we still have not been liberated by September 5, then please see to it that we receive a parcel with the shoes and a sweater in a separate package.

Many among us have stomach trouble, Bep is also suffering a little from it. Mien van Dantzig has had fever with it. Last night everything became just too much for her. She is usually so courageous. But this eventually gets to all of us.

I have found a dear friend in Mimi Lans, the daughter of Professor Lans.

Sunday we had about 60 people for our sermon. It's like there is an awakening. God's Spirit is working. Oh, if there could be a revival here! There is so much unspeakable anguish in this place.

Give my regards to Ellie and Kees Hage. Are they safe? There must be so much danger where you are, too! It is so wonderful that we can pray for you all the time. Oh, and Flip, is he in school as usual? And all the boys? When I come home I won't be able to stop asking questions!

Where is Bep's ID card?

Give my regards to Annie, Stien, Jap, Fie and all the others. Oh, Elske, how wonderful it will be to see you

again. But Nollie, I long most of all for you. I do so hope
that we may still enjoy being with each other for a long
time to come. A half year is a long time, isn't it? But I believe that I have learned a lot.

I am no longer so tired in body and soul. Forgetting
what lies behind I press on toward the goal for the prize of
the upward call of God in Christ Jesus. It's the Saviour who
has a task for us. He will lead us. Therefore how wonderful our life will be whatever the future may bring.

Piet, Aty, Leendert, Cocky—everybody—I so hope that
we will be able to do some positive work together again in
the future. I am longing for rest and for action at the same
time. And on Sundays we will be singing again in the Liberty room [at home]. Here in the evenings we sing all the
well-known songs so nicely when we close the day, and so
often I think of Father—also of the Sunday afternoons at
home.

How long still?

Club girls, be brave and work and help wherever you
can. Bea, did you still get a chance to take an exam this
year? Oh, how much I long to be in our clubhouse. But I
am here and here is where I have to be and it is *well.*

We have a lot of sun here, much more than at home. I
am writing at my workbench and in a little while Bep will
be waiting for me and she'll get half of my Phillips-mash.

They say there'll be bag inspection, so first of all, everything has to be hidden well. Annie van Bavel, a communist, is walking around the workroom with a Jehovah's
Witness to the beat of the whining music from the radio.
Then all of a sudden a concert by Handel sounds through
the workroom. How did the record get hidden in between
that clamoring music? It was nearly too much for me! I did
like Dr. Brouwer did when she was here and pressed my

ear against the loudspeaker post to hear better. You may
tell her this when you see her. See you.

YOUR KEES

Sharing.

The latrine is the most important room in the barracks, a space
with 10 toilets, 3 or more of which are usually out of order and
are covered with a large piece of cardboard, such as is used to
cover the windows at night so no light can shine out for planes to
see. In the camp, the latrine is the place where we have our most
interesting political discussions. In the latrine, you comb yourself
with a fine comb, you give secret messages or rest for a moment.
You hide there when "the air is thick." [This phrase was used to
warn that a guard was near.] Of course, when the danger is one of
the female guards, this is no solution, for she follows you into the
latrine, too.

You meet acquaintances in the latrine. You pass on dangerous
news to others and you also do gymnastics. The latrine has 4
large open windows. There is one faucet over a little hole in the
floor and that hole is always closed. Sitting next to each other in
the latrine are communists, criminals, Jehovah's Witnesses, Christian Reformed, liberals, prostitutes. The bravest heroines who
have made the greatest sacrifices are sitting there side-by-side
with the degenerates of society.

Just a short while ago, right at lunch time, there was an air
battle directly overhead. We lay in the sand watching. First,
hundreds of airplanes flew over us like silver birds. They shone
like diamonds in the sun's reflection. Then, suddenly, a crackling
noise and shell fragments were flying all around us . . . bullets,
too! We could not identify the planes. I ran and stretched out on
the ground up against the barracks for shelter. I was not afraid
and only later realized the seriousness of the moment. Five of us
were wounded and have been hospitalized. Yesterday, somebody
who had just arrived here from Barrack 4 said that everywhere

over there in 4 you find underwear with our name, ten Boom, on them. [We always embroidered our underwear and shared it with other prisoners.] I pray that our words of consolation may also be shared. God's Word will not return empty.

"I am longing for all of you."

Bibi Kijzer, Bachplein 4. Amsterdam Z.

August 25, 1944

Dear Nollie,

Will you send the enclosed letters to the above address? A little note has been found—not on me—but we will have to be more careful.

During the last few weeks we have not heard anything from you. However, I hope and pray that you received our notes. Also, Mien has not received a parcel. Mien is completely well again. Bep looks a bit pale. Oh, may the Lord grant that we may come home soon. That would be more wonderful than I can imagine.

This morning Number 1 was called. She had been here the longest of us all. Even the guard, who brought the list from headquarters and apparently had not yet seen the numbers, exclaimed with some distress, *"Ach liebe, Numero Eins."* The prisoner came forward from the group where we were standing in rows of 5 awaiting work commands. She swayed while she was standing in front of the office. We called to her, "Sit down, quick!" She dropped down on the uncomfortable bench made of birch trees, her arm on the back, her head on her arm. She was still sitting there when we marched away, *"eins, zwei, drei, vier."*

The sun colored the clouds in the east so brilliantly that they illuminate us.

Leendert, will you copy the poems which are enclosed and send them on to Amsterdam? How is Dientje ten Boom? Give her my regards and, also Henri.

Oh, Bob, I long so much for you. Are you still studying German? I am longing for all of you, but we will be able to hold out.

"Daybreak in the east." It's such a blessing that this is such a beautiful month of August. Health by the spoonful!

Jap, will you type the portions of my letters which are important? Pencil writing fades so easily. You can decipher my scribbles. Is Rie Luitingh getting married soon? Give them my best wishes. His brother is fine. Also regards to Bob W.

My Bible verse for today is, "That I may see the good . . . . Lord, lift thou up the light of thy countenance upon us."

We cannot make the people here see the good in all this, but we can pray—Lift up Thy Light—Psalms 4:6.

YOUR CORRIE

This was my last letter from Vught. Shortly after I wrote it, many male prisoners were shot and killed. All women prisoners were transported to Ravensbruck concentration camp in the heart of Germany.

Bep and I were shipped to Ravensbruck on a train. As we passed out of Holland we managed to slip a scrap of paper through a crack in our boxcar. The paper said:

Corrie and Betsie ten Boom.
Being transported to Ravensbruck
concentration camp.

I asked the finder to please send the note to Nollie
in Haarlem.
During my confinement in Ravensbruck, where
mail was nonexistent, I felt a great emptiness. This
was compounded when Betsie became one of 97,000
women to die there. When Betsie died in camp in the
winter of 1944, she left this world with a smile on her
face, the smile of one who knows the Saviour. She
was gone, but I knew she experienced the happiness
of Eternity.
The horrors of Ravensbruck, especially Betsie's
death, caused me to wake up to reality. When I did, I
was able to see that when all the securities of the
world are falling away, then you realize, like never
before, what it means to have your security in Jesus.
It was not until December 28, 1944, when, through
a miracle, I was set free, just one week before all
women my age and older were put to death. I was
free and knew then as I know now it was my chance
to take to the world God's message of the victory of
Jesus Christ in the midst of the deepest evil of man.

After being released from prison, I felt the need to write
one final letter . . . to the person who had originally revealed our family's work to the Germans.

Haarlem, June 19, 1945

Dear Sir,

Today I heard that most probably you are the one who betrayed me. I went through 10 months of concentration camp. My father died after 9 days of imprisonment. My sister died in prison, too.

The harm you planned was turned into good for me by God. I came nearer to Him. A severe punishment is awaiting you. I have prayed for you, that the Lord may accept you if you will repent. Think that the Lord Jesus on the Cross also took your sins upon Himself. If you accept this and want to be His child, you are saved for Eternity.

I have forgiven you everything. God will also forgive you everything, if you ask Him. He loves you and He Himself sent His Son to earth to reconcile your sins, which meant to suffer the punishment for you and me. You, on your part have to give an answer to this. If He says: "Come unto Me, give Me your heart," then your answer must be: "Yes, Lord, I come, make me Your child." If it is difficult for you to pray, then ask if God will give you His Spirit, who works the faith in your heart.

Never doubt the Lord Jesus' love. He is standing with His arms spread out to receive you.

I hope that the path which you will now take may work for your eternal salvation.

CORRIE TEN BOOM

Here are some of our "watches" (code name for Jewish guests) in the Beje with underground workers. *Left:* My beloved father, who said, "I am too old for prison life, but if that should happen, then it would be, for me, an honor to give my life for God's ancient people, the Jews." He died after nine days in prison.

Willem, my only brother, who wrote to Betsie, "What a blessing when you may witness about Him by word and deed in surroundings where sorrow and privation open hearts so easily."

My oldest sister, Nollie, who sent wonderful letters and packages to us in prison. It was Nollie who saved our notes—every scrap of paper—and gave them to me after the war.

My nephew Kik, Willem's son, who worked with the underground.

Our beautiful Betsie who died at Ravensbruck. She wrote to Nollie, "The Lord leads me every minute and second. That gives me courage now that I have to wait and wait. I am longing so much for you, for freedom, and for work."

Afterword

The letters and notes in this book do not, of course, tell the whole story of what happened. I met many wonderful people while in prison, but because of the circumstances I do not have records of them to pass on. One person, however, does stand out in my mind. He is Hans Rahms, mentioned only briefly in 2 letters.

Hans Rahms was an official in Scheveningen prison during Betsie's and my interrogations. He was instrumental in helping my brother Willem be freed from Scheveningen after only a short stay. Willem was originally arrested with us at the Beje for teaching a Bible study.

But it was while we were in prison that the Lord touched Mr. Rahms's heart so that Betsie and I were both able to tell him about Jesus and His love. Later, in camp at Vught, Betsie told me that she had been able to say, "Mr. Rahms, it is important to talk about Jesus but it is more important to talk with Him. Would you mind if I prayed with you?" Five times she was ordered to report to this man for interrogation and five times she prayed with him . . . she, the prisoner and he, her judge. Through this, Hans Rahms became a friend instead of an enemy and we were recipients of his help several times during our imprisonment.

One morning, just before a hearing, he showed some papers to me. When I saw them, I knew that many lives were in great danger, for the papers contained detailed information about my underground activities. I could see on them the names of friends, Jews, and underground workers. When he asked me to explain the papers, I could not. The silence that followed was one of the most agonizing moments of my life. Then, suddenly, that moment was transformed into joy, for the judge took all the papers, opened the stove door, and threw them into the fire! Before my eyes, I saw the flames destroying every name and, at that instant, I understood the verse, Colossians 2:14, "Blotting out the handwriting of ordinances that was against us, which was contrary to us, and took it out of the way, nailing it to his cross."

That is what Christ did for us, and for me. After the war, I had the privilege of meeting Hans Rahms several times and he once said, "Corrie, I shall never forget your sister's prayers."

There were many things for which I needed to thank Mr. Rahms, for it was he who helped free my friends and some of my family from prison. Because he did many good deeds for people, it was difficult for him to see that he needed a Saviour, but, during one of our later meetings, he saw that he was a sinner and that he needed Jesus. Together we had experienced many dark moments and, occasionally, a light one, but the moment he accepted the Lord Jesus was one of life's richest experiences for me, for on that day I glimpsed a little of God's side of the pattern of my life.

God has only plans, no problems, in the life of a child of God. I have experienced God's love.

Love knows no limit to its endurance, no end to its trust, no fading of its hope: it can outlast anything. It is, in fact, the one thing that still stands when all else has fallen.

1 Corinthians 13:7, 8 PHILLIPS

IN THE PRESENCE OF MINE ENEMIES
1965-1973

IN THE PRESENCE OF
MINE ENEMIES

1965-1973

A PRISONER OF WAR

HOWARD AND PHYLLIS RUTLEDGE
WITH
MEL AND LYLA WHITE

Illustrations by Gerald Coffee

FLEMING H. REVELL COMPANY
Old Tappan, New Jersey

Scripture quotations in this volume are from the King James Version of the Bible.

Library of Congress Cataloging in Publication Data

Rutledge, Howard.
    In the presence of mine enemies, 1965–1973.

    1. Vietnamese Conflict, 1961–   —Prisoners and prisons, North Vietnamese. 2. Vietnamese Conflict, 1961–   —Personal narratives, American. 3. Rutledge, Howard. 4. Prisoners of war—Religious life. I. Rutledge, Phyllis. II. White, Mel. III. White, Lyla. IV. Title.
DS557.A675R87   959.704'37   73–7986
ISBN 0–8007–0624–2

To all who never stopped hoping and praying for our return, and to God who answered those prayers.

Contents

Illustrations are by Gerald Coffee,
who was also a prisoner of war
in the "Hanoi Hilton."

Part I
Captain Howard E. Rutledge
1965-1973
Prisoner of War

1

Shot Down and Captured

My freedom ended November 28, 1965. I was the Executive Officer of Fighter Squadron 191 aboard the attack Carrier USS *Bon Homme Richard* in the Gulf of Tonkin. We were conducting round-the-clock missions over North Vietnam. This day I was a flight leader in a large force of fighter and attack aircraft. Our mission was to destroy a strategic bridge just northwest of Thanh Hoa. My F-8 Crusader jet, armed with two 2,000 lb. bombs, two air-to-air missiles, and four 20mm cannons, had catapulted from the carrier, rendezvoused with the squadron, refueled in the air, and approached the target as planned.

As I crossed from the safety of the sea to the enemy beaches, I signaled FEET DRY to the pilots of my flight and reported the overcast weather conditions to the strike leader. At almost 600 mph I broke through the haze at 5,000 feet and off to my right got a clear view of our target.

We suspected the area might be heavily protected and immediately I faced a fierce barrage of antiaircraft fire. I could see the guns below belching flame and knew that shells were exploding all around me; but after over 200 safe missions over Korea and North and South Vietnam, the thought of being hit never crossed my mind.

As I approached the roll-in point for my drop, two antiaircraft shells exploded somewhere in the tail section behind me. The pilot of a Crusader fighter sits right in the nose and cannot really see the fuselage aft. Because the plane responded satisfactorily and because I would be headed toward the safety of the sea at the end of the bombing run, I selected my afterburner and continued my attack on the target almost at the speed of sound. I dropped my bombs, and, still accelerating, turned to a heading toward the sea.

It was then my fighter received another hit. This time I knew it was a mortal blow. The plane pitched down about 20° and commenced an uncontrollable roll to the left.

I heard my wingman on the radio, "They are really shooting in here!"

I tried a quick transmission in reply, "I am hit! I am hit and bailing out!"

The plane was traveling like lightning and rolling uncontrollably. The stick went dead in my hands. The horizon spun past. We rolled 360°, and a few degrees before top-dead center I jerked at the ejection curtain. My escape seat hurled into the air as another shell burst under the cockpit itself. A fragment tore into my leg. I made one 360° tumble and saw the horizon pass. The chute deployed automatically, and I watched with horror as my plane exploded into a ball of flame before me.

"Thank You, God!" I prayed for the first time in twenty years, dangling 1,000 feet above North Vietnam. It was a short prayer of thanks. If I had waited another second to eject, I would have died in that explosion of bombs, jet fuel, and cannon shells. My grateful reveries were interrupted by a new danger.

Remember how bullets zing past the good guys in B-grade television westerns and old war movies? I could hear bullets singing past me and could see the holes they were making in my parachute. Instinctively, I hung limp in the shrouds to make the enemy believe I had been mortally wounded. Still curious

I watched with horror as my plane exploded into a ball of flame before me.

to see who could be firing, I cracked open my eyes, slowly turned my head downwards and, to my horror, discovered I was descending rapidly into the town square of a rather large village. A crowd was gathering. Everyone was gesturing in my direction, and I could hear them shouting excitedly.

Resurrected by the sight, I reached up and pulled the two front risers that altered my course and sent me drifting faster toward the flooded rice fields at the edge of town, and away from the welcoming committee that was forming there.

I had never parachuted from a plane before that day, and though it all seemed terribly unreal, I was functioning on instinct carefully trained into me by the U.S. Navy survival schools. In the last few seconds of descent, I could see that I was going to land about twenty yards to the north of a huge dike that ran east and west to the sea. For a navy pilot, the sea is friendly. I was hoping that those big, beautiful, search-and-rescue helicopters had been notified of my plight and were on their way to lift me back to safety. I had seen my wingman, Lt. Ken Masat, risk his own life to circle through the antiaircraft fire to check out my chute and get a sighting on my descent. He would notify them. If I could just stay free long enough to reach the dike and run for the sea, they would find me. But already I could count perhaps fifty men running in my direction. I landed standing up. Fortunately, I was knee-deep in mud; without that my legs would have broken almost certainly. Instinctively, I released my lower rocket fittings to get rid of the raft and survival paraphernalia. One release rocket wouldn't fire, and I struggled desperately to free myself.

By now I could hear voices shouting from all sides. In the two minutes it took to break free, only one young Vietnamese militiaman had gotten between me and that important dike. He was in his early twenties and carried a machete which he waved threateningly. Yelling at the top of his voice, he ran toward me, blocking my escape to the sea.

I jerked my 38 revolver from my survival gear, pulled back the hammer and pointed it at his chest, hoping to frighten him away. He didn't waver. Still screaming and wielding the machete high over his head, he ran to point-blank range. I pulled the trigger, and he fell dead at my feet. I will never forget the look on his face as he slumped forward or my own horror as he fell. By now, a large crowd was running toward me from every direction. There were no military weapons on these farmer-militiamen, but they carried knives, long, sharp-pointed sticks, and machetes wired to poles prepared for just such an occasion. Everyone was shouting in a cacophony of Vietnamese curses and threats. They stopped about fifteen feet from me and formed a ring, completely blocking my escape. They could see the young man in the water at my feet and were afraid to come any closer. I circled, aiming my gun towards each man as I turned. We were at a strange impasse—each eyeing the other—each afraid.

Perhaps a minute passed. During those long seconds, I realized this was going to be my final appearance on the earth. It was perhaps the first time I had seriously contemplated death. Then an old, gray-haired Vietnamese stepped out from the ring.

I bore down on him with the 38. He dropped his machete and put his arms down at his side. Then he raised them for silence. The crowd obeyed and an eerie silence followed. The next two minutes were critical for me. I couldn't speak Vietnamese; he couldn't speak English. But through gestures and signs, he promised me that if I would not shoot again, he, their leader, would guarantee my safety.

To this day I cannot believe that those few wild gestures could make that complex message clear. Looking back, I believe the hands of God were gesturing through the hands of my enemy to save my life, and I am grateful.

Realizing that to trust the old man was the best of some very bad options, I threw my five remaining shells as far as I could in one direction and the revolver in the other. If they were going to kill me, it wouldn't be with my survival weapon.

Then, the brief silence was broken by a unison scream of revenge, and the crowd was on me. They pounded me to my knees. I felt a shower of blows on my head and shoulders from their bamboo clubs. Each man and boy, feeling years of pent-up anger and hatred, took this moment of revenge. Each got his blow, and for a moment I feared that I had made the wrong decision. I had been deceived. Then—just before unconsciousness—the old man intervened. The blows and kicks and curses ceased, and I was dragged to my feet.

At that moment the village commissar arrived, wielding a vintage German luger. His was the first uniform I had seen that day, and he was obviously in charge. He took one arm, the old man took the other, and together they half-dragged, half-walked me toward the village. In the confusion a boy about twelve years old slipped out of the crowd, deftly lifted my watch right off my arm and ran off with it. Later in the crowd I saw him passing out the twenty-dollar bills I had been carrying in my flight jacket. He had no idea how much those green bills were worth.

The crowd was jubilant. They had captured a valuable prisoner. They were returning to their village in triumph. Suddenly, I felt afraid. Everyone was looking toward the village. Instinctively, I looked backward and saw, to my horror, a man, his face twisted in anger, running towards me. A huge scar ran down the right side of his face; his right eye was missing; he was running at me full-tilt, carrying a three-foot-long rusty harpoon. He had every intention of planting that lance deep into my back. I lunged in front of the commissar who, upon realizing my predicament, felled the man with one strong blow to the face with that old German luger. What made me feel the danger and turn? I believe it was God at work again.

By now we had crossed to the edge of the village. The whole town had gathered. For a moment they just stood and looked at this strange man from another world. They were peasants dressed uniformly in simple, black, pajama outfits. I stood before them in full-battle dress, armed with a flare gun, sheath knives, a two-way radio, life vest, compass, navigational watch, and miscellaneous survival paraphernalia. I must have looked like a man from the moon to them. For one long moment we stood in open-mouthed unbelief seeing each other close up for the first time. Then they laid me spread-eagle on the dirt path and commenced to undress me and relieve me of my treasures.

They didn't use any of the zippers on my flight clothing. They took knives and machetes and cut off everything, including my boots. In seconds I was completely naked. Someone tossed me short, ragged pants and a child's short-sleeved shirt with no buttons. I struggled into my new uniform and sat back exhausted on a low rock wall, wiped my arm across my face and was quite surprised when it came back covered with blood. I must have been a sight, almost naked, covered with mud, beaten to a pulp, my leg wounded and bleeding.

The commissar held the crowd back, unsure what to do with his unexpected prize. Then the crowd parted and a little Vietnamese man approached carrying a black medic bag. A woman followed with a basin of water. Together they washed my wounds, wrapped a bandage around my head, and gave me a shot in each arm. I recognized the syringe of morphine from my survival gear and supposed the other was a tetanus shot. This moment of compassion that probably saved my life seemed even then an act of God. These people had every reason to hate me. If it hadn't been for the commissar, I believe they would have killed me on the spot. This medic went about his work without a smile or friendly gesture as if compelled by a force of compassion that outweighed any hatred and desire for revenge.

When the medic finished his hasty repairs, the commissar dragged me through the crowd to a little shelter just off the central village square. I lay on my back on a hard, wooden pallet on the dirt floor. The room was dark, with no windows; a kerosene lamp burned nearby, lighting the room in flickering semi-darkness. All afternoon and into the night the commissar let the villagers enter the room in groups of three or four. No one showed particular hostility. They were mainly curious. No one did me any harm. Now and then a teen-ager would spit on me, say something in anger, and punch me with his finger, I suppose to tell his young friends he had touched the fallen American pilot. Few tried to speak. Most simply looked, then hurried on. I thought of funerals back in Tulsa and how mourners approached the casket, stared for a moment, and then walked on. This time the corpse stared back. Then the crowds stopped coming. I was alone for the first time since my capture. I had not thought about God much since dropping out of Sunday school in my late teens, but lying on the floor, I could not help but think of Him then.

I had come close to death so many times in that one day and each time I had felt the hand of God. Pictures flooded my mind: the plane exploding into a ball of flame moments after I had ejected—shots zinging by me, making holes in my parachute—the crowd of angry men beating and kicking me, intent upon my death—that unforgettable face twisted by anger and by war, running at me with the rusty lance—the medic—the commissar—the old man.

I was a prisoner of war. I had no idea what my fate would be, but the Lord had made Himself abundantly clear. He was there with me in the presence of my enemies, and I breathed my second prayer of thanks that day.

2

New Guy Village

My first day in captivity had left me exhausted but grateful to be alive. I had survived the day on grace and my adrenalin. Now, the adrenalin was wearing off, and the morphine was taking hold. My thoughts slowed to a halt, and I floated in a drugged stupor on the floor of that village shelter. A loud commotion in the village square jolted me back to my senses. It was the sound of a crowd of cheering peasants running along behind a large truck. The truck stopped outside.

The door burst open, and in marched eight or nine North Vietnamese regular soldiers in army uniforms. They hauled me to my feet. It was then I learned my badly sprained leg could not support my weight, so the soldiers dragged me between them through the crowd outside. There were no electric lights in the village, but makeshift torches lit the night. The people cheered the soldiers as they loaded me onto the back of a half-ton military truck. I lay spread-eagle on the slats, while one young soldier blindfolded me and lay a tarpaulin over my shivering body. Unfortunately, the tarpaulin wasn't meant for warmth but to guarantee that I could not see anything on the coming journey.

The truck pulled out of that village and sped toward Hanoi.

We drove the entire night on a very rough road, stopping every few hours for the soldiers to unveil me to another cluster of applauding peasants carrying torches and cheering the soldiers loudly. One particular stop was unforgettable. There were no crowds this time; in fact, we were parked on a pontoon bridge in the middle of a wide river. The soldiers took off my blindfold and pointed thirty feet above me to the Ham Rong bridge which they thought had been my target. It was still standing. I noticed that our truck's wheels were submerged beneath the water and that the pontoon bridge was totally hidden from the surface to camouflage it. My enemy was proud, and boisterous, and confident.

At about dawn the next morning, I could hear traffic and the sounds of a city. The truck stopped and my blindfold was removed; then, we drove into a large fortress in the heart of Hanoi, In the few seconds I had to survey my surroundings, it was perfectly clear that this was a prison that would permit no escape.

A series of huge concrete walls fifteen to twenty feet high surrounded the inner buildings. Broken glass was cemented into the surface, and hot, electric wires ran the length of the walls. There was a dry moat around the prison separating one tall wall from the other.

We drove through iron gates and stopped before an ominous structure of concrete brick and mortar approximately thirty-five feet long and twenty-five feet wide. Inside this tomblike building were eight individual cells, 6 x 6 feet. Each held two concrete bunks, one on each side, with barely enough room to walk between them. The bunks were about two feet wide and at the bottom of each, imbedded in cement, was a set of iron stocks. A prisoner would put his feet in place, and another iron bar was forced down across the top with an iron pin to lock them. There were seven cells with an eighth prepared as a kind of washing place. This was Heartbreak Hotel. It was one of many cell blocks of the huge Hoa Lo prison complex. Built by the French early in the century, American aircrews housed there had nicknamed the prison the "Hanoi Hilton." Needless to say, this was no hotel.

I saw no other prisoners as I was dragged into Cell 7. Only minutes passed before the guards moved me again from Heartbreak Hotel into a completely different section of the prison. Later I learned my second stop was nicknamed New Guy Village, for almost every new prisoner was housed temporarily in its cells.

The retaining room I now found myself in had knobby plaster walls that gave the place a cavelike appearance. Nicknamed the "Knobby Room," it was small and the filthiest place I had seen to date. It was like the worst of slums in miniature. I sat down on a pile of debris in the center of this mess and took stock of my condition.

I had no clothes. I was freezing cold. I had eaten nothing for twenty-four exhausting hours. My body ached. My leg and wrist were sprained and swelling badly. I was covered with caked blood and filth. The officers' quarters on the *Bon Homme Richard,* a warm bath, a hot cup of coffee, that emergency first-aid kit I hadn't opened in ten years seemed a million miles away.

No sooner had I begun to collect my thoughts than I was interrupted by a burly Vietnamese officer who led me from the Knobby Room into an interrogation center nearby. I knew this moment was coming. I had been trained in survival school and was well versed in the Code of Conduct. I was to answer only four questions. The questions began almost politely.

"Your name?"

"Howard Rutledge," I answered, teeth chattering in the morning chill.

"Your rank and serial number?" he continued.

"Commander; 506435," I replied.

"Your date of birth?"

"13 November 1928."

The questions continued without pause. "Your squadron and ship?"

I refused to answer further, explaining the American fighting man's code and the International Conventions at Geneva, 1949.

His reply was calm and quiet. "You are not a prisoner of war," he said. "Your government has not declared war upon the Vietnamese people. You must answer my questions. You are protected by no international law." I continued to refuse to answer any of his questions.

Suddenly, the interrogator closed his notebook, leaned over toward me and said, "Commander Rutledge, you are a criminal, guilty of high crimes against the Vietnamese people. If you do not answer my questions, you will be severely punished."

With that I was led back into the Knobby Room and given thirty minutes to decide. The guard returned, and I was taken back into the interrogation room and asked the first four questions, which I answered again. The fifth I refused to answer. I was threatened again and returned to the Knobby Room. This little charade happened every thirty minutes for the entire day. The verbal lashings increased each time I refused to cooperate. But every time I returned to the Knobby Room, I felt I had beaten them again.

Meanwhile my body ached with growing ferocity. I had received no clothing, and I was beginning to "cold soak." My body temperature was dropping to the temperature of the North Vietnamese winter evening; my swollen wrist and leg were throbbing, but I was going to win. Survival school had taught me well. Again I was called to the interrogation room.

This time when I refused to answer the threat of punishment sounded like a promise. "Now, Commander Rutledge," the interrogator said, "you will be severely punished."

I was taken back to the Knobby Room. The officer who spoke English was joined by a guard we named Pigeye and three men in civilian clothes. Pigeye probably tortured more Americans than any other North Vietnamese. The others looked like criminals off the street. A guard with a burp gun closed the door on the six of us and stood watching through the bars.

The officer told me to sit on the floor and extend my legs straight out. My left leg was so badly swollen that I could not straighten it, so one of the interrogator's accomplices planted his heavy boot on my knee and forced the swollen leg onto the cement floor. I felt a flash of pain and simultaneously felt my leg pop. That guard probably did me a real favor by forcing into place my badly dislocated leg. It may seem strange to thank God for this sadistic act, but I don't know what would have happened to my leg if that guard hadn't acted.

Then they forced my legs into spurlike shackles and used a pipe and strong rope to lock both ankles firmly into place. Next they forced my arms into a long-sleeved shirt and began to tie them behind me from above my elbows to my wrists. One guard put his foot on my back, forcing the laces tight enough to cut off all circulation and pulling my shoulder blades almost apart. I could see the rope cut through my wrists all the way to the bone, but they did not bleed, because the bindings acted like a tourniquet, cutting off circulation entirely into my arms and hands.

I began to have severe pains in my arms; by forcing myself on my side, I could see my arms and hands had turned a deep shade of blue. It slowly dawned on me that they were going to leave me in this miserable position until I answered their questions. For a while I thought that I would die. I never prayed for death, but I did pray for unconsciousness. For at least three hours I lay in this position, my prayer unanswered.

Then the guards returned, unlaced my arms and legs, and left again. I had a terrible fear that my arms would never function normally, but an hour or so later feeling began to return, and except for deep cuts and bruises they soon moved quite normally. My first contact with torture as a weapon of war had left me a

One guard put his foot on my back, forcing the laces tight enough to cut off all circulation and pulling my shoulder blades almost apart.

bit unnerved, and when they brought me once again to the interrogation room, it took all the strength I could muster to refuse to answer their questions once again.

All they wanted was for me to answer question number five— my squadron, airwing, and ship. If I didn't answer, I would be hogtied again and probably lose the use of my arms and hands, if not my life.

"Commander Rutledge, you have committed high crimes against our people. You will be severely punished if you do not answer our questions."

My explanation was interrupted; I was returned to the Knobby Room, placed in shackles, tightly bound, and left again to ponder my resistance. This time the guards slapped me several times before they left. And each time during the night, as I refused to answer, their blows increased. Around dawn the interrogator was relieved by a high-ranking officer. Later I learned the prisoners called him Colonel Nam.

I had been through an entire night of punishment, and the more I had refused, the more angry and impatient everyone had become. Now, everyone was tense and angry. When Colonel Nam repeated the questions and then the threats, I exploded in anger.

"Why don't you go ahead and kill me, because I will *not* answer your questions!" Colonel Nam did not reply. He just watched as the guards dragged me away. This time they would have their answers.

I was shackled; the laces were pulled unbearably tight. I had not eaten for two days, and my requests for medical care for my wrist and legs and head were ignored. I had not even been permitted to have a normal kidney or bowel movement in the entire time. I still had no clothes and was truly cold.

This time they laced the rope from my ankles up around my neck through my handcuffed wrists. This forced me into a pretzel-like position; if I bent forward or leaned backward, the rope would choke me. I had to sit in a perfectly upright position, with arms laced tightly behind my back. One guard repeatedly struck my head and shoulders with a bamboo pole; another jumped up and down on the rope binding my legs, cutting deep into my ankles. I prayed for unconsciousness. I asked God to give me strength. I thought about my wife Phyllis and my family, and knew I would never see them again. I knew my ability to endure any more physical or mental pain was rapidly ending. I determined that before I cracked completely, I would volunteer to answer their questions, hoping that while I still had some control, I could lie and deceive them and so survive.

"Stop." My voice was no more than a whisper. "I will answer."

Immediately, they undid my bindings and unshackled me. As I lay there on the floor, the interrogator entered and politely asked me question number five.

"What is your service?" he said.

"The United States Navy," I replied.

Then he was gone. They had their fifth answer. It was all they wanted.

Guards brought a blanket and a suit of long prison clothes. At last I was allowed to relieve myself. I could not eat. I received no medical attention, not even Mercurochrome, but I lay back on that concrete slab and slept.

3

Heartbreak Hotel

On the morning of December 1, 1965, two guards roused me from a fitful sleep and marched me out of New Guy Village across the prison into Cell 2, Heartbreak Hotel. When the door slammed and the key turned in that rusty, iron lock, a feeling of utter loneliness swept over me. I lay down on that cold cement slab in my 6 x 6 prison. The smell of human excrement burned my nostrils. A rat, large as a small cat, scampered across the slab beside me. The walls and floors and ceilings were caked with filth. Bars covered a tiny window high above the door. I was cold and hungry; my body ached from the swollen joints and sprained muscles.

I felt guilty for having answered more. Worst of all, I felt totally alone. I seldom cry, but that day tears of self-pity and of fear welled up in my eyes, and I fought them back. This was my first taste of solitary confinement. The war against my nerves had begun.

Then I heard a voice.

"New guy that just moved in, what's your name? What ship are you from?"

I literally sprang to that window and pressed my face against the cold iron bars. Down the narrow passageway staring back at me were other Americans. Commander James Stockdale, air-wing commander downed in September had spoken. I was not alone!

At great personal risk he briefed me quickly and clearly about the other men in Heartbreak. In a cell across the way was Commander Harry Jenkins, a squadron commander in Airwing 16. To the left was Air Force Captain George McNight, downed only weeks before. In Cell 4 was Lt. Comdr. Duffy Hutton from a photo-recon squadron, and across from him Marine Captain Harley Chapman off the attack carrier USS *Oriskany*, and Air Force Lt. Jerry Singleton, a helicopter pilot downed in November.

In quiet, rapid phrases, Commander Stockdale told me that to clear the area of guards, the person wanting to communicate would whistle "Mary Had a Little Lamb." Everyone would immediately get down on his hands and knees and look through a small crack under his door to insure that his own immediate space was clear of guards. If you saw a Vietnamese in the corridor, you'd cough, the danger signal not to communicate.

Then I spoke. The words poured out of me. I was a traitor. I had answered more questions than name, rank, serial number, and date of birth.

Commander Stockdale heard my brief confession. When I had finished he simply said, "Don't feel like the Lone Ranger." Someone coughed; then all was silent.

The silence lasted throughout the entire day and night that followed. Soon I learned that communication was risky business. We could get off only snatches of conversation in an entire day. The rest of the time we sat alone in our cells. It's hard to describe what solitary confinement can do to unnerve and defeat a man. You quickly tire of standing up or sitting down, sleeping or being awake. There are no books, no paper or pencils, no magazines or newspapers. The only colors you see are drab gray and dirty brown. Months or years may go by when you don't see the sunrise or the moon, green grass or flowers. You are locked in, alone

I literally sprang to that window and pressed my face against
the cold iron bars.

and silent in your filthy little cell breathing stale, rotten air and trying to keep your sanity.

I remembered Edgar Allan Poe's vision of hell in "The Pit and the Pendulum." Poe's hero saw the walls slowly moving toward him, threatening to crush him to death. In Heartbreak Hotel I realized Poe's walls may not have moved at all. It is something in one's head that moves to crush him. I had the best of survival training in the navy, and it got me through that first long day of interrogation. But after that I was alone, and no survival training can prepare a man for years of solitary confinement. What sustains a man in prison is something that he has going for him inside his heart and head—something that happened, or did not happen—back in childhood in the home and church and school. Nobody can teach you to survive the brutality of being alone. At first you panic. You want to cry out. You fight back waves of fear. You want to die, to confess, to do anything to get out of that ever-shrinking world. Then, gradually a plan of defense takes shape. Being alone is another kind of war, but slowly I learned that it, too, can be won. Like a blind man who is forced to develop other senses to replace his useless eyes, a man in solitary confinement must quit regretting what he cannot do and build a new life around what he can do.

Since I couldn't move more than a few feet in any direction, I lay on my bunk and moved my eyes, searching out interesting cracks or scratches in the plaster. Who had made them? What could they mean? Immediately I learned that though no human being shared my tiny space, I was not really alone. The walls were crawling with interesting vermin. Ants fascinated me, and even the rats made entertaining though ugly roommates. These North Vietnamese rats were unlike any I had ever seen; they were over a foot long and looked like opossums. One old rat was so big I fantasized his stepping out into the corridor and calling, "Here, Kitty, Kitty!" Because I couldn't force myself to eat the bowl of cold seaweed soup with sowbelly fat on the top and could only nibble at the stale French loaf during those first lonely days, my cell was preferred territory to these large, ugly rodents.

More friendly and more agile than the rats were the geckos, six-to-nine-inch-long multicolored lizards with suction cups on their legs. These prehistoric little monsters were wonderful entertainment. They could dart across a wall and snatch an unsuspecting fly or mosquito in mid-flight. I played a game with geckos; lying on my slab, I tried to herd the flies in their direction, celebrating every gecko conquest and keeping score, competing one gecko's accuracy against another.

I developed all kinds of mental games that kept me entertained and edified by the hours. In those thirty-four days in Heartbreak, I also disciplined myself to reconstruct my life, year by year, month by month, day by day. I worked hard to reconstruct and evaluate each event. My memory had rusted over, and I set about scraping the rust away.

In prison I discovered how important regular times of reflection can be. Living in America, one becomes preoccupied with family and career. When I was free, I seldom thought seriously about what I was doing or why I was doing it. When days are filled by travel, conversation, books, papers, movies, television, meals, radio, billboards, and the like, the mind is constantly looking outward and dealing with the world outside and around. But when suddenly all that is taken away, it is forced to deal with the world inside.

At first, this process of remembering was torture; all I could think about was food. I thought of Wednesday steak night in the officers' mess on the *Bon Homme Richard:* a six-inch baked potato swimming in butter, sour cream, and chives; hot apple pie with cheese and hot coffee, all I could drink. I thought of Mom's chocolate pie or my wife's cooking—anything and everything she put on the table. Then I would see the bowl of rotting pumpkin or seaweed soup and the small loaf of stale French bread in my cell. The thought of swallowing that cold, greasy, repugnant stuff was nauseating. Day by day I refused to eat until my own body fat had been depleted, and my weight began to drop. Soon it became clear that if I didn't eat, I would starve. If I didn't get the necessary protein, I could not survive. Already I was weak and getting weaker.

One day I decided to eat it all. I never really felt full the entire seven years in Vietnam; but every bite of seaweed soup, every small piece of sowbelly fat, every bowl of sewer greens kept me a little closer to health and survival. When one is dying from starvation, a bowl of sewer greens is a gift from God. Before every meal during my captivity, I offered a prayer of thanks. In the past, when others prayed my mind wandered over the day's events or simply waited impatiently for the prayer to end. But in prison, grace was not a routine endured out of habit, guilt, or pressure. To thank God for life seemed the natural thing to do.

During those long periods of enforced reflection, it became so much easier to separate the important from the trivial, the worthwhile from the waste. For example, in the past, I usually worked or played hard on Sundays and had no time for church. For years Phyllis encouraged me to join the family at church. She never nagged or scolded—she just kept hoping. But I was too busy, too preoccupied, to spend one or two short hours a week thinking about the really important things.

Now the sights and sounds and smells of death were all around me. My hunger for spiritual food soon outdid my hunger for a steak. Now I wanted to know about that part of me that will never die. Now I wanted to talk about God and Christ and the church. But in Heartbreak solitary confinement there was no pastor, no Sunday-school teacher, no Bible, no hymnbook, no community of believers to guide and sustain me. I had completely neglected the spiritual dimension of my life. It took prison to show me how empty life is without God, and so I had to go back in my memory to those Sunday-school days in the Nogales Avenue Baptist Church, Tulsa, Oklahoma. If I couldn't have a Bible and hymnbook, I would try to rebuild them in my mind.

I tried desperately to recall snatches of Scripture, sermons, the gospel choruses from childhood, and the hymns we sang in church. The first three dozen songs were relatively easy. Every day I'd try to recall another verse or a new song. One night there was a huge thunderstorm—it was the season of the monsoon rains—and a bolt of lightning knocked out the lights and plunged the entire prison into darkness. I had been going over hymn tunes in my mind and stopped to lie down and sleep when the rains began to fall. The darkened prison echoed with wave after wave of water. Suddenly, I was humming my thirty-seventh song, one I had entirely forgotten since childhood.

> Showers of blessings,
> Showers of blessing we need!
> Mercy drops round us are falling,
> But for the showers we plead.

I no sooner had recalled those words than another song popped into my mind, the theme song of a radio program my mother listened to when I was just a kid.

> Heavenly sunshine, heavenly sunshine
> Flooding my soul with glory divine.
> Heavenly sunshine, heavenly sunshine.
> Hallelujah! Jesus is mine!

Most of my fellow prisoners were struggling like me to re-discover faith, to reconstruct workable value systems. Harry Jenkins lived in a cell nearby during much of my captivity. Often we would use those priceless seconds of communication in a day to help one another recall Scripture verses and stories.

One day I heard him whistle. When the cell block was clear, I waited for his communication, thinking it to be some important news. "I got a new one," he said. "I don't know where it comes from or why I remember it, but it's a story about Ruth and Naomi." He then went on to tell that ancient story of Ruth following Naomi into a hostile new land and finding God's presence and protection there. Harry's urgent news was two thousand years old. It may not seem important to prison life, but we lived off that story for days, rebuilding it, thinking about what it meant, and applying God's ancient words to our predicament.

Everyone knew the Lord's Prayer and the Twenty-Third Psalm, but the camp favorite verse that everyone recalled first and quoted most often is found in the Book of John, third chapter, sixteenth verse.

> For God so loved the world, that he gave his only begotten Son, that whosoever believeth in him should not perish, but have everlasting life.

With Harry's help I even reconstructed the seventeenth and eighteenth verses.

> For God sent not his Son into the world to condemn the world; but that the world through him might be saved. He that believeth on him is not condemned: but he that believeth not is condemned already, because he hath not believed in the name of the only begotten Son of God.

How I struggled to recall those Scriptures and hymns! I had spent my first eighteen years in a Southern Baptist Sunday school, and I was amazed at how much I could recall; regrettably, I had not seen then the importance of memorizing verses from the Bible or learning gospel songs. Now, when I needed them, it was too late. I never dreamed that I would spend almost seven years (five of them in solitary confinement) in a prison in North Vietnam or that thinking about one memorized verse could have made a whole day bearable. One portion of a verse I did remember was, "Thy word have I hid in my heart." How often I wished I had really worked to hide God's Word in my heart. I put my mind to work. Every day I planned to accomplish certain tasks. I woke early, did my physical exercises, cleaned up as best I could, then began a period of devotional prayer and meditation. I would pray, hum hymns silently, quote Scripture, and think about what the verses meant to me.

Remember, we weren't playing games. The enemy knew that the best way to break a man's resistance was to crush his spirit in a lonely cell. In other wars, some of our POWs after solitary confinement lay down in a fetal position and died. All this talk of Scripture and hymns may seem boring to some, but it was the way we conquered our enemy and overcame the power of death around us.

It looked as though I would spend my first Christmas in captivity in Heartbreak Hotel; but about 8 P.M. Christmas Eve, 1965, guards entered my cell, blindfolded me, roped me into a jeep with Lt. Commander Duffy Hutton, and drove us across Hanoi to another prison. POWs called it the Zoo, and it would be my home for two torturously long years.

4

The Zoo

To the southwest of downtown Hanoi, there is an old French art colony complete with race track, swimming pool, theater, and assorted living quarters, and service buildings. It must have been quite a showplace at the height of French colonialism. However, by that Christmas Eve, 1965, when I was taken there, some changes had been made.

American prisoners had named this art-colony-turned-prison, the Zoo. Around the place there was a foreboding wall, with guard towers and massive gates. The outbuildings had been stripped of furnishings, the windows had been bricked over, bars covered any opening that remained, individual cells had been constructed in every building, the pool was being used to grow fish for camp officials, the place was overgrown with weeds, and piles of filth were crawling with vermin and rodents. Each building had a name that best indicated the change: the Stable, the Outhouse, and the Pigsty.

Our guards took off our blindfolds and marched me to the Pigsty where I first met the English-speaking interrogator POWs called the Dog. He was large for a Vietnamese and wore a Chinese-type cap with a red star; a cardboard collar-insignia on his olive-drab uniform indicated his rank. I immediately recognized the hated Pigeye standing at his side. It would not be long before I experienced his torture skills again.

The Dog asked me my name and rank. Hoping there might be other Americans present, I shouted out my reply, "Commander Howard Rutledge!" He scribbled on a yellow pad and walked away. Seconds passed.

Then, in the darkness I heard a voice. "Commander Rutledge, come towards the front window." Commander Bill Franke had heard me call out my name. Quickly and quietly he explained where I was. Because it was dark, he couldn't clear the area of guards but promised to communicate the next day.

Cell 4, Pigsty, was approximately 15 x 15 feet. It seemed huge after one month in the closet at Heartbreak. But there was no bed or furnishings, just a cold cement floor. The windows had not yet been bricked in on Cell 4, and the winter cold made my prison feel like an icehouse. Still, I lay back on that cement floor with some hope. After all, I was "on the line"—communicating within thirty seconds of my arrival.

I'll not forget that first Christmas Eve in captivity. It was terribly cold, and though I knew of at least one other American nearby, I was still alone. My body still ached, and my wounds were only beginning to heal. As I lay there in my ice-cold misery, somewhere in my cell a Christmas carol began to play. It was an incredible surprise; I sat up and searched the cell. For a moment I thought my mind was playing treacherous tricks— "Silent Night, Holy Night." The fidelity was awful, but it was the first song I had heard since bailing out more than a month ago. Scratches and all, that carol was beautiful beyond describing.

Then the carol ended, and the voice of Hanoi Hanna came on with a barrage of propaganda. Later I learned that in the walls every cell had a speaker that broadcast bizarre programming for the prisoners. Many of the programs were recorded in the United States, and were designed to agitate homesick Americans. "Radio Stateside" may have been a tool to break us down, but the snatches of American music, especially that carol on Christmas Eve, backfired and really boosted my spirits.

I hadn't thought about Christmas carols for my growing list of hymns and gospel songs, but on that strange Christmas Eve, with Hanoi Hanna ranting in the background, I recalled at least eight or ten carols, verse by verse. It was like discovering hidden treasure, and I reveled in it.

On Christmas morning we were awakened early by the camp gong. I hadn't shaved in thirty-two days, and my hair was dirty and extra-long. I was taken to the bathing area and given a haircut and shave. It was primitive but rejuvenating. Americans were not allowed to mix, so the one-by-one trip to the latrine took all of Christmas morning.

Around noon in North Vietnam, the turnkeys (jailers) take a nap. The minimal crew of guards was fairly easy to clear, and in that short hour we could communicate with others without great fear of being caught and punished.

Because I was the new guy at the Zoo, immediately upon clearing the area, everyone wanted to know the latest news from the outside world.

Commander Franke, imprisoned already for five to six months, peered through the crack above his door and whispered the question everyone wanted answered.

"When do you think the war will end?"

Later I learned that across the way listening was Everett Alvarez, the first American POW, downed eighteen months before. How could I tell them it might go on for years? I tried to give them a straightforward message that wouldn't shatter spirits and destroy morale.

"Hang on. We might be here next Christmas."

I could hear the groan pass from cell to cell. Immediately I felt guilty for bringing such bad news, especially at Christmas.

Even I never dreamed it would be seven more long years before release.

The next question Bill Franke asked me was, "Do you know the code?"

The first regulation in all the prisons of North Vietnam was DO NOT COMMUNICATE WITH YOUR FELLOW AMERICANS. The enemy knew that if he could isolate a man—make him feel abandoned—cut off—forgotten—he could more easily destroy his resistance and break down his morale. To win this war against our nerves, we had to devise all kinds of ingenious systems to keep the lines open among our fellow prisoners. We learned to think like criminals, to devise ways to lie, cheat, and deceive.

The tap code Commander Franke asked me about was a series of taps and pauses, representing each letter in the alphabet. A man would get down on his hands and knees, wrap himself in a blanket to cut down noise a guard might hear, and tap out messages to the man in an adjoining cell. This man would receive the message, then pass it on to the man next door. Sometimes a message could sweep around the cell block faster than a guard could walk.

"Yes, Bill, I know the code." I had overheard the code being whispered to another prisoner during my short stay at Heartbreak and had memorized it, never realizing I would spend the next seven years using this simple code to tap out messages almost every day.

Communicating was our major weapon against the enemy. Each cell block had a key man who initiated most communication efforts. He usually was located in a place which allowed him the best view of the area. When he gave the signal to clear, each of us would scramble for a position to see if any guards were about. If there were two men in a cell, one would climb on the other's shoulders and look through the high, transom-like windows above the solid wooden doors. Though most of us were kept in solitary confinement, it was advantageous for many

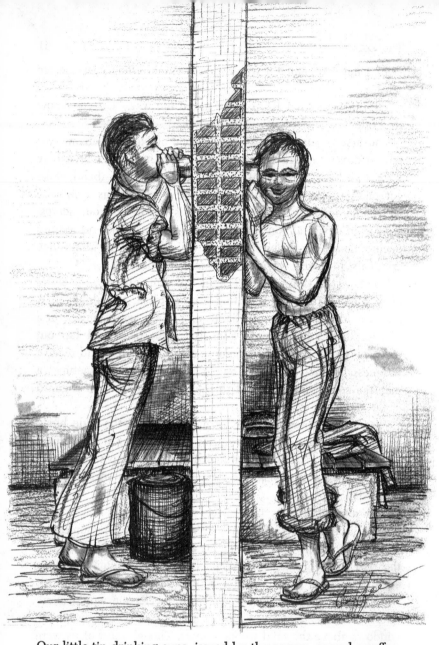

Our little tin drinking cups, issued by the enemy, served as effective transducers to get voice or tapped messages through solid walls.

reasons to be with another prisoner. You could send messages on the wall, while the other maintained security. Many prisoners in solitary risked punishment daily to send messages and keep the line clear. Often in the midst of communicating, a lone prisoner would be surprised by a guard and severely punished.

Our little tin drinking cups, issued by the enemy, served as effective transducers to get voice or tap messages through solid, cement walls. Every time a new man would enter a prison, his name and rank would be passed quickly to the entire camp and memorized. That way we protected each other. If we knew each other's names, the enemy could not lie or claim they never knew us. I can still reel off more than four hundred names and serial numbers memorized in prison.

That Christmas Day was memorable for more than my first bath and shave. We were fed a turkey dinner. There were many pictures taken by the enemy that day to show how well we were being treated. But perhaps a year went by between those few real meals that we had.

That first New Year's Day of captivity I made at least three resolutions that I repeated each year:

1. I would try never to be cold again.
2. I would try never to be hungry again.
3. I would never be without the Bible again. (This I would put in my mind and my heart.)

Early in January the Dog asked me for a written autobiographical sketch. Surprisingly, when I refused, he let me go. I was moved from the Pigsty down to a small, solitary cell with no windows where I remained alone until August 1966. Living in a cement box with cement floors, cement walls, and bricked-in windows is like living in a cold-storage vault in the winter and a hotbox in the summer.

Alone in the cell, I continued my devotional periods searching my mind for Scriptures, going over the more than fifty hymns I had recalled. My wrist and leg were almost back to normal. In spite of almost no medical care, my cuts and bruises from the first interrogation had healed. I knew my turn for interrogation would come again. I waited and wondered when.

Early in August the guards came for me. They took me to the "Auditorium," an old theater dressing room, and again the Dog demanded that I write a confession and a biographical sketch. When I refused, they shackled me to the spot and left. A tiny bulb was the only source of light in this spooky torture room. As my eyes became accustomed to the dimness, I could see spiders as big as my fist hanging all around me. They may have been friendly spiders, but they created quite a terrifying effect in the semidarkness. Ants crawled all over me, and nine million mosquitoes were trapped inside. Gecko lizards scurried through the filth, and large rats looked me over hungrily. It is a helpless sensation to be shackled, hands and feet, in such a place. I had no way to kill the mosquitoes or frighten off the rats. I just sat and watched and trembled.

I sat for four days and nights hardly moving. I remember the third day, August 7, because for two days and nights it had been stifling hot. The third day it rained and those showers of blessings cooled off the cell, and made it almost bearable. Also, August 7 was the day I married Phyllis eighteen years before. Was she well? Did she know I was alive? I missed her so. I breathed a prayer that God would get us through and, if He willed, let me hold her in my arms again.

Each day the Dog or Spot, his assistant, came in to demand a confession, anything in writing the enemy could use against us. I continued to refuse, and on August 8, 1966, the Dog visited me again and insisted once more upon my writing a confession or this time to suffer the punishment of death.

I took the pen, and wrote my choice on the paper, and handed it back to him. DEATH!

They slapped me around and cursed and threatened and demanded something useful in writing.

So I took the pen and wrote again. "I support my country, its government, and its people. I always will." Then I signed it.

August 8, 1966, Pigeye and his friends shackled me, hands and feet, in another torture room, dubbed by those who suffered there, the Outhouse. The Outhouse was located on the south wall of the camp just behind Pigsty. It was a squat, flat-roofed, concrete, bunkerlike room with no windows. The filth in that small room was far beyond anything I had seen to date. In fact, the ants were so plentiful and so large that I am sure by now they've eaten up the entire cement building.

Because it was out in the sun, the temperature inside—and I believe I'm estimating conservatively—was 100 or 110 degrees at midnight.

As I sat there in a pile of human excrement crawling with countless moving things, I thought back upon my "bravery." It was not bravery to ask for death when the enemy needed us alive, but I knew the cost I would pay for my resistance. Again it took all the courage I could muster. Now I sat staring into the darkness, gagging on the odor, my skin crawling with pests that bit and pinched in the dark. My courage waned. Maybe they wouldn't kill me. Maybe they would just abuse me until I died.

I remained in the Outhouse, my hands cuffed behind my back, my legs in irons. They gave me only a small bowl of rice each day and two cups of filthy water. It was unbearably hot, and by the end of the first week I was very sick with dysentery and couldn't eat. For almost three weeks I sat getting weaker each day from the constant diarrhea and the lack of food and water. There was a bucket in the room in which to perform the bodily functions, but it is difficult when you're handcuffed with your arms behind your back and your legs in irons, and you're too weak to move. So I and the prisoners before me just relieved ourselves in our clothing and on the floor. No one ever cleaned the Outhouse. To keep us lying in that filth was part of the plan.

By the third week I had developed a heat rash that itched and bled, and left me feeling close to despair. Our camp policy was to hold on until just short of losing touch with reality and then volunteer to confess in writing. While we still had some senses left, we could usually write a confession anyone but our enemy could tell was false. I decided that if each of us could take thirty days in that torture room in one year, only twelve would suffer, and some men might even be spared.

Each night was getting harder and harder to endure. I would work my mind furiously in the daytime, hoping to be tired enough at night to sleep in spite of heat rash, dysentery, hunger, and pain. All day I planned to get through just one more night and then confess, but in the morning I would feel new strength to bear one more day and night.

On August 31, after twenty-eight days of torture, I could remember I had children but not how many. I said Phyllis's name over and over again so I would not forget. I prayed for strength. It was on that twenty-eighth night I made God a promise. If I survived this ordeal, the first Sunday back in freedom I would take Phyllis and my family to their church and at the close of the service confess my faith in Christ and join the church. This wasn't a deal with God to get me through that last miserable night. It was a promise made after months of thought. It took prison and hours of painful reflection to realize how much I needed God and the community of believers. After I made God that promise, again I prayed for strength to make it through the night.

When the morning dawned through the crack in the bottom of that solid prison door, I thanked God for His mercy and called the guard.

Immediately upon hearing my willingness to write, the guards released me. I was taken to a bath and cleaned, then taken to the Fox, the commander of the Zoo, to sign my "confession."

"I am a Yankee imperialist aggressor," I wrote, parroting their text, knowing how little those words sounded like anything an American would write. I knew they had not released my name yet after nine months and that confession could be used against me to humiliate me in the camp and as propaganda around the world. I hoped my friends and family would understand.

5

Las Vegas

In January 1967 I left the Zoo with nineteen other men and traveled back across Hanoi to the Hanoi Hilton. The enemy had opened a new section, promptly dubbed *Las Vegas* by the prisoners, in the immense Hoa Lo prison complex. Six cell blocks ringed a courtyard area. On the north wall was the Thunderbird. On the Northeast corner was the Mint. Then came the Desert Inn and the Stardust along the east wall. The Riviera, on the south wall, and the Golden Nugget on the west completed the square.

In the courtyard were ten small bathing areas appropriately named the Sands. You can imagine what kind of baths they were. In fact, by May there was no water at all to fill the basins, so the enemy dug three wells in the Las Vegas courtyard. Because there was no sewer system, everything was dumped in holes beside the wells; therefore, the water we dipped to wash our clothes and to bathe was ultimately sewage, filthy with fungus and crawling with worms.

Inside each cell block was an assortment of cells ranging from 4-man units in a 9 x 9 foot space, to 2-men units in a 4 x 8 foot space, and in the Mint the smallest cells I had ever seen—total space 3 feet wide and just over 6 feet long. A hardwood bed on one wall left less than a 1 x 6 foot space to walk and exercise in.

At the foot of every bed in Las Vegas was a set of stocks to shackle an offending prisoner to his slab.

Apparently the enemy knew how effective our communication systems had become and had built Las Vegas to cut down our wall-tap system. They left a two-foot dead space between the cells so that prisoners could no longer share a common wall. We just continued tapping on the floor or common perimeter wall, and all their extra work didn't ever slow us down. We continued to communicate, to organize, and resist.

By now communication among the prisoners had become immensely effective. The enemy needed prisoner cooperation to make its propaganda tapes and to meet its press and protest delegations. The easiest victim was the new guy freshly captured who walked innocently into the enemy's trap. However, no sooner had the new guy entered the Hanoi Hilton than the prisoner-communication network got to him, briefed him on in-camp resistance policy, and turned him almost overnight into a seasoned resister.

During those long years of captivity, we learned to communicate with anything and everything. Under ideal circumstances—which seldom came—we could grab off a few minutes of face-to-face communications. As I explained earlier, we used tin cups as transducers to tap or talk coded messages through solid walls. For short distances we tapped with fingers; for longer distances we tapped with the ball of fist or elbows against the floor. Other legitimate noises were never wasted—a cough, a sniff, spitting, and/or clearing the throat were converted into simple communication efforts. One specially effective ruse was to sweep through a compound, using the broom movement to signal messages to the entire area. Or, if a man walked by another's cell, he could drag his little Ho-Chi-Minh sandals in code. When he cleaned out his "honey bucket," he swept and cleaned it with a bamboo broom. Often with the guards looking on, men pounded out messages on those pails with the enemy none the wiser.

We were shackled in our leg irons, handcuffed behind our backs in this position day and night.

We began to think like criminals. I have spent as much as ten hours a day staring at a two-inch drain hole trying to track and clear a guard so that I could grab five minutes of conversation on the wall. Tracking a guard revealed his habits, identified his routines. In two-man cells one prisoner sat on another's shoulder watching the guard, memorizing every regular move he made. When we had visual sightings of each other, we communicated with semaphore code or hand flash movements like the deaf use. If someone could see under the door opposite (through the crack), he could tap out messages with his toe to the prisoner across the corridor.

We even wrote coded messages to each other, using any scrap paper, including toilet paper, and writing with ink made of cigarette ashes or blood and water. We would take a piece of wire from a screen or a stick from the floor, tear off the bottom of old lead toothpaste rolls, and make a pencil. Charcoal and lye soap mixed together in the right proportions make an excellent crayon.

The enemy realized our communications system was beating them. We were isolated into small cells, yet the whole camp was organized and informed. I often fantasized about how I would enjoy taking a high North Vietnamese visitor through all the cell blocks, pointing out the name, rank, serial number, place of birth, date of capture, and even the favorite Scripture or food of every man in every cell block, even those areas I had never visited because through covert communications we could know almost that much.

However, our successes led eventually to painful reprisal. The enemy began a vicious crackdown, punishing men caught in the act of communicating with swift and unforgettable vengeance. There were small portholes in the cell doors; a guard could flip that door and catch a man without warning. Little child-size handcuffs would force the elbows together painfully, and we would be left in them for weeks at a time; or we were shackled in leg irons, handcuffed behind our backs, and left on our beds in this position day and night.

Later on, this cruelty was compounded by blindfolding a prisoner. If he cried out, he would be gagged with a rag. Also there were the little milking stools the prisoners sat on during interrogation. An offender would be forced to sit on the stool as long as he could, seven, maybe ten days. Of course, without sleep or rest, hallucinations start. If the offender moved, the guard would beat him. It was very severe punishment.

April 24, 1967, after only four months in Las Vegas, I was called to interrogation by an English-speaking officer we had dubbed the Rat. He surprised me with the news that after 540 days of solitary confinement I would have a roommate. That day I moved into Cell 6 of the Desert Inn, with Air Force Captain George McKnight, whom I had covertly talked with back in Heartbreak an eternity ago. Both of us were incorrigible. He had been at another camp near Hanoi, nicknamed the Briarpatch, and had suffered treatment similar to my own. Like my twenty-eight days in the Outhouse and the Auditorium, George had spent thirty-four days, hands cuffed behind his back, in a hole in the ground before he finally gave up and wrote his "confession."

For eighteen months I had experienced only snatches of covert conversation with anyone. He, too, had suffered under silence. The result was hilarious. We talked nonstop for three days and nights. In seventy-two hours of conversation, you can learn a lot about a man. One of the first things I asked him was, "George, do you know any Scripture?"

There was a long pause, and for a moment I thought I had landed a roommate totally uninterested in such things. Then slowly he replied, "No, I don't! I'm sorry." So during those next days together he listened to mine.

George is a bachelor. Apparently he was quite a swinger and called himself Peck's Bad Boy. But in prison he, too, had thought a lot about Christ and his church. He was a Catholic and had tied knots in a string to create a makeshift rosary. Every morning he would pray using the rosary, pacing in the little walk space we had. I would sit on the bed for my devotional.

Perhaps before I was shot down I had some prejudices against Catholics based on childhood misconceptions. I remembered talk of purgatory and limbo and the pope. But locked together in a tiny cell in a North Vietnamese prison, it didn't take the two of us long to get past such things that separated us to the common faith we felt in Christ.

Don't misunderstand. We weren't two fully-developed saints sitting dispassionately through the day discussing theology. There probably wasn't a thimbleful of serious theology between us. We just knew that without our faith in God, without our common belief that He was with us, we could not have made it through.

Prison life was rough. We were treated like animals, so, I am afraid, we developed some rather crude behavior in the process. One example was our constant use of four-letter words. Even covert communications were sometimes sprinkled with rough language. George and I both were quick-tempered and took pleasure in throwing out a curse to a guard. Because he couldn't understand English, we could smile and tell him in no uncertain terms how we felt about his brutality, and he had no idea how thoroughly he had been insulted. Swearing was one of the few pleasures we had. Nevertheless, we both knew that profanity was a crutch and a bad habit that needed breaking.

One day George and I made a pact. We would start on Sunday and go seven days; we would each keep track of the other's swear words, numbering them, and the person with the fewest slips would receive a precious banana at the end of the week. We may have had to steal the banana from a careless guard, but we weren't working on a cure for stealing that week!

After I had spent a year and a half alone, George McKnight, a Catholic brother-in-Christ, brought me new strength to face the years of prison that lay ahead. If I can help it, I will never try again to "go it alone." Those wild, hilarious, stimulating, prayerful nights of sharing we spent together in Las Vegas made me realize how much we need each other. The experience renewed my resolution made in the Outhouse, to join my family's church as one of my first acts upon reaching freedom and to take again my responsible place in Christ's body on earth.

On May 19 I was called before the senior interrogator at Las Vegas and asked to say something nice about prison treatment. I told him simply and clearly that the year and a half that Captain McKnight and I had spent in solitary confinement was the severest form of mental cruelty. Needless to say, he didn't take kindly to my remarks.

I'll not forget that night. Tensions were high. The heat had been miserable and our communications system was ruining the enemy's plans to use us in its propaganda war. The lights blinked on and off. Apparently the interrogator was a chain smoker, and cigarette rations were down, so he was trying in the semidarkness to roll his own. Suddenly our bombers struck Hanoi with unusual fury. The sirens sounded wildly, and the bombs began to fall around us, splitting the silence and rocking nearby targets. He exploded into a rage. I knew my days of living with the luxury of a roommate had ended. Two days later the guards entered my cell and took me to one of those 3 x 6 cells in the Mint. The pressure was on again.

The Mint was a filthy place. The enemy had built a pigpen in the alley around the cells to house the camp's pigs. The smell of those pigs slopping through the filth outside my window, together with the din of squealing that they made, was quite a change from the long nights of quiet conversation with George.

But being alone again was even more of a shock. I knew that (for my sanity's sake) I had to reestablish my system of discipline immediately. By May of 1967 I had developed over one hundred hymns and Scriptures by memory. Of course, they weren't perfect; in fact, back in freedom now I'm having to check them out and rememorize them correctly. But they were mine, and I had a regular program each day in my cell to go over them one by one.

My routine included rising early and charting my day. The key was to plan more tasks than I could possibly accomplish. I spent the morning pacing the cell in three steps, then turning around and pacing back again—back and forth every morning, humming quietly every hymn I knew, repeating the words, verse by verse in my mind. I had arranged the songs in groups of five. I would wind up each group with a prayer, first for my daughters Peggy and Barbara, then another group of five hymns and prayers for my oldest daughter Sondra, then five more hymns for my son John, then five more for my wife Phyllis, and then my mother, and so forth. I would quote through my Scriptures or pick a word and try to develop that word into another hymn or Scripture buried deep in my memory, waiting to be discovered.

One day I thought of the word cymbal and the phrase "sounding brass and tinkling cymbal," fell into place. Eventually I reconstructed that whole love poem in 1 Corinthians 13, but the Apostle Paul would have looked with horror at my arrangement of his masterpiece. I began with "Now abideth faith, hope and love, but the greatest of these is love," and went backwards from there through a dozen or so verses, ending with "sounding brass and tinkling cymbal." I had the whole thing totally out of order; the first verse was the last; the last, first. So, I messed up, but the thoughts were right, and often those verses sustained me.

My system was a mind-saver; but after twenty-seven days of conversation with another human being, I had to get "on the line" again. I guess I was out of practice and tapped out a message to a cell nearby before the area had been thoroughly cleared. A guard surprised me in the act, and I was punished.

He shackled me to my slab in rear cuffs and irons. For five days I couldn't move. It was summer and very hot. The humidity must have been in the 90s, the temperature in the 100s. I developed one of those severe heat rashes where the red welts turn to blisters and ultimately to boils. At first I wasn't too concerned about the boils. But they wouldn't come to a head, so I'd have to pick them to stop the swelling. I didn't know the pus was contagious or that the bug inside the poison caused the boils to spread. In a few days I counted at least sixty boils about one inch in diameter over my entire body—under my arms, in my nose, in my hair, on my ears, legs, arms, hands, and fingers.

I couldn't bathe. The water itself was crawling with filth to infect the open sores. I tried putting lye soap on the boils, but that only seemed to irritate them more.

Finally the boils got so bad I felt like Job. They began to attack my spirit. I prayed often through those miserable nights for God to heal them. I don't know why God answers some prayers with relief and others with silence. But like Job I could only go on trusting Him. The alternatives are too bleak to consider. It wasn't long until I received my second act of kindness from the enemy; a medic gave me some sulfa pills, and in a few days the boils were gone.

6

Alcatraz

In the absolute center of Hanoi, right behind the National Ministry of Defense, is a walled, island-like prison called Alcatraz. No more than 50 x 50 feet in size, this maximal security area contains only two buildings—one housing three cells; the other housing ten. Alcatraz had been a high-security prison built by the French for their VIP prisoners.

On October 25, 1967, eleven of us with reputations as POW incorrigibles were chosen by the enemy to be transported immediately to Alcatraz. We were, for the most part, senior officers who had taken active resistance roles, establishing communications and encouraging noncooperation. The North Vietnamese isolated us in the heart of their capital to put us out of circulation and to help curtail the resistance movement. We promptly nicknamed ourselves "The Alcatraz Gang."

There was Commander Jim Stockdale from Illinois, the senior ranking naval officer whose policies in Las Vegas during the summer of '67 had been so effective; and Commander Jerry Denton from Mobile, Alabama, second senior naval officer whose great leadership organized the Zoo in '66. Both men were active communicators and aggressive leaders. Commander Harry Jenkins, Washington, D.C.; Capt. Jim Mulligan, Lawrence,

Massachusetts; and I were also senior naval officers and each had resistance as reasons for our sentence.

Air Force Captain Ron Storz was there, another effective communicator from New York, who administered Jim Stockdale's policies in Las Vegas, as was Comdr. Bob Shumaker, second pilot captured in 1965, a resister who gave the enemy nothing but trouble. Then there was Air Force Capt. George McKnight, my old roommate, and Navy Lt. George Coker. Both earned their ticket for having escaped from Dirty Bird Prison in October '67. Upon recapture they were singled out for the honor of joining us at Alcatraz.

The last two men were Major Sam Johnson from Texas, a hard resister, and Lt. Commander Nels Tanner, a navy man from Tennessee. Nels had earned his ticket to Alcatraz in a press conference in Hanoi where he "confessed" with a straight face and sincere voice that there were at least two turncoat pilots in his squadron. They were Ben Casey and Clark Kent! Of course television audiences around the world immediately recognized Doctor Casey and Superman from a popular TV show and comic-page fame and laughed that propaganda bulletin to shame.

But there was nothing funny about Alcatraz. Each cell had a cement sleeping slab and a walking area no more than four feet square. There were no windows, and the small transom-like space above the solid iron door had been very neatly secured with a steel plate. At last we knew the truth about that old refrigerator joke—when the guards closed the door, the light really did go out. In the winter the cells were refrigerator cold, and in the summer they were stifling.

To make matters worse, we spent fifteen hours a day with our legs in shackles. Every night we slept in those 10- to 20-pound leg irons. In the winter they got icy-cold beneath our thin blankets, and in summer they cooked us. We were unshackled on the Tet holiday and at Christmas, but for sixteen months we wore them almost every day.

Immediately, in spite of the handicaps, we set up a communication system. Through covert communication techniques—tapping, semaphore, quick snatches of conversation, coded notes, coughs, sneezes, and the tapping broom or sliding Ho-Chi-Minh sandals—we talked to each other every day. Soon we were sharing intimate details about each other's family life, military career, and religious faith. There may have been cement and iron walls separating each man from the next, but by now we had all learned how important each man was to the other. Our circle of friendship grew strong and intimate. I think I can honestly say, the more we knew about each man's strengths or weaknesses, the more we loved each other.

The Vietnamese tried to exploit us one against the other. They tried to get us to contribute propaganda statements or tapes, and when we refused, we were punished. The interrogation room was also used for torture; and when one of us went inside, we all suffered with him. We had no secrets, and the bonds of friendship built there will last an eternity.

By now, most of us had suffered from torture and deprivation. We received almost no medicine during our entire prison terms, and because our two daily meals consisted primarily of pumpkin or cabbage soup with a few pieces of pig fat floating on the greasy surface, our protein intake was extremely low. Therefore, our resistance to disease and infection was down; we had to be extremely careful. If we stubbed a toe, we knew we would lose a toenail. Because we received little, if any, medical assistance during those long years of prison, we had to devise home remedies.

For the ever-present diarrhea, dysentery, or flu, pieces of charcoal salvaged from a dump pile might help. For skin infections or serious cuts and scratches, we washed with lye soap and bore the irritation to achieve healing. Our intestines were crawling with worms that would work their way out through our system in surprising ways. One night Harry woke up with what he thought was a piece of string in his mouth. He pulled out a six-inch worm! Now and then the enemy would throw a red pepper into our soup. We soon discovered that the pepper cleaned out worms. When no peppers were available, we tried to steal a drink of kerosene from a lantern. That quick snort of stolen kerosene fixed the worms and almost fixed the thief who had them.

We did what we could to keep each other's spirits high. One favorite method was to sweep out messages of encouragement to the entire compound with our broom. Each morning one by one we would dump our bucket in the hole near the latrine. Jerry Denton would be the last man down, and he would sweep out the latrine area, slowly using each stroke to communicate in code.

One day in 1968 we were all believing the war must end soon; the bombing had increased, and we were looking for a sign of hope. Day by day we waited, and day by day no sign came. The morale was down when Jerry went to clean that day. We listened as he tapped, "In Thy gentle hands, we are smiling our thanks!" It was a strange message but an important reminder that in spite of our hopelessness, we could be thankful. Jerry helped me remember my blessings, though small, for gratitude was the way to defeat the power of loneliness and fear. I found, even in Alcatraz, plenty to be thankful for, and it made all the difference.

During those days I worked my mind double time to stave off the temptation to lie down and die. I built five houses in my imagination during my seven years in North Vietnam. Carefully I selected the site, then negotiated with its owner for purchase. Personally, I cleared the ground, dug the foundations, laid the cement, put up the walls, shingled the roof, and landscaped the property. After I had carefully furnished the home, I sold it, took my profit, and began the entire process once again. I'll probably never build my own home in freedom, but in solitary confinement I enjoyed the mental exercise, nail by nail, and can recall today each stage of every house I built.

I also reconstructed, day by day, my childhood in Tulsa, my marriage to Phyllis, and the growth of our family. I soon realized how insensitive I had been with my family and how preoccupied I had become with my own interests. I had dropped out of church almost immediately after marriage and left my family to develop their spiritual life on their own. One memory that especially haunted me was a trip to El Paso that I made with Phyllis and the children. I was feeling guilty for paying them so little attention, and so to compensate, I offered them money to buy any Mexican merchandise they desired. I showed John the beautiful leather goods, the elaborate stone chess sets, and the colorful peasant shirts and sandals. He chose a rather amateurish sketch of Jesus in a rough wooden frame. I had offered him anything, and when he chose that rather ugly picture, I plainly showed my disappointment. Every time in prison I recalled my thoughtless, insensitive reaction, I got a knot in my stomach.

Here my young son was already showing interest in something more than baseball and routine chores. He was sending me signals loud and clear, and I missed them. How many signals I must have missed from Phyllis, Sondra, Peggy, Barbara, as well as John. I was too busy doing "other things" to really be a dad. How I regretted those late-night cocktail parties that seemed strategic to my life. I decided in Vietnam that if I were ever free again, I would try to listen, try to understand, and try to show spiritual leadership in my home and with my family.

Every day in Alcatraz I repeated my devotional routine, my prayers, Scripture quoting, and my songs. By now I could quote about 120 hymns and Scriptures. But every day it got harder to believe we would ever really be free again. It seemed the war would never end. I remember Alcatraz as a time of loneliness and misery, constant harassment, torture, and interrogation; but I

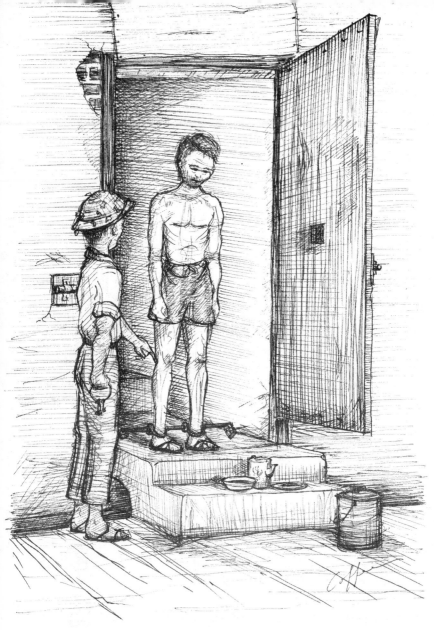

I remember Alcatraz as a time of loneliness and misery, constant
harassment, torture, and interrogation.

don't remember one of the Alcatraz Gang ever losing faith in God or in his country.

Alcatraz is the source of my saddest memory of all my POW experiences. Eleven of us went in. Only ten came back. Ron Storz, the sensitive, young, air force captain from New York, was not really well upon arrival at Alcatraz; but in spite of physical weakness, he was a real leader. His message by example was "unity over self." An able, aggressive communicator, Ron loved to tap out messages with the broom. He was an Episcopalian and a sensitive Christian brother. One day in 1969 he swept through that compound a message that was perhaps the most effective sermon I have ever heard. "Seek God here! This is where you'll find Him."

Like all of us he was probably wrestling with his increasing anxiety to get out of that miserable place and into the light again. But when freedom didn't come, he reminded us all plainly to quit sulking and get down to the important business of seeking God now, rather than waiting for some better time or place.

One day Ron swept a very different kind of message. With his broom he tapped, "God, hear my cries." We all knew Ron was very ill. He was getting weaker and his weight had dropped from around 175 pounds to just over 100. He was quite emaciated, and even the enemy was growing aware of his plight. One day Frenchy, our interrogator, approached Ron in our corridor and told him he would have to move to the larger interrogation room and out of the tiny cell.

Ron argued loudly to stay with his friends. All he wanted was a roommate. After months of solitary confinement, he needed to talk to someone. The enemy had permitted Ron no letters from home and now even though they knew his mental and physical strengths were depreciating rapidly they would not give him a roommate. They tried to separate Ron from the rest of us, but Ron would not go.

Finally, Frenchy had to explain that in a few short hours his friends would be leaving Alcatraz and that he would have to remain. The Vietnamese were not hard on Ron that night. They did not make him move. All of us had heard it. Frenchy said tonight we would be moving out. After almost two years in Alcatraz, we would be leaving. That night we moved, one at a time, into a waiting truck, past Ron in his lonely cell. It was one of the hardest moments of my life as a POW. The worst part of being a prisoner is the helplessness to reach out and lift up another man in need. We couldn't even say good-by. They had the burp guns. They had the power.

War is like that for both sides. I'm sure the enemy had families who bled and died. I'm sure the enemy cried when loved ones went away and did not return. I'm sure they, too, were tempted to give way to anger and hatred. But revenge is God's business. Anger and hatred can destroy us all. When it's over, we must try to forget and to forgive.

We never stopped praying for Ron and for his family, but we knew we would probably never see him again until that day God chose to reunite the Alcatraz Gang in another world free from such pain and sorrow.

7

Stardust

As the enemy's trucks carted us away from Alcatraz that cold, winter night in December 1969 we dared to hope that the nightmare was ending and that we were going home. But when the blindfolds were removed and we were standing once again beneath the walls of the Hanoi Hilton, our hope died. The guards escorted us past New Guy Village and Heartbreak Hotel, and the iron doors of Las Vegas swung open to receive us once again.

Everything seemed the same. The place was as bleak and cold and filthy as ever. The waters of the Sands still ran thick with sewage, alive with parasites of every description. Men were still crowded into cells not big enough for animals, and the pigs still slopped in troughs around the Mint, my wretched home in '67.

I felt agony and anger as the turnkey slammed that iron door and I found myself once again in solitary confinement. This time my home was a cramped cell in Cell Block Stardust. It was like repeating a bad dream. Would it all begin again, the long interrogations, the threats, the torture? Had nothing changed?

Little by little it dawned that something had changed at Las Vegas. There were no agonizing cries in the night from torture rooms. There were no fresh rope burns, no new broken bones. Physical torture had ended, or so it seemed. The rumor spread. Hope mounted.

Soon the Cat himself confirmed our suspicions. Major Bai, chief North Vietnamese staff officer and supervisor of the various prison-camp commanders throughout Hanoi, told Jerry Denton and me that prisoners would no longer suffer physical torture and abuse. Speaking quietly and in broken English, his former cocky manner subdued, his spirit broken, the Cat explained the reason.

"I have misinterpreted the will of the Vietnamese people," he told us. "For four thousand years the policy of the people has been humane and lenient treatment toward prisoners. I have misread and misinterpreted the party's will. I have gone before the people and confessed." Soon after his strange confession, Major Bai disappeared from the Hoa Lo prison complex, and, to my knowledge, he has not been seen again.

Was the Cat speaking truth? Would the torture end? Why had the policy been changed? With growing excitement, the questions raced through our minds. We didn't know about the volunteer organizations in America that were working so hard through bracelets and bumper stickers to keep our plight before the public. We hadn't heard about the strenuous efforts on our behalf by the world's leaders, the International Red Cross, and patriotic organizations all across our country. We couldn't know about the thousands of letters and cables the North Vietnamese were receiving from the little people all around the world. We only knew that the Cat had spoken to a few of us, and the word needed to be spread.

However, most senior officers were still living in solitary confinement, and it would be no small task to get such news spread quickly and convincingly from our cell block to other cell blocks within the Hanoi Hilton and throughout Hanoi to the other prisons: the Plantation, the Son Tay Camps Faith and Hope, and the Zoo. But to get the word out was imperative, because the enemy was still using threats of torture and coercion to get us to submit and to cooperate in its propaganda campaign.

Alan Paton once wrote in his *Cry the Beloved Country* that men are held "by chains of fear and fear of chains." We had to put the prisoners' minds at rest. We didn't need to fear. Resistance would not be met with torture. Fortunately, the Alcatraz Gang had gone to work immediately to establish lines of communication, and it wasn't long until the word was out.

The Asian flu was spreading through Hanoi about this time, and at least 75 to 80 percent of the prisoners in the camp came down with high fever and dysentery. For three days I couldn't move off my plank bed. Then, just as I was getting strong enough to sit up and stare another bowl of rotten-cabbage soup in the face, a guard opened my door, and in walked Harry Jenkins. It was Wednesday night, February 25, 1970, and during more than four years of captivity, I had lived outside of solitary confinement for only twenty-seven wonderful days with George McKnight. During all my years in prison, I had not been more than thirty feet away from Commander Jenkins, and we knew each other intimately through our covert communication efforts. But after four years, to shake his hand and know that when the turnkey walked away, I would be face-to-face with another human being—and not alone—was something else!

We talked nonstop for several days and nights. It may have been in whispers, but the sound of our voices was like music. Sometimes we would go for years without using our voices in prison. Several times I honestly was afraid that when I tried to speak again, nothing would happen. But during those next thirty days with Jenkins it happened around the clock. Even with the thousands of words we got off during those first days, few were wasted. Fighting doesn't end because a man's plane is shot down or his squad is captured. The war isn't over for a man thrown into a high security, escape-proof prison. The prisoner of war works round the clock to beat the enemy, and Harry and I had much to accomplish in the short time we had together.

A prisoner in the Desert Inn cell block in Las Vegas was hav-

I followed last, lagging behind just long enough to whisper the code.

ing trouble getting "on the line." He didn't know the code and needed tutoring; this was our chance to teach him letter by letter how to communicate. Fortunately Waldo, one of our regular camp guards, was not too bright. With Waldo's help we could get the new man "on the line" and mend the broken communications link.

The plan was simple. On our daily walks to the latrine dumping area, Harry would try walking so close to Waldo that the poor, unsuspecting guard would never see me lagging back just long enough to whisper the code, bit by bit, to the new man in Desert Inn.

It worked! The sight must have caused a lot of stifled laughter to any prisoner who might have been watching this charade through transom slit or barred window. First came Waldo, shuffling along, mumbling to himself. Then Harry followed, literally tripping over Waldo's heels, clicking our honey pots together now and then, and making sufficient heavy breathing and noisy footsteps for the two of us. I followed last, lagging behind just long enough to whisper the code, then running madly to catch up before Waldo got the wiser. He never suspected a thing, and in a matter of days the new man was "on the line."

We assigned ourselves, or were assigned, important tasks to accomplish every day. Surveillance of the camp area became an art form. We determined to know the perimeters of each prison with considerable more detail than the enemy knew them. Every POW's trip to an interrogation room became a mission to sight, memorize, and report back on specific areas of the prison. We knew every rusty nail that might support a rope or wire. We knew which windows were barred and which were large enough for a man to crawl through. We knew the location of every cell, cell block, guard post, administration building, even the immediate area outside the walls.

Although escape was always in the back of our minds, it wasn't the primary goal of disciplined surveillance. Knowing the intricate details of the prisons had practical day-by-day importance for survival. For example, in July of '66 a new guy, Lt. Commander Cole Black, a neighbor of mine in San Diego, was spotted through a crack in the door in a cell in the Zoo. No one knew that he was down, yet somehow the enemy had him. He wasn't "on the line," didn't know the code. We had to get it to him.

On an earlier surveillance trip, a fellow prisoner had noticed that a clothesline was attached to one end of the new man's cell. Prisoners hanging clothes could whisper the code to Commander Black in segments until he knew it all. From that moment a lot of prisoners used filthy water to wash clothes that would have been better off dirty so that piece by piece the new guy could learn the code and get "on the line." The effort required elaborate preparation and coordination by three different cells, but once again surveillance paid off.

By the time we left that vile prison complex, I could sit down and draw an intricate, detailed description of the entire prison, many sections of which I had never even seen. Surveillance and covert communication helped defeat the enemy's painstaking effort to keep us isolated, confined, and hidden. Isolation is a terrible weapon. Strong men have been destroyed by it. I was constantly amazed at how the loneliness could break my own willingness to resist. Physical torture may have ended, but there is still no torture worse than years of solitary confinement. Our successful struggle to communicate with each other turned a group of prisoners, isolated by cement and steel walls, into a community, and through that community we survived.

Harry Jenkins and I were separated four months later. I spent the last six months of 1970 living alone again. The days after one loses a friend are the hardest days to bear. Immediately I had to develop all kinds of new mental projects to fill those lonely hours. I worked for months trying to recall the names and faces of every member of my high-school graduating class. While trying to remember faces forgotten twenty-four years, I was reminded again how generous God has been in giving man wonderful and mysterious powers.

At night, exhausted from my mental search for high-school friends and asleep at last, I would suddenly awaken with a new name or face recalled. While my body slept, my brain worked on. This computerlike miracle between our ears seems so strong a proof of a loving Father behind creation. In spite of my problems in prison, it became easier to thank God for His gifts. It almost seemed that the less possessions I had, the more significant His really worthwhile gifts became to me.

We didn't have much in the way of possessions during those first five years in prison—a blanket, a pajamalike prison suit, a drinking cup, a honey bucket, and a mosquito net. We had no books, no Bible (every New Year's Eve for seven years, I repeated my resolution that after my release I would never be without a Bible again), no newspapers. (In fact, I didn't learn that Neil Armstrong had walked on the moon until three years after his return!) We missed pencils and notebooks, and radios and soft pillows, but most of all, I think, we missed decent food —let alone home cooking. Our food was basically the same those first five years. We ate two meals a day. It was either rice or hard French bread with a liter of boiled water. Also, we had a bowl of soup, the rotten cabbage or seaweed varieties, and in the summer sewer greens, little green shoots that grew around sewers. These were thrown on top of the soup, with a piece or two of sowbelly—all fat—plus skin and hair. We didn't eat very high off the hog; you can believe that! Now and then we would get a fish head or tail, all scrap, maybe a hamster, and, if lucky, dog meat or fragged duck. (The men called it "fragged duck" because the duck had been cleavered—bones and all—into tiny fragments.)

Most of what we ate I considered inedible before prison, but meat—even dog meat—is the prime source of protein, and to survive we ate it, hair and all. On special days the enemy might prepare a very edible meal. Usually photographers would be on hand to use our enjoyment of the meal as propaganda, but we all gave in and ate gratefully. On rare occasions a package from home would get through. Everyone would share this unexpected bonanza. If a man got a bottle of vitamins, everyone in camp would get a vitamin that day until the bottle was empty. Our motto was UNITY BEFORE SELF. We shared and in the sharing kept each other alive.

It's important to remember that the North Vietnamese are terribly poor people. Our bombing and blockades had cut down all supplies, including foodstuff; and though we suffered extraordinarily, we weren't the only ones who went to bed hungry in that land.

I lost more than forty pounds in captivity, and I was skinny when captured. The last two years the food increased in quality and quantity. I gained back twenty pounds primarily because the enemy initiated a third meal—the Vietnamese version of breakfast—a cup of hot powdered milk or sugar and a piece of bread. If the war had ended three years earlier, you would have seen a different crew of survivors—skinnier, leaner, and meaner perhaps. That added breakfast those last few years did a lot to mellow us and to fatten us for release.

Perhaps the greatest boost to our morale came during the last few weeks in Stardust. November 21, 1970, the prison and its immediate environs exploded into activity—trucks, troops, and tanks moving in all directions. We saw lights in the night and new construction in the prison. By the evening of November 24, more than two hundred downed American air crews had moved into the western section of the Hanoi Hilton, trucked there blindfolded from camps all around Hanoi.

Finally, we learned what happened that historic night, November 21, 1970. Colonel Bull Simons and his group of seventy had invaded North Vietnam in jet-powered helicopters to search out and rescue prisoners. They landed in the area of Son Tay, about fifteen miles west of Hanoi, and besieged a POW camp there. Unfortunately, at that time there were no Americans being held in that area; but when the word got out that such a mission had taken place, we had concrete evidence that we were not forgotten—that our nation was really trying to bring us home. After that invasion things were never the same at the Hanoi Hilton.

8

Camp Unity

Pacing my 4 x 8 foot cell in Cell Block Stardust at the Hanoi Hilton, my mind busy recalling a verse of some forgotten hymn, I suddenly remembered this was Christmas Day. My memory flashed to our home in San Diego at Christmas. It had been six years since our family had gathered together around a tree loaded with gifts for a day of food and fun. I pictured Phyllis carrying the Christmas turkey to our table and ten-year-old John jumping up and down, begging to carve it. My daughters Sondra, Peggy, and Barbara, looking beautiful and proud, had set the table in our Christmas finest. How we had enjoyed those feasts together! Earlier that day the children had torn into our endless pile of presents, heaping the torn wrappings into a growing pile, squealing with feigned surprise over gifts they had spied out earlier, hidden in closets and underneath their parents' bed.

Six years had passed since our family had been together around the Christmas tree, and my eyes filled with tears prompted by those happy memories; but in my cell that day, I was astounded to realize how unaware I had been of the real meaning of Christmas on those days so long ago. Oh, I knew it was Christ's birthday and I knew He was God's Son—Someone very special. That was nice, but it took prison to help me to see what Christmas really meant. All the world was a prison, and every man a prisoner until He came. On that night two thousand years ago, God had invaded my world. Like Colonel Bull Simons and his brave group of seventy, God came down to search out and rescue prisoners. Baby Jesus, lying in a filthy manger, surrounded by the smells and sounds of the barnyard, was more than a cute, cuddly kid, as Christmas cards portray Him. He was God Himself come down. He would grow to manhood. He would risk His life to break open prison doors. He would die to set men free. Christmas Day would be the beginning of freedom for men who would believe. I spent that day thinking of the freedom I felt in Christ and wishing to be free to celebrate His birth again with my family.

That Christmas night my devotional reveries were disturbed by the sounds of guards entering Las Vegas, throwing open cellblock doors. Without warning all of us in Las Vegas were herded one-by-one out of that stinking place and into one large area we promptly dubbed Camp Unity. Talk about a celebration! We laughed and hugged and chatted excitedly. We had no idea why we were together or what it meant—but we were together. And if it were only for a night, we would enjoy it.

Up to that point I had spent fifty-eight months in solitary confinement with only a few short breaks; that is 1,740 days alone. Other men had spent over four years in solitary, too; and here we were, milling about in a big room, shaking hands with men we had known and loved for years—men we knew intimately, yet had never seen. For years it had taken as much as twenty-four hours to get a message around that crowd and twenty-four hours to get the answer back. Men had risked and suffered much to communicate a sentence in a day. Now, suddenly, we were face-to-face. Everybody wanted to talk to everybody else simultaneously. It was a wild and happy Christmas night.

Here we were milling about in a big room, shaking hands with men we had known and loved for years.

The enemy had gathered all the downed American aircrews into this one prison. There were nine cell blocks around Camp Unity. Each of them had about forty men. One of the first things we did in Camp Unity was to begin regular church services in every cell block. In the past five years we had sent covert devotional messages from cell to cell, but now we would sit down and worship together in groups. We sang a hymn, someone quoted Scripture, another prayed, a third man shared a meditation. Everything was from memory. There were no hymnbooks, no Bibles, no pews. The service was imperfect but beautiful and very important to our morale. Almost every prisoner entered into worship wholeheartedly.

The enemy immediately decided that church services would be interrupted and the worshipers disbanded. To the North Vietnamese, most of whom didn't speak our language, this was a political meeting. Asians, friends and foes alike, use singing and speeches in group gatherings like our church services for political purposes. Our service was immediately suspected of being a dangerous rallying point. Of course, we tried to explain that we had assembled simply to worship God. We even invited the English-speaking enemy officers to join us in our service so that they would convince our guards that this was church and nothing else. They refused.

The pressure to discontinue worship mounted. Though the torture had ended, threats were made. Reprisals were promised. The guards would heckle us, trying to drown out the words of those who led—but we refused to give up our right to worship God. It seemed the most natural and proper issue on which to take our stand. We enjoyed this new taste of communal life, but we would risk the privilege to keep our right to worship together. A showdown was inevitable.

The cell blocks in Camp Unity were divided more or less by seniority. I was in the senior cell block during that first wonderful month of communal living. We knew that if the enemy had to be confronted with our right to hold church services on Sunday morning, that confrontation would be our task. So, for two weeks we invited the Vietnamese (those who spoke English and their officers) to join us in church to see what we were doing and to prove we were doing nothing to endanger the internal security of their prison. They continued to refuse, and by the third Sunday the confrontation was imminent.

February 7, 1971, all the guards in camp hung around the senior cell block. This was it. George Coker, the young navy lieutenant from Alcatraz, was acting as the chaplain in our cell block that Sunday. He was the junior officer in the building, yet it was his morning to conduct the service and address the group. We had a small choir to sing a familiar hymn. I was going to recite the 101st Psalm, and Lt. Colonel Risner was going to lead the benediction.

As we began the morning's hymn, the doors opened, and the guards poured in. We had already decided to continue the worship at any cost, and we all looked straight at Lieutenant Coker as he spoke. The guards tried to keep him quiet. They argued and cursed angrily; Lieutenant Coker just kept talking.

Then it was my turn. The guards tried to interfere in every way they could short of physical abuse. I continued quoting Psalm 101; they kept yelling for me to stop. The choir sang and Lt. Colonel Risner gave the benediction prayer. By now the guards were embarrassed and angry and determined to have revenge.

The service ended, but no one moved except the guards who stalked out angrily. The "church riot" had been heard by everyone, and we all waited for the ax to fall. Fifteen minutes passed before the guards returned. Then they reentered Cell Block 7 and called out Lieutenant Coker, Lt. Colonel Risner, and myself; the three of us were herded into the courtyard just outside the cell-block gate.

Everyone watched as we nervously awaited our fate. I must

confess the memories of past torture and abuse were still vivid in my mind. What did the enemy have planned? What would that short service cost us?

As we stood, each alone with his own questions, each handling his own anxieties, a fantastic thing happened. Somewhere in Cell Block 7 someone began to sing the first verse of "The Star-Spangled Banner." It had not been sung (on penalty of severe punishment) for five long years, but somewhere, someone was singing it. Others joined in. Before one line had passed, all of Cell Block 7 was alive with that song; and by the time the officer returned to march us away, it seemed that every cell block in Camp Unity was singing.

O say, can you see, by the dawn's early light,
What so proudly we hailed at the twilight's last gleaming,
Whose broad stripes and bright stars, through the perilous fight,
O'er the ramparts we watched were so gallantly streaming?
And the rockets' red glare, the bombs bursting in air,
Gave proof through the night that our flag was still there;
O say, does that Star-Spangled Banner yet wave
O'er the land of the free and the home of the brave?

There was a lump in my throat as we were marched away from our friends, the sounds of the national anthem ringing through that old French prison in Hanoi. Of course, we had no idea where we were going or what we would find when we got there. So that march and the months that followed were torturous. Alone again after a taste of communal living, locked in Heartbreak-sized small cells, forced to communicate covertly again was torture, indeed. But we had conquered! From that Sunday until the prisoners were released, church services were held throughout the prison with little, if any, interference from the enemy.

Junior officers remained in communal-living status for the rest of their imprisonment, but the senior officers were eventually locked into what we called Building Zero. When Lt. Colonel Risner and I arrived in Zero, we found small cells, appalling filth, and extreme heat. At least ten men were in irons; sometimes two on a bunk. They weren't permitted out and had to perform all their bodily functions with their legs shackled to the slab. Lt. Colonel Risner and I were not in irons, so we set about to clear the guards, begin communications, and raise the spirits of the men who suffered there.

Here in Building Zero—code name Rawhide—I talked for the first time through closed doors to Col. John Flynn, the senior prisoner in North Vietnam. John is an extremely strong yet sensitive man and proved an outstanding leader. He had been informed of the church riot in Cell Block 7 and had decided for us to have church in Building Zero. Remember, Rawhide imprisoned men in cells, isolated from each other, shackled in solitary or small groups; but Colonel Flynn knew how much even a brief time of prayer and worship would mean.

We plotted carefully to clear the area and conduct the service. Robby Risner prayed a magnificent prayer, and I quoted imperfectly but with enthusiasm, the 101st Psalm; Jack Finley, an air force lieutenant colonel, whistled "Ave Maria." I don't remember hearing anything so beautiful in my life as Jack's version of that great old Catholic song. We worshiped regularly in Rawhide in spite of barriers of brick and cement; in fact, we even formed a choir with individual members separated by their cells. Those men could really sing. We were all denominations. All the things that could have divided us didn't matter in Building Zero. We were united in our faith in God and in each other. Nothing else mattered.

March 19, 1971, I moved into a 6 x 7 foot cell with my old and great friends Harry Jenkins, Jim Stockdale, and Jerry Denton. There were only two concrete bunks, no ventilation, no windows; we were four men locked together in a room with little or no space to walk; it was hot and filthy and crowded. Each of us carefully organized his daily schedule, trying to be sensitive to each other without giving up the discipline, physical and mental, long established. It was easy to be irritable. None of us had any saintly inclinations. There were harsh words and embarrassing silences, but we were united against a common enemy. The enemy was more than ignorant and abusive guards. The enemy was loneliness and fear and death. We would survive, and we would survive with honor. Any anger or impatience between us quickly dissolved in our common task—to survive—and in our love for one another.

I never stopped doing my daily routines. Some part of each day was filled with Scripture recall. We worked together to find more. Every man found some floating in his memory and contributed to the pile. Daily I would pray for my family, and renew my resolve to make my commitment to Christ, and join my family's church upon return to freedom. In prison I firmly believed that there was a God who loved me and was working in my life. I cannot explain with reason or proof why my faith was central to my survival. But it was. Other men went in unbelieving and came out the same. I didn't, and for me my faith in Christ made all the difference.

Somehow we all survived that long hot summer of '71, and in September, nine of us were moved into Cell Block 8. These were the nine senior officers under Colonel Flynn. We had already organized the cell blocks into a complete, sophisticated command structure much like an air force wing command, with Colonel Flynn as the wing commander. Every building in our covert communications system was given a code name. If the enemy intercepted our traffic, he had no idea what it meant, who originated it, or who was to receive the message. Cell Block 8 became our headquarters. We gave it code name BLUE. The wing commander's code was SKY. So any man who received a message from SKY BLUE knew that Wing Commander Flynn was sending it from headquarters.

My responsibility as wing communications officer was to keep communications open, to keep every man "on the line." If we could keep every man alert and informed, he would not fall to angry interrogators pushing for propaganda statements or military information. When one man went to interrogation, we all knew immediately and sent waves of support in his direction. We were working at maximal resistance and had one united goal: **RELEASE WITH HONOR.** We wanted to leave that place as men, standing tall and proud, not broken and bent. Our goal was to produce men who had more than survived—men who had conquered.

Besides promoting mental activity, the wing worked to get us back in good physical health. Every man ate everything he could. Exercise programs were part of the wing's organization, and even those men with broken bones worked hard to get and keep their bodies in shape. Cellmates would walk their rooms for miles a day in line, do push-ups, sit-ups, and run in place. The organization worked to get us ready for that day we hoped lay ahead—*Freedom!*

Remember, all our communications were still covert. It took time and effort. The enemy knew of this underground wing organization and did everything short of physical torture to chop communications and kill our system. But the enemy could not stop us. It was a great and exciting effort on the part of many men that kept our wing command strong and effective during those last long months of imprisonment.

Moving then, in September of '71, was a big move up for all of us. It was the first time in six years that I had been in a cell with an open window—there were bars, but it was a window. It wasn't dark in that cell, and now and then breezes made breathing bearable. In fact, often in the daytime we were allowed into a small

12 x 12 foot courtyard area for two or three hours a day; for the first time in 75 months I felt the sunshine on my face. The walls around me were 15 feet high and broken glass was imbedded in their surface, but I could look up past those walls and see the sun. It was a glorious sight.

We even had a kind of Vietnamese toilet. It was only a hole with a squatting place, but it was a luxury. I still dreamed of beautiful white toilet seats, white pillow cases, a soft bed with clean sheets, and chocolate-covered peanuts! We weren't home yet, and the conditions, though improved, were still frightful by any standards. There were still the mosquitoes, the insects, the lice, the parasites that lived on and in our bodies, and the rats that surprised us by nibbling on our toes at night.

As I was stretched out on my hardwood bed in Cell Block 8 one night, I was awakened by the feeling that something was gnawing on the end of my thumb. It was a rat the size of a small opossum; and when I yelled, I scared him as much as he had scared me. Unfortunately, we were both trapped in my mosquito net. We rolled together biting and bashing, but with the help of my cellmates, I finally did him in. Those experiences look funny to me now. They didn't then!

My friends in prison had all been Americans until Cell Block 8. There I met three outstanding men from Thailand and one South Vietnamese pilot, allies shot down, captured, and imprisoned like ourselves. The South Vietnamese could speak English, French, Spanish and Thai. He was a brilliant young man, an able friend and conspirator against the enemy. The Thais were industrious and friendly, but they couldn't speak English, so at first we couldn't communicate. I must confess at first we were suspicious of them because we didn't know who or what they were. As trustees who worked around the compound, they had access to all our secrets. We watched and waited and wondered if they were friends or foes. Then one day the South Vietnamese pilot spoke out.

"Commander, do you trust me?" he asked through the wall that separated us.

I didn't hesitate. "Of course, I trust you. We are allies. You were shot down fighting with us. Why shouldn't I trust you?"

He paused and then continued. "If you trust me," he said, "know this; the three Thais are true and loyal friends. You must trust them too."

That ended the matter, and immediately we set about teaching the Thais English and the code. They learned them both, and we were constantly amazed and grateful for their skills and friendship. We always ended our communications in code throughout the wing sending R.W.H.S.W.D.G.B.U!, which translates: RELEASE WITH HONOR. STICK WITH DICK. GOD BLESS YOU!

The Thais were Buddhists, and I was surprised to get a message one day that ended with the part of that sign-off that they could not really understand: GOD BLESS YOU! On Christmas and Easter I had spent time tapping out the meaning of these holidays. Perhaps they had understood.

We worked hard those last months of 1972, contacting new people, maintaining our organization, and operating covertly inside of the Hoa Lo prison complex. People may wonder why we didn't attempt escape. Unfortunately, they believe that prison life is like the world of "Hogan's Heroes," that slapstick television series featuring imaginary American prisoners in World War II.

There had been at least two attempts by Americans to escape from North Vietnamese prisons. George McKnight and Lieutenant Coker earned their way to Alcatraz through their escape from Dirty Bird, October 1, 1967. Ed Atterberry and John Dramesi escaped from the Zoo, May 10, 1969, but were recaptured shortly and brought back to that prison in the same truck. There they shook hands, wished each other luck and were parted. No one has ever seen Ed Atterberry again.

There were heavy reprisals for escape attempts; and though we thought about it, diagrammed the area, and made various plans in '71 and '72, our plans were never tried. We were locked in cells, inside of cell blocks, inside of a series of jagged glass and hot-wire walls, in a massive prison with inner and outer walls, with twenty-four-hour guard surveillance, in the heart of the capital city. Even if a prisoner survived an escape he would have no friends and no place to hide in downtown Hanoi. So, until 1973 we waited for the miracle of freedom to happen from the outside. One day we would be taken through the gates of the Hanoi Hilton to freedom or to death. Until that day we had to pray and work and wait.

9

Gia Lam Airport, Hanoi

On January 31, 1973, it seemed our prayers for freedom had been answered. Still living in Cell Block 8, we had learned of the agreement signed in Paris on January 28. As an important part of that agreement, the United States had demanded that the North Vietnamese deliver into prisoner hands a copy of the protocol describing our release. When we heard the news, Colonel Flynn asked the nine of us to stop our work so that we could thank God for His mercy. We had hoped and prayed for so long; now freedom was in sight. We didn't say much. I suppose we didn't have to. A look of relief and joy was on everybody's face. I am sure the good Lord could look into our hearts and see the gratitude that was there as we prayed.

I had never prayed much after dropping out of church twenty years before—never with Phyllis. But in prison many of my most important memories are associated with prayer. There were frightening prayers; for example, the prayer of thanks I whispered dangling one thousand feet over enemy land just after my jet exploded only yards before me and only moments before I was captured. There were dramatic prayers like the one Colonel Risner prayed, with the enemy cursing and yelling at him during the church riot of '71. There were prayers of great sadness like those prayers we prayed for our comrade dying and alone in Alcatraz. There were even funny prayers. One example I recall occurred in Cell Block 7. We were digging a hole between two cell blocks to help us communicate by voice between them; unfortunately the hole had to be dug with the diggers lying in the latrine. The smell was terrible. One day at grace John Dramesi prayed, "God, help them get that hole dug through the latrine before it's my turn to dig again." Talking to God became a natural process, like eating and breathing.

There were eloquent prayers by men like Commander Chuck Gillespie or Col. Norman Gaddis or Col. Dave Winn who were strong Christians and who had obviously developed seasoned prayer lives, but praying was a new experience for me. I'm still not very good at it. Words don't come easy when I pray. But even we amateurs discovered in prison the incredibly powerful force prayer can be in our lives. I learned I could talk to God anyplace, dangling from a parachute or shackled in a cesspool. I learned He could hear me whether in worship with a crowd of men or alone in solitary confinement. I learned He understood even if I fumbled the words, spoke with rotten grammar, or asked Him to do crazy, unreasonable things.

There was a time when I might have thought that men who prayed a lot were milquetoasts or sissy types. Now I know differently. There were times I thought prayer was a silly ritual we did from guilt or pressure, an act of piety we performed in church, or family worship that really didn't have much meaning. Now I know the truth. Prayer really works! I still don't pray aloud very well. But I have tested prayer and found God hears and answers. So when Colonel Flynn, the senior officer in Vietnam, asked us to stop and pray, it seemed the right and natural thing to do.

February 6, 1973, we were moved together into a large room in Cell Block 6. It was there I met for the first time since our capture Denny Moore, a man from my old squadron, who had been shot down exactly one month before I was. I thought he was dead until I learned he was being held in a cell block next to mine. To walk up to Denny and say, "Hello! Glad you are alive," to shake hands again with old friends separated for years by iron and cement was a real thrill.

We enjoyed a lot of things about Cell Block 6. I played my first volleyball game in seven years in prison; I spent wonderful hours in long conversations with old and new friends, and we had great spiritual experiences there. We gathered for worship. Howie Dunn, a marine lieutenant colonel, led a five- or six-man choir that was terrific (by now choirs were common to all the cell blocks, and on an average Sunday one could hear hymns of praise echoing through that entire prison complex).

Norm McDaniels, a very profound and sincere, black air force officer, led the worship and preached the morning meditation. He had been in a cell block where a Bible had been available for a short time, and he quoted a psalm. Then he spoke to each of us. We knew this might be our last service in prison. His subject was right on target. Being a pilot himself, he knew that none of us had ever gone into combat thinking we would be shot down, captured and imprisoned, certainly not for seven long years. Now that release was in sight, he knew we all were asking, "Why me?" He listed the reasons many of us had already been thinking. "Am I here because I have committed some ugly sin and God is punishing me for it?" "Am I here as a test of faith, a trial by fire?" "Or is it all a mistake? I accidentally got in the way of enemy fire and now God's helping me make the best of it." Each of us had to come to terms with these questions.

As I looked into my own life, I thought, "Yes, I was a sinner," and, "Yes, this has been a test of my faith," and, "Yes, God has really helped to bring something to me from those long prison years." After all, I was shot down, a church dropout, disinterested in Christian truth. I would return to freedom aware of God and anxious to stay "on the line" with Him.

Earlier in the service we had sung the Doxology.

> Praise God from whom all blessings flow;
> Praise Him, all creatures here below;
> Praise Him above, ye heavenly host;
> Praise Father, Son, and Holy Ghost.

Norm McDaniels ended his closing prayer; the choir sang the benediction hymn:

> Hear our prayer, O Lord,
> Hear our prayer, O Lord,
> Incline Thine ear to us,
> And grant us Thy peace.

Sunday, February 11, 1973, was the end of the two-week period outlined in the protocol we had received. We arose that morning wondering if this might be the day. That afternoon the North Vietnamese chopped up eight turkeys and fed them to the 200 airmen in that prison. Having turkey was not common to everyday life. Our excitement mounted.

At sunset the guards entered our cell blocks and took us, six or seven at a time, to Heartbreak. There was a moment of fear as the first group entered that ugly place filled with so many terrible memories, but quickly our spirits soared as we were issued new clothing for release. There were 115 of us chosen for this first increment, and now we had our clothing ready and our release bags packed. Sitting around that night, unable to sleep, we felt the next day to be almost anticlimactic.

We were going to leave as we had come—*with dignity.* We would go home with honor! The torture had ended; we had kept the faith. Finally, the sun rose above Hanoi. No gong was needed to get that crew of excited airmen up and dressed for this occasion. We were going home!

By 8 A.M. we were lined up outside our cells. A guard checked off our names, and we walked out of the gates of the Hanoi Hilton. There were six buses waiting. We watched and waited as the men on stretchers were loaded and driven away towards Gia Lam Airport. Then the rest of us, less ill, wounds almost healed, climbed on board with heads high. It was the first time in seven years that I had sat in a vehicle without my hands in rear cuffs and my eyes blindfolded. I watched the prison through my window as we pulled away. It had been a kind of tomb for seven years, and now I felt resurrected from the dead, driving away to life again.

Hanoi was in ruins. It is a poverty-stricken place—hard to describe. Long years of war had taken an effective toll. The city was a mess, but the streets were alive with people. Apparently the news of our release had been broadcast over Radio Hanoi. The people lined the streets, stopped their work, and watched as we drove by. There were many friendly gestures and happy waves. Everyone was smiling, obviously aware of our great joy. We didn't smile back.

When we arrived at the airport, we didn't feel particularly joyful. There were no airplanes. The airport was bombed and gutted. On one of the few buildings that remained, a Red Cross flag was flying—the first we had seen in seven years. We unloaded the buses. Our guards told us that there would be a delay as both sides hammered out the final details of the turnover.

We stood around nervously. At first there were feeble attempts at joking about our predicament. Then we lapsed into silence. About noon the Vietnamese brought us something to drink and some stale sandwiches. We ate them, hoping this was our last meal in Vietnam. No one wanted any trouble. There was too much to lose. We wanted the release to go smoothly. Others were still in prison and our actions could affect their release.

We could see the international control teams scurrying around. There was nothing to do but wait. Suddenly the guards loaded us back on the buses and we drove towards loading ramps on the runway. A cheer went up as the first C-141 transport broke

We saluted the air force colonel standing there.

through the overcast and landed. By now each of us calculated in his mind how many men per plane and which plane we would pull. It was obvious that I would be on the second C-141. It had not appeared, and as the first plane was loaded, I just knew there would be no second plane—that I would end up driving back through Hanoi to spend more time in prison.

Then the second C-141 broke through the haze and made its final approach. Suddenly the pilot added power and went back up again. I knew perfectly well this wasn't some new form of torture, but oh, how it hurt to see that plane fly by! We sweated his second approach inch by inch; and when he was finally down, we allowed ourselves a cheer. We knew now that in minutes our nightmare would be over.

The first C-141 taxied out and took off toward Clark Air Force Base in the Philippines. Then it was our turn. An especially hated North Vietnamese officer—nicknamed Slick or Soft Soap Ferry—came to our bus with a binder containing a list of names. He was one of the most dangerous men I had ever seen, known as a consummate liar and an extortioner, guilty of torture and death, and personally responsible for a great deal of our misery. There he was, calling out names. I am sure every man that crossed the line to freedom felt a flash of bitterness as Slick called each name.

Then we were walking towards the ramp. We saluted the air force colonel standing there, and one by one we were escorted to the plane. I shivered when I finally stood inside that beautiful rescue ship. Harry Jenkins and I chose the last seat in the plane and slumped gratefully into its cushions for the long ride home.

10

San Diego

A few hours in an airplane can seem an eternity to a prisoner homeward bound. Fortunately, the first hours were filled with pleasant new sights and sounds on the C-141 that carried us. This was a medic plane, and it was manned inside by a couple of beautiful American flight nurses. We hadn't seen American women for more than seven years. I must confess that all of us, including me, just stared at them with delight as they arranged our pillows and plied us with creature comforts. Their bright smiles and sweet smells after seven years of living in an all-male prison, with the smell of death in the air, were almost too much to bear.

Early in the flight we flew over the attack carrier *Enterprise* on maneuvers in the South China Sea. An old friend, Jack Christianson, was the carrier division commander now just a few thousand feet below. There was a moment of silence as we passed that beautiful ship. There wasn't a man aboard our plane who wouldn't have given his right arm to be down there operating that great carrier. All of us were professionals, and it felt so good to be back in our own world of ships and planes and pilots.

The sleek new C-141 that was carrying us provided another source of inspiration and conversation for a bunch of old flyers who had almost lost touch with their profession—in my case, for the last seven years. In fact, the airplane, the pilot and copilot had all been commissioned after I was shot down. The copilot wasn't even in high school when I was taken captive and here he was the one chosen to fly us home! I felt a bit like Rip Van Winkle waking up in the middle of an unfamiliar world. While I had been locked away in a concrete prison cell, the world had changed. My children had grown up, graduated, married, had children of their own, and I had missed it all. Men had gone to school, won their wings, flown their missions and been given commands while I had paced beneath a prison wall. It wasn't long before the cheering and the celebrating died down, and we were left alone with our memories and our questions.

What would we face at home? Who had died? Who had gone away? Men thought of wives, sweethearts, friends, parents. Many were flying home to face divorce or death in their families. Others would require extensive hospitalization; some needed surgery. There were broken bones to be reset, teeth that needed care. Many needed counseling. We all needed rest. What tragic surprises would greet us? Could we face the coming days? Could we begin again?

What would we face in America? We had heard about the antiwar activities, the demonstrations, and marches. I felt some anger at those who had opposed the war; but I had been fighting to defend their right to oppose it. But how would they feel about me now? Would we be booed in the streets? Would our families be humiliated, our children scorned? We had no idea of what our reception would be.

It was a long flight home, but all too soon it ended. The wheels touched down on the runways of Clark Air Force Base, the Philippines. We had no idea of the reception that awaited us.

Harry and I hung back as the men deplaned. I was the last one to leave the C-141, and imagine my surprise at our reception. There was a long red carpet, a clear sign of welcome known

It wasn't long before the cheering and the celebrating died down, and we were left alone with our memories and our questions.

round the world. At the head of that carpet stood Admiral Noel Gayler, Commander in Chief of the Pacific. If we had had any fears about our reception, they ended in that bus ride to Clark Hospital. The road was lined with children and adults. They carried hand-painted signs: WELCOME HOME! GOD BLESS YOU! YOU HAVE KEPT THE FAITH! It seems like a dream now—the friendly smiles—the children waving, held high on Father's shoulders—women crying—and young people cheering.

We arrived at the hospital at dinnertime and immediately got in line. The men who had arrived on the first flight were standing in hospital pajamas and wearing LIGHT DIET tags pinned to their shirts. They were glumly receiving their bowls of soup, jello, and custard when we stepped up to order steaks, and pie, and banana splits. The flawless planning of Operation Homecoming had included special diets for us all. But we had not received our tags, and needless to say, the medical officer saw that all of us could stand the shock of good American cooking, so he tore up the light diet order and we all dug in.

For three days we remained at Clark Air Force Base, and I suspect my total amount of sleep was less than three hours in that entire period. It was time to be debriefed. The names and serial numbers we had memorized were taken down by debriefing officers and compared, one list against the other. If there were men still in prison and not on the lists, our government was determined to find them. They wanted to know everything we knew about how many Americans were still in prison. What was their condition? Who were missing? Who had died?

At last I was alone in my hospital room, and the operator on my bedside phone informed me that my call to America and my family was ready. I had received only four cards of the hundreds of letters and packages she had mailed. I had waited six years before I received that first seven-line card the enemy finally granted me. Phyllis was on the line seven thousand miles away. What would she say? How would she feel about me?

"Hello, Phyllis?"

That warm voice of the woman I love, with her slight Oklahoma drawl, was full of love and welcome. She tried to put my mind at ease that everyone was well and waiting anxiously for my return. But I could sense she was holding back. Finally, she told me of my son John's accident four years before. He had been swimming with friends near our home in La Jolla and had dived into the ocean and struck his head against a rock hidden just beneath the surface. Phyllis told me quietly, calmly that he had been permanently paralyzed from the neck down but was as smart and witty as ever and couldn't wait to see his dad. Finally, after talking briefly to my daughters and learning some happy news about my grandson, I hung up and tried to sleep.

My mind went back to George Air Force Base, Victorville, California. John was only two years old when we were stationed there. One hot summer afternoon I went with him to an ice-cream truck; we bought a half-dozen frozen popsicles. He ran excitedly in front of me back into the house. We had a powerful air cooler that kicked up quite a suction draft. As Johnny went through the door, the suction slammed it shut on his hand. I dropped those popsicles, yanked open the door, and wrapped his finger, dangling by a thread of skin, in the palm of my hand. Phyllis drove us to the emergency hospital, and the surgeon spent more than an hour sewing Johnny's little finger back on his hand.

I paced the hospital waiting room, reliving that moment, seeing the door slam, hearing his cries of pain. I would gladly have given every finger on both my hands to save my son's precious little finger. When the doctors finally came in, they said we had very little chance that he would use it again. But when a child is two years old, miracles often happen, and the finger grew back. By the time he was ten, Johnny was one great Little Leaguer.

Now he lay paralyzed from the neck down. But for a miracle, John would never move again. That night in Clark I would gladly have taken the next flight back to Hanoi and locked myself in Heartbreak if it would have given Johnny the use of his arms and legs. It was like being locked away again in solitary, powerless to change what desperately needed changing.

God had been so real to me in prison. This time when I prayed, there was no clear answer. I don't understand these things. I don't know why God seems to intervene so plainly in one event and seems so absent in another. But I refuse to let my questions overpower my faith in Him. To not believe there is a God at work in the world is a grim and unacceptable option. I do believe God is working in John's life just as he is working in mine. He has a plan for both of us. Now, John and I would have to find it together.

I don't think I slept that night. The next morning a young hospital orderly passed me the third note from one of the nurses saying she would like an interview. Security at Clark was at a maximum. We ex-POWs had determined among ourselves not to speak of prison life or conditions to anyone until all the other men were free. But this note was accompanied by a scribbled sentence from the orderly: YOU'D BETTER SEE HER, SIR. SHE'S VERY PRETTY.

So, curious, I asked the orderly to bring the nurse to the waiting room on my floor. I'll not forget that meeting. The orderly was right. Miss Ronalyn Thompson was very pretty. She also had a gift for me. It was an aluminum bracelet with my name, rank, and the date of my captivity printed on it. I'll never forget what she said when she gave me my bracelet that afternoon.

"Captain Rutledge, for many months I've worn your bracelet, without taking it off night or day. Every day I've prayed for your safe return. Now these prayers are answered. I just wanted to tell you how glad I am you're home again." Then she was gone. Later I learned that millions of Americans, young and old, from all walks of life, had been wearing ID bracelets like this one to keep the memories of the POW and MIA men clear in the public's mind and to remind them daily to pray for our safe return. I believe those prayers had everything to do with my return and, again, I am grateful.

The last leg of that journey home began February 15 as our giant transport flew towards San Diego and reunion with the ones we loved. There was so much I wanted to tell my family. There was even more I wanted to hear from them. In prison I had plenty of time to decide on the things I wanted to change in my life.

I had gone away a church dropout. I was returning transformed by what I'd seen God do in prison. I was sure that Phyllis would be happy but skeptical. In the past I hadn't even gone with her to church. Now, I wanted to be a real Christian husband and father to my family. On the plane I rehearsed what I would say.

First, I would tell her of my resolution made that torturous night in the Outhouse, when I promised God that the first Sunday of my return to freedom I would take my family to their home church. At the close of the service I would walk to the front, confess my faith in Christ, and take my responsible place as a member there with my family. In prison I had learned what it means to be isolated, struggling to build my faith alone. I had resolved never to be outside the community of Christian believers again.

Second, I had heard Colonel Flynn in a meditation at Cell 8 in Camp Unity talk about the Scripture, "Let not the sun go down upon your wrath" (Ephesians 4:26). He told how he and his wife Mary Margaret had determined in their marriage never to go to bed before an argument had been settled, the apology made, the angry words forgiven. That brief passage from God's Word really made sense to me, for often I had lain awake at night too proud to say, "I'm sorry," and both of us could feel the hurt.

That first New Year's Eve in Heartbreak Hotel I had resolved never to be without a Bible again. Those verses of God's Word that I had memorized or that I had scrounged from other prisoners' memories had been a living source of strength in my life. I was determined to begin applying God's Word in our family's life together, even in the smallest things.

Third, I can't remember ever praying with Phyllis during our entire married life. In fact, the more involved I got in my career and she in our family, the less we ever really talked with each other, let alone with God. This had to change and change fast. In prison I had worked months trying to get another man "on the line," communicating. Now I had to get my wife and family "on the line" with me. Prayer seemed the perfect way to start. So I resolved to end each day with Phyllis, talking over the day's activities and thanking God for the love we felt from each other and from Him.

Frankly, I was unsure what my wife's reaction to these resolutions might be. I determined on that long flight home to tell her the moment I landed, before we got caught up in the whirl of being together again and before my nervous pride drove me into silence.

On that plane to San Diego, flying across the Pacific Ocean, I practiced every move I would make during our reunion. This wasn't the first time we would be dramatically reunited. Phyllis was a good navy wife. We had spent much of our lifetime waiting to see each other after long tours of duty aboard a carrier or in a foreign base. No matter where I left her, she was always there waiting for me when I returned. When I would walk across the pier or runway to greet her, every reunion was the same. She would come roaring out of the crowd to embrace me in a kind of feet-off-the-ground, full-body tackle.

This time I wanted it to be different. I wanted to hold her at arm's length for one long moment, look into her eyes, tell her that I love her—and then let her tackle me. I had plans, too, for that first moment with my family. During the flight I would ask the stewardess to lend me six napkins. I was going to step off the plane, kiss Phyllis, and then hand each person in my family a napkin to kneel on. Then and there we would thank God for uniting us again. On the runway we would end this drought of prayer in our family once and for all. I had no idea that the television camera would be on us every step of the way, that all my family but Phyllis would await my arrival in the privacy of the beautiful hospital suite, or that there we would say our prayer of thanks together!

We fastened our seat belts for our final descent. The wheels touched the runway. There was a band playing, and cameras were everywhere. It seems like yesterday. I walked down the steps, saluted Admiral Joe Williams and the colors, and heard the crowd's welcome-home applause. Then out of the crowd she ran and planted her own full-body tackle on me. Her feet left the ground and almost knocked me over. All my plans to hold her at arm's length for one long moment, to tell her that I loved her, were forgotten. Thank God! Things were back to normal for the Rutledge family, but they would *never* be the same.

Part II
Phyllis Rutledge
1965-1973

II

Missing in Action

Sunday morning, November 28, 1965, my four young children and I worshiped together in the Clairemont First Southern Baptist Church of San Diego. No one remembers what happened in the service that day, but we had been inspired by the music and by the Reverend Charles W. Foley's sermon. We stopped at a supermarket nearby to pick up groceries. The children unloaded the trunk and were already in the house when our friends Jack Snyder and Merle Gorder drove into the driveway beside me. I didn't think anything strange about their visit until I saw the navy chaplain getting out of the back seat and walking toward me. Then I knew instantly. Howard was dead!

"No, no, no," I said, over and over, denying what I feared the most. I didn't faint, but my knees did give way. Immediately Merle had his arm around me, guiding me towards the house.

My tears began to flow. I wanted to be brave, a stoic navy wife, a Christian saint, but the tears came anyway. For a while there seemed to be no end of crying. As we walked in the back door, Merle was trying to comfort me.

"No, it's not that bad, Phyllis. We think he's all right. His wing-man saw a chute before the plane exploded."

Inside the back door my oldest daughter Sondra, fifteen,

approached and put her arm around me. The look in her face told me that she knew. There was no need to explain. My tears kept falling. I wanted to stop and gather the family around. I wanted to explain calmly and quietly that Daddy had been shot down and was missing in action, but no words came. The older children knew without being told. John, twelve, disappeared immediately into his bedroom, and Peggy, seven, and Barbara, six, were too young to really understand.

Soon, Merle's wife Kay and Jennie Speer, another family friend, dropped by. Within minutes it seemed the house was filled with people. Pastor Foley was there and folks from the church, navy friends and neighbors. Their eyes were wet, their faces reflected how deeply they shared our anguish.

As if walking in a daze, I found myself fixing refreshments, making coffee and hopeful conversation with my friends and neighbors. I was in a state of shock, answering the door, putting flowers into vases, thanking people for their concern, and somehow carrying on.

I was too busy to notice that John had not come out of his room. He was all alone in there and really suffering. Until the last few years, John had felt his dad had always favored the girls in our family. Recently, through their common interest in Little League, John and his dad had become good friends. Now, his father was missing in action. In my preoccupation with the house filled with company, I never went near his bedroom door, and still, today, deeply regret letting him face his sadness alone.

The crowd of friends, the noisy kitchen, the little girls playing at my feet made it seem almost like any other day. Then the sun went down. My body began to ache with tiredness but my dear, thoughtful friends just would not go away. I wanted desperately to be alone, to have a moment by myself to think it through. Then, at last they were gone. The kids were asleep. I walked into our bedroom and slumped down on the bed.

The first thing I noticed was Howard's picture smiling down

on me. I took the picture off the wall and held it close asking all those endless questions countless military wives have always asked.

Is he alive? Is he lying wounded somewhere in the jungle? Was he captured, even executed, or is he locked up already in an enemy prison somewhere? Will he survive?

Looking into the dark brown eyes on that photograph, I knew Howard was in the hands of God. There was nothing I could do about him but hope and pray. The real question to face now was how could we survive? In the rooms nearby were four young children who needed a father's love and attention. In the bedroom file were piles of papers, insurance policies, wills and records I could not begin to understand. In my kitchen desk were all the bills accumulating in his absence that he could straighten out in one long frantic evening when he returned. But now he wasn't coming back. I had to face those problems alone.

Being alone was nothing new. The career military wife spends a large part of her life alone. When Sondra was born, Howard was practicing jet landings on a carrier somewhere in the Pacific. When John was born, Howard was standing watch for a good friend whose basement had been flooded. When Peggy was born, my husband was stationed on a ship deployed in the Mediterranean. I've spent half my life—or so it seemed that night—waiting for him to come home and straighten out the messes I had made. Now, I didn't have a husband to take care of me or my messes. This time he wasn't coming home.

12

Despair

The morning after we learned that Howard had been shot down over North Vietnam we all made brave attempts to go on living. I fixed the children breakfast and sent them to school. I put on the coffeepot, sat down to read the morning paper, and the headlines shouted out the news again.

LOCAL NAVY PILOT—MISSING IN ACTION

For the third time in less than twenty-four hours, I was crying. To be honest, I wasn't crying only for Howard. I was also crying for Howard's wife—me. I felt lonely and deserted and afraid I couldn't handle those next long days ahead.

Then I remembered the night only eight weeks before when Howard sat me down on our bed, took out a household ledger from his briefcase and a whole notebook of instructions. Patiently, he told me how to pay bills, insurance premiums, car payments, and the like. It probably sounds silly, but this was one of the most beautiful nights of our marriage, sitting on our bed at midnight with papers spread in all directions, talking business. For the first time in our life together, he had really sat down to share all these things with me.

Maybe he had a premonition. His squadron had been flying

round-the-clock missions over North Vietnam. Several of his friends had been killed or captured. Three days before, his father had died and Howard had been forced to think of death and those whom death left behind. Apparently, Howard was trying to prepare me.

The next morning he flew to Travis Air Force Base and took a trans-Pacific flight to catch his ship. Now he was gone, and I had the ledger.

It's hard to be the head of a household with no real preparation. I started dating Howard when I was just fourteen, and he was a senior in high school. Dependence set in early. He made almost all the decisions. Even when he was stationed on a ship halfway round the world, I knew I could call him or write a letter and ask how to handle this or settle that. Now he couldn't tell me what to do.

Fortunately, in the days and months ahead, there was little time to waste regretting. The children were growing up fast, and I had to be both mom and dad to all of them. Sondra was a teen-ager with boyfriends and dates to think about. Helping her through those awkward teen-age years was an awesome responsibility. I've always been too easygoing. Howard had always disciplined the children. He made the rules. He enforced them. Now with Howard gone, it was my task to get my daughters through. Fortunately, I had been a teen-age girl once and had some experience to fall back on.

Raising John was something else. He was a wonderful boy, and like his father he was full of energy and strong-willed. He was often in trouble for his temper. John was lonely and angry. He missed his father very much and needed a man in his life.

I knew how he felt. I needed a man in my life, too. But Howard was not dead. He was missing. So, I was not a wife. I was not a widow. I was nothing. I still loved Howard and never thought once of ending our marriage. So John, Sondra, the little girls, and their unhappy mother would just have to wait and see what happened next.

I got really despondent during those first two years. I would pray and pray and nothing would happen. Often I would ask God, "Just let me have anything to know that Howard is alive and that all of this suffering is good for something." It seemed my prayers went unanswered.

There were some little answers we clung to along the way, hoping that God had heard our prayers. For example, my mother-in-law received an envelope with a foreign tea bag inside. It was addressed to Howard's dad who had passed away just before Howard had been shot down. We wondered if someone was trying to send us a message. I knew if Howard were trying to communicate in code, it might possibly be from the Bible. So, scratching at straws, I looked up *tea* in our Bible concordance. I found one Scripture in the Book of Haggai. The verse included such lines as "I have just enough to eat to keep from being hungry. I have just enough clothing to keep from being cold." That fit our idea of prison perfectly so our hopes soared. Then I realized that Howard hadn't read the Bible in years. Surely he wouldn't begin using it with a passage from an obscure Old Testament book like Haggai!

Finally, we sent the bag to navy authorities who reported back that some crackpot was sending them around indiscriminately to other families.

I was really desperate. It seemed that God had abandoned us. Our church attendance and our spirits fell.

Howard and I were both reared in loyal Southern Baptist households. In our homes, as children, it was family tradition to attend church every time the church doors opened. We would go to Sunday school faithfully and stay for morning worship. Sunday nights the family would all go back for choir practice and Baptist Training Union. On Wednesday nights we went to

Bible study and prayer meeting, while Thursday nights we often joined the evangelism visitation teams.

But something happened when Howard and I got married. Stationed at Pensacola, Howard only went to church three or four times and then dropped out completely. Every time I asked him to join us at church, he would answer, "Not today, Honey. I'm too tired," or "I think I'll just stay at home and read the paper," or "There's a ball game on TV, and it's my only chance to relax and see one."

He was never sarcastic, nor did he try to get me to stop going. He just lost interest himself. Howard's career was really climbing. He said he couldn't be active in church the way he should be and still be a good fighter pilot. He got active in the happy-hour cocktail circuit on Friday nights and eventually threw off all the constraints his parents had enforced during those teen-age years.

We never had liquor in our homes as children. We never went to shows on Sundays, never even played cards, and any kind of swearing was rewarded with a mouthful of soap or a switching. Now, Howard was boss in his own family, and he rebelled against his strict Oklahoma Baptist background.

By the time we had children, the only services Howard would attend were the memorial services for his friends lost in battle.

For a while, in Jacksonville, I had a friend whose pilot husband also was losing interest in the church. We would plot and scheme to get our husbands there. Every Sunday morning I would look around the congregation to see if she had her husband in tow. She would give the A-OK sign if her husband was there or look discouraged and shake her head if he wasn't. It was kind of comical at first. Eventually, we both quit trying.

I was worried what his not attending church would do to our children. When Sundays came around and I went through the house saying, "Get up, it's time for Sunday school," I was answered by a series of groans. "Daddy's not going; why should we go?" After Howard disappeared, I grew more and more depressed. Feeling pity for myself, it was easier just to stay in bed on Sundays. Eventually I dropped out of church, too.

One afternoon two years after Howard was shot down, I was visiting my mother when she became very ill. She had had a stroke; and only days after the operation to save her, she died. During her funeral I cried tears of guilt for all those things I should have done. I should have written more; I should have called more. I loved my mother, but in my preoccupation with survival, I had seldom even seen her in the past few years. Now I felt guilty and even more alone. First Howard is shot down— now this! What tragedy would strike us next?

The third tragic blow fell on July 4, 1968. School was out. The children were restless. The house was full of John's and Sondra's teen-age friends. I had planned on sending John to Oklahoma to spend the summer with my sister and her son, but she beat me to the punch and sent her boy to spend the summer with me. We planned a July 4 picnic at the beach. The summer before, at a similar picnic in Tulsa, my sister had been injured in the head by a firework tossed from a crowd, so we tried to find a quiet beach away from holiday dangers.

John was like a fish in the ocean. He and his visiting cousin, Mark, loved to see which one could hold his breath the longest under water. They were diving and swimming and having a great time. On one particular dive John stayed under far too long. Suddenly, I could see a black boy pulling a white boy through the surf, one arm around his waist and the other around his neck. It was John, and it looked as if he had drowned. I ran to his side in panic. Apparently, he had dived into the water and struck his head on a rock beneath the surface. The stranger saved my boy from drowning. I never even had the opportunity to thank him.

We called an ambulance and rushed John to the emergency

hospital. The first person I thought to call was Pastor Foley. He came immediately. An outstanding young neurosurgeon happened to be on the staff of that hospital and recommended immediate surgery. Brother Foley had been a medic in World War II. He explained the options and after he prayed, I decided to permit the operation. Then we waited. During those endless hours, I prayed. It was the first time I had prayed in months, but I prayed hard. "Don't let John die!" It seemed the past few years I had had to watch all my family suffer. I felt so helpless. I wanted to bear their pain, but all that I could do was stand helplessly by.

Finally, the surgeons walked out of the operating room and sat down beside me. I could tell their news was bad news.

"Mrs. Rutledge, your son is paralyzed from the neck down. He is alive but will probably never move again."

John was only fifteen years old. He was just becoming a man. He had so much life ahead of him, and now he was paralyzed. How much grief were we to bear? Where was God in all this? Was He punishing us for something I had or hadn't done? Was He testing me?

Brother Foley talked softly of a God who stood helplessly by as His own Son, Jesus, died on a Roman cross. With tears in his eyes, Pastor Foley talked about a heavenly Father who understood our pain and shared our sorrow. We can't understand the mystery of suffering. But we can know that God has promised never to leave us or forsake us. The words poured out, and somehow I got hold of hope. I didn't understand the tragedy that struck my son that day. I felt guilty and responsible, but I prayed for strength, and God heard my prayer.

13

Hope

For the next few months after John's accident, I went overboard trying to help him. He lay helplessly on his bed, needing total care day and night. I worked around the clock to make him feel comfortable and entertained. If he called, I was there. After all, he was only fifteen years old and needed all the attention I could give him. Besides, I was feeling more and more responsible for the accident. Often, while feeding or bathing my son, I asked myself hard and useless questions. Could the accident have been avoided? If I had been more careful, would John be well today? Will his father think I failed him, that his son is crippled because of my neglect?

The guilty feelings multiplied as I grew tense and overworked. Peggy and Barbara needed more of my time. Sondra was going steady and also needed attention. I was working day and night and gradually falling apart. I knew something had to change as my own frustration mounted to a dangerous level.

All during this time, Pastor Foley and the people of Clairemont First Southern Baptist Church were praying. During the seven years of imprisonment, our family was mentioned in public prayer every Sunday morning faithfully. There were cards and calls of encouragement, cookies and candy for John. I wasn't attending church, but Pastor Foley and his wife still visited often. They didn't berate or badger me. On every visit they would chat a while, share words of encouragement, and say a brief prayer. Then, usually on the way to the door, Brother Foley would invite us to church on Sunday. I never felt pressured. Somehow I knew he understood. Even if we didn't attend, the people at First Church never gave up on us. They were faithful when I wasn't, just as God is faithful when we aren't.

It was my two young ones, Peggy and Barbara, who got me going back to church. They became very active in the youth group and loved singing in the choir. Their enthusiasm was contagious. I went to church when I could be sure John was well taken care of, and, the house cleaned, the dishes done, the bills paid, the records kept, the girls ready, and myself presentable. I was trying to do everything and ended up getting more and more irritable with John, impatient with the girls, and angry at myself.

The tension of not hearing anything about my husband for five long years was getting to me. I still didn't know if he were alive or dead. I was trying to be both mom and dad to my growing brood; eventually, I realized that unless something happened I couldn't keep it all together. For a while we had an attendant for John. When he left and my health failed, I had to put John in a nursing home where he could get professional care.

I have to admit that I wasn't aware that God was working in my life during those first years of waiting. But as I look back, it is plain to see that God was working, even then. He was working through people who cared enough to reach out and lift us up. Howard's mother was really used by God to help us survive. She visited us from Tulsa and helped clean up the house, fixed roasts and stews and chocolate pies. She would talk with John and play with the girls. At night, when we couldn't sleep, she would pray and quote promises of hope from the Bible. Before John's accident, she had been the one who noticed him crying during an invitation at church and together they went forward to pray and commit John's life to Christ. He was only eleven, but he and his grandma did important spiritual business that day. No one makes mother-in-law jokes around me anymore. I've seen what a god-send a mother-in-law can be.

LaVerne Barger, one of my Sunday-school teachers at First Church, was another important friend God used. She always seemed to know when I needed her. Invariably she would appear at our door with food or flowers or books just when I was getting low. She and the pastor often visited John and talked with him about the Bible and baseball. Brother Foley once told me that John could ask deeper questions about the Bible than any boy his age. It was good to see my son take an interest in God's Word.

Ken Masat, Howard's wingman who saw his chute that day, also visited John and talked enthusiastically about airplanes and flying. Ken is a Catholic, and I was pleased to learn from him one day that his church, too, was praying for us.

Other people helped. The city of Bellflower, California, adopted Howard as their prisoner of war and sent the family gifts and gave John a thousand-dollar scholarship.

God was using all kinds of people to help fill the emptiness in our lives, but nothing could really satisfy until we heard from Howard.

About Thanksgiving 1970 I went to my mailbox and pulled out a handful of bills and fourth-class ads. There was a POW folder and like all the other folders I had gotten I supposed it contained news reprints and important speeches about the prisoners or the war. Usually I just opened these folders, skimmed their contents, and tossed them in the trash. This time a strange-looking letter fell out. There were Vietnamese words printed on the cover and inside in a square there were seven beautiful handwritten lines from Howard.

I screamed with delight and ran into the house yelling at the top of my voice, "He's alive. Your daddy is alive." Of course, our joy was tempered slightly by his words "very minor injury." Was he

NGƯỜI NHẬN (Addressee)

HỌ TÊN (Name in full):

Mrs. Phyllis Jean Rutledge

ĐỊA CHỈ (Address):

4525 Mt. La Plata Ct
San Diego, California
U.S.A.

NGƯỜI GỬI (Addressor)

HỌ TÊN (Name in full):

Howard Elmer Rutledge

SỐ LÍNH (Service number): *506435*

TRẠI GIAM PHI CÔNG MỸ BỊ BẮT TẠI
NƯỚC VIỆT-NAM DÂN CHỦ CỘNG HÒA

(Camp of detention for U.S. pilots captured
in the DEMOCRATIC REPUBLIC of VIETNAM)

NGÀY VIẾT (Dated) *12 October 1970*

Dear Phyllis, I had only very minor injury and
am today in fair health. I am, therefor, living testimony
to the power of your prayers, your love, and faith.
I know, in my heart, that you and ours are equally
well, and for the same reasons. Keep faith, for we
will have our reunion, whether in this world or the next.
If you write use this form. Send pictures, gifts. Love all.

CHI CHÚ (N.B.):

1. Phải viết rõ và chỉ được viết trên những dòng kẻ sẵn (*Write legibly and only on the lines*).
2. Gia đình gửi đến cung phải theo dung mau, khuon kho va quy dinh này (*Notes from families should also conform to this proforma*)

A reproduction of the first letter Phyllis Rutledge received from her husband—five years after he was captured.

just hiding the truth from us, or was he really well? But the handwriting was obviously his. He was alive for sure. After five years of being suspended between hope and despair, hope tipped the scales.

That Thanksgiving Sunday my family and I took the letter to church and Pastor Foley read it from the pulpit. When he finished reading those seven short lines, he bowed his head and said a prayer of thanks. I will always remember that Thanksgiving and the gratitude I felt to God and to this pastor and his people for the love they had shown to me and my family.

In the next two years there were only a dozen or so other letters from Howard, but it was easy to read between the lines. My husband's Christian life was growing. He had shown almost no spiritual leadership in our home in the past twenty years, but it sounded as if something had happened to him to change all that. It got me thinking about my own spiritual growth. I began to read the Bible. I read books on prayer, and I began to pray again. The family went to church regularly and found our real friends were there. People like Virginia Smith and Yvonne Boling were quick to help out in a crisis and never expected to be thanked for their thoughtfulness. I don't know what I would have done without the people at First Church.

Meanwhile, John was really losing ground in the nursing home. Surrounded by old people who were dying, constantly aware of the sadness and despair around him, John's morale was sinking fast. One afternoon I walked out of the nursing home knowing that if I didn't get him out of there soon, we would lose our son. I was afraid he might get on drugs or even try suicide. He had every reason to be depressed. But I had no idea where to take him.

The next morning I decided something must be done. In Sunday-school class one of my friends had told of a recent experience when she and her family "let Jesus take them out to dinner." It may sound farfetched, but they got into their car and asked God to lead them to a restaurant. They drove through the streets of La Jolla, turning down one street and up another. Then they felt it was time to stop. There was a restaurant nearby that they had never tried. So they went in, had a wonderful evening, a delicious meal, paid the bill, and thanked God for His guidance.

So I thought to myself, "What can I lose?" If God cares about dinner, surely He cares about my son's suffering! I'll try trusting God to lead me to a place that can help John. So I got up, got dressed, climbed into the car, and prayed for guidance. There was a new rehabilitation center nearby and it seemed natural to start there. So, I drove towards Clairemont Mesa Boulevard and Sharps Hospital. I got out of the car, walked into the brand-new reception area, and to my surprise found John's doctor in the corridor as if waiting for me. I don't know about your experience trying to catch a doctor in, but this was something new for me.

I walked up to Dr. A. J. Russell and said, "I have to talk with you."

Surprised, he answered, "Fine!" We sat down on a bench, and I told him my fears about John's living in that place, surrounded by death and the dying, growing more and more depressed.

He answered with concern. "I've just been talking with some old med-school friends of mine who are starting an experimental rehabilitation center for young people in Tempe, Arizona. I'll call them about John, and we'll see what they can do." I mumbled words of thanks and made a hasty retreat from the hospital.

I don't pretend my faith was strong. I didn't even know for sure he would call me back. But he did, and not long after, John was flown to Tempe, Arizona, and the Good Samaritan Rehabilitation Center. It was a miracle, and it came just in time. And though he is still paralyzed, today he is studying at University of California at Berkeley.

Thanks to God and all the people who cared, we were making headway. I even got the checkbook balanced now and then. But the big question remained. When would the war end so that Howard could come home?

POW AND MIA wives around the country were beginning to feel that it might never end. We organized our small informal groups into a national organization and worked to keep the prisoners' plight before the public. It's easy to forget a man when he has been in prison seven years. We could not let the public forget.

The National League of Families of POW and MIA in Southeast Asia worked hard writing congressmen, the military, and the press. Other groups sold bracelets with the prisoner's name, rank, and date of capture to raise money to help our cause and, again, to keep our men remembered. Thousands of people wore those bracelets. Hundreds of them wrote me that they were praying for Howard and for his safe return.

As the talks in Paris continued and Dr. Henry Kissinger dashed around the world, we held our breath and prayed for our president. He was only human and had a superhuman task to perform. Like all of us, he would make mistakes, but he tried, as we were trying, to get our men home again.

One Christmas would come and go, and we would say, "Next Christmas they'll be home." Then another twelve months would slowly pass with no real hope in sight. I tried to be casual about the whole thing, but my excitement mounted as the talks in Paris and the secret visits to Peking, Moscow, and Hanoi were made known. Then, unbelievably, the peace was signed. Sunday, January 28, 1973, early in the morning we got a call—Howard was coming home!

14

Reunion

After learning from Operation Homecoming that Howard would soon be released, I rushed down to the church, told Pastor Foley that this would be our day, and then rushed home to await further news. Again, the church service stopped and the people thanked God together for answer to prayer. Every time the phone rang, I thought I'd faint with excitement. First, it was Howard's mom calling from Tulsa. She had just hung up, disappointed that there had been no more news, when the phone rang again. The navy was calling to officially notify me that Howard was to be included in the first group coming out of Hanoi.

I didn't let myself get too excited. He wasn't free yet. All we had been told was that he would be flown to Clark Air Force Base in the Philippines. We were also told that there would be no press there, but that we would be sent a picture immediately when he arrived.

Two weeks passed. They were the longest weeks of my life. Would Howard be the same? How had prison changed him? Would he be well? How would he react when I told him of John's accident and paralysis? Would he blame me? Would he approve of the new house I had bought and of the way I had managed the ledger he gave me seven years ago?

Then my phone rang again. An excited neighbor reported the first plane was landing at Clark. The girls ran to the television, and together we watched the first load of men climb down. No Howard. Our phone was ringing off the hook. The people at First Church had been praying seven years, and they really got involved in their praying. Now in homes all over the neighborhood, they were waiting to see the man they had been praying for. We were all going crazy with excitement by the time the second plane landed.

Thirty-nine men got off, one by one they said their words of thanks, saluted the military officers, then walked the long red carpet to freedom. Still no Howard. Then a slender, black-haired man climbed off the plane. The newsman's voice grew silent. Then we heard him say, with a kind of laugh, "Captain Howard Rutledge; he says his name is Howie."

A cheer that God couldn't help but hear went up that day from the Rutledge house and from the houses of the people of First Church. A thousand voices hoarse with hollering, two thousand hands back-slapping, and a thousand people dancing with joy around their living rooms! Howard's home! I'm sure that God knew that those cheers were our way of saying thanks for bringing Howard home.

The cameras were close. We all saw him clearly. He looked thin, but he was walking, head high; and when he saluted Admiral Gayler, we could tell he was all right. He called me three times from the Philippines during the next three days. Each time it was about 3 A.M., I think. He talked very low and very slowly. And the conversations were a bit strained. You know how it is when you've been storing up things to say for years, and then when it's time to say them, you freeze with excitement.

When I finally had the courage to tell him about John, he

paused for one long moment. Then he spoke. "Phyllis, do you blame yourself for Johnny's accident?" I mumbled something tearfully; then slowly, calmly, as though we were back on that bed the midnight I had seen him last, he said, "Phyllis, I trust you in all things. I know you did your very best. That's all anyone can ask."

I learned a lot about God that day. Howard's voice went on, "We can do all things through Christ which strengtheneth us" (*see* Philippians 4:13).

The day Howard was due home in San Diego, the doorbell rang, and a deliveryman handed me a beautiful orchid. It was from my husband. Not since high school had he sent me orchids. Then the government limousine arrived to take us down to Miramar.

It was a dreary, rainy day. I wondered on that short drive to the airport why the sun wasn't shining and the birds singing for Howard's return. The weather got worse as we approached the airport. Imagine San Diego with hail so heavy that it left the golf course looking as if it were covered with snow!

When we arrived at the operations building at Miramar there were TV and radio reporters, cameras, microphones, and mobs of excited people. The plane was due any minute. We were told to wait for our husbands in our limousine, but when I saw another wife standing on the field, I jumped out and ran across the VIP area to get a closer look. Other wives saw me and followed. Suddenly, the sun broke through the clouds, and the silver plane bearing my husband landed and taxied to the waiting crowd. One by one the men got down, and then, as if in a dream, he was standing there. How often I had seen him across crowded waiting rooms, piers, and runways! How often my heart had skipped a beat as he smiled and held out his arms in greeting. But he had been gone so long. Would he smile? Would he hold out his arms again?

Then I heard his name. "Captain Howard Rutledge!" I waited. He saluted Admiral Williams, greeted the press, looked into the crowd. Our eyes met. He smiled and held out his arms. I ran and felt his embrace, my heart crying out its thanks to the God who brought us back together again.

Faith in God Sustained Him, Ex-POW Tells Congregation

BY HAROLD KEEN .
Times Staff Writer

SAN DIEGO—A Navy flier imprisoned more than seven years in Vietnam went to church Sunday to thank those who had prayed for his freedom.

Capt. Howard Rutledge came home Thursday and was released from a Navy hospital—as were 10 of 15 ex-prisoners in San Diego—to spend the weekend as he wished. Some of the men went for drives or visits. Some went shopping.

Rutledge went to church.

Word had spread that he would be at the First Southern Baptist Church of Clairemont and there was a crowd of 700 filling the church for the late morning worship service when he arrived.

Rutledge, 44, wore his khaki uniform. His mother, his wife, his two teen-age daughters, and his married daughter and his grandson accompanied him. His family belongs to the church, but Rutledge left for Asia before he could have his membership transferred here.

The pastor, the Rev. Charles W. Foley Jr., asked Rutledge to speak to the congregation. He was given an ovation which lasted almost five minutes. He stood in front of the congregation and told the crowd:

"I was able to sustain life and hope through the faith I have in God. I am here today also because of the prayers of Christian people while I was in prison."

He urged everyone to place their trust in God—because, he said, there was no other place to put it. He thanked the congregation for its prayers on his behalf.

Please Turn to Page 20, Col. 1

FAITH IN GOD

Continued from First Page

He officially joined the church at the Sunday service. He had been a member of another Southern Baptist congregation before being transferred to San Diego.

Mr. Foley said that five others in the audience, moved by the captain's testimonial, "were inspired to accept the Lord."

Afterward, Rutledge gathered with members of his family at the home in the University City district which his wife had bought in his absence. He had not seen his grandson —the 3-year-old son of his oldest daughter, Sondra Tollison—before his return from Vietnam.

Rutledge was one of the former prisoners who got what the Navy called an "open gangway" for the weekend after passing preliminary medical examinations.

My Anchor Held

MY ANCHOR HELD

Lt. Comdr. Stephen R. Harris, U.S. Navy

as told to James C. Hefley

FLEMING H. REVELL COMPANY
Old Tappan, New Jersey

Scripture quotations in this volume are from the *King James Version of the Bible*.

Quotation from *Markings* by Dag Hammarskjold © 1964 are used by permission of Alfred A. Knopf, Inc., publisher.

SBN—8007-0402-9

Copyright © 1970 by Fleming H. Revell Company
All Rights Reserved
Library of Congress Catalog Card Number: 75-123058
Printed in the United States of America

Contents

Foreword

On January 23, 1968, the U.S.S. *Pueblo,* an American ship on an intelligence-gathering mission for the U.S. Navy, was harassed, boarded and ultimately taken captive by ships and sailors of the Democratic People's Republic of North Korea. One American crew member died of injuries sustained in an exchange of shots during the boarding; the eighty-two other crew members were taken ashore to face charges of espionage. Ahead of them were eleven months in North Korean prisons. Each day, each hour, carried the threat of death.

Physically these men suffered beatings, malnutrition, illness left unattended. Mentally they endured interrogation from their captors and separation from everything familiar: their families, their country, their way of life. Emotionally they were ravaged by fear repeatedly and deliberately induced.

On December 23, 1968, these eighty-two men were released from captivity after long and complex diplomatic negotiations that to this day are regarded with strong and conflicting opinions. But on one thing people everywhere in the free world were in agreement—that these men should not remain prisoners. Their reunion with their families and loved ones was beyond joy; it was an exaltation. All of us shared in it, for all of us knew that their ordeal might have happened to any of us in this hostile, tormented world.

The story of the U.S.S. *Pueblo*—its mission, its capture, and the events leading to the release of the crew—will be a controversial one to the end of time. It can be told in at least eighty-two different ways, all of them true, all of them honest, and no two of them identical. For each person involved was an individual human being who lived a distinct experience. Each of these men has his own story to tell.

This is Lt. Commander Stephen Harris' story. It is more than a story about a dramatic event in recent history; it is more than a description of human survival under unbelievably brutal conditions; it is an inspiring account of what happens to a man when he is cut off from everything this world has to offer, when body and mind give way under agonizing pressure, and only the spirit is left to do battle with the enemy. This story tells of a spiritual victory. This book is about a Saviour.

THE PUBLISHERS

8

⌐⊏⊐⌐⊏⊐⌐⊏⊐⌐⊏⊐⌐⊏⊐⌐⊏⊐⌐⊏⊐⌐⊏⊐⌐⊏⊐⌐⊏⊐⌐⊏⊐⌐⊏⊐

Captured!

Lunch seemed a nice break on this hazy, zero degree day, January 23, 1968—turkey, peas, and mashed potatoes. Chop suey was on the menu for supper. I glanced down at my ample stomach and thought, "This is almost as good as Esther's cooking."

Suddenly the wardroom phone rang for the captain. He listened, then announced to the five of us, "Law has a visual contact about seven miles away. Might be a torpedo boat or subchaser."

We went topside and the captain threw the ship's "big eyes" (twenty-two inch binoculars) on the visitor which had begun circling us. We identified it as a 147-foot SO-1 subchaser with 57-mm guns. The crew was on deck in full battle dress with their guns trained on us.

I went below to see what my men had learned through electronic surveillance. The communications shack contained the most advanced electronic systems to date. In here, I was the officer in charge of twenty-nine navy personnel, but it was off limits to most of the ship's crew.

At 1,000 yards the SO-1 signaled, HEAVE TO OR I'LL FIRE, then, FOLLOW IN MY WAKE. I HAVE A PILOT ABOARD.

The captain ordered our signalman to signal back, I AM IN INTERNATIONAL WATERS.

Three torpedo boats began closing on us. MIGs were seen overhead by the bridge watch.

One of the ship's radio operators notified headquarters in Japan that we had "company."

From my spaces, I heard the ship's engines start up. We had been lying to more than sixteen miles off the North Korean coast, over four miles beyond their claimed territorial limits. The captain, I figured, would be heading east and out of the area.

Word came from the skipper that we should make preparations to destroy classified material. There was an emergency destruction procedure posted in my area.

About 1:30 we heard the first salvo explode over the deck. We had already started destroying materials. Suddenly there came the chilling clatter-clatter-clatter of machine-gun bullets hitting the sides. The MIGs screeched over us and fired rockets up ahead.

The radioman made a desperate call for help.

"If you guys know any prayers," Communications Technician First Class Frank Ginther shouted to my group, "now is the time to say them." Ginther was one of only two *Pueblo* crewmen who had attended the single service I had tried to hold as Protestant lay leader of the ship.

The firing kept up. We were swinging sledges and fire

10

axes, shredding paper, burning documents, and doing all we could to destroy the classified material and the advanced electronic system.

It seemed that the unexpected was about to happen. We on the U.S.S. *Pueblo* had presumed that the Soviets' little brother, North Korea, wouldn't interfere with us. We were doing nothing illegal in this "listening game" that may someday be the price of survival. What's in the air is free for the taking.

I knew our ship didn't have a breath of a chance in resisting. There were two 50-caliber machine guns mounted on deck—peashooters compared to the big guns of the subchaser. And we had about a dozen Thompson submachine guns and a few grenades. In our role as a noncombatant "environmental research" ship, we were not equipped for hostilities.

At 2:32 P.M., Korean time, the *Pueblo* sent its last message:

HAVE BEEN DIRECTED TO COME TO ALL STOP AND BEING BOARDED AT THIS TIME. FOUR MEN INJURED, ONE CRITICALLY. GOING OFF THE AIR NOW AND DESTROYING THIS GEAR.

From the pilot house Captain Bucher, in frustration, threw a coffee cup at the pirates who were clambering onto the deck. Not since 1807 had an American commander surrendered his ship in peacetime.

The "KORCOMS" (Korean Communists) began running through the ship, rounding up their captives. I was in a group of about thirty whom they herded to the well deck area in the forward part of the ship. They pulled sheets from bunks and ripped them into blindfolds. Then they ordered us below deck and out of the bitter cold.

As I prepared to step through the door leading off the weather deck, a KORCOM stopped me. I noticed that the ear flaps and strings from his fur cap were flapping in the bitter breeze.

He pushed the bayonet on the end of his machine gun against my stomach and grunted. He had noticed the bulge under my flight jacket.

I shrugged and pulled out the leather-bound Bible which my grandmother had given me in Boston when I was eleven years old. Other than my rings, watch, ID card, and Geneva Convention card, it was the only personal possession I had tried to keep with me. I hated to give the Bible up, but the sharp point of the bayonet and the KORCOM's twitchy trigger finger presented enough persuasion. The North Korean took the Bible, briefly flipped the pages, then motioned me on. I never saw it or any other printed Scripture for the next eleven months.

A guard motioned for us to sit on bunks in the crew quarters and to put the blindfolds on. We could hear men rummaging through lockers—pilfering, I guessed. For the next two hours we heard nothing else except the gentle throbbing of the ship's engines and an occasional KORCOM scream over the ship's general announcing system. I guessed correctly that we were being led into the port of Wonsan. Later I noticed that Wonsan is on a latitude line that runs almost exactly through Washington, D.C. With Esther living there, this seemed a strange coincidence.

Unanswered questions tumbled through my mind. Why had the North Koreans risked war? Why did they want us and the ship? Would our government make an attempt to rescue the ship and crew?

By five o'clock on that dismal January 23, 1968, we were moored to a pier in an alien and hostile land. The KORCOMS took us one by one up the ladder from the compartment to the main deck where they bound our wrists in front of us and pushed us toward the gangway. A guard discovered a knife in Signalman Roy Maggard's pocket and beat him viciously. Another sailor moved too slowly and got a rifle butt in his teeth.

I felt a springy plank under my feet and moved carefully straight ahead, thinking how easy it would be to step over the side and drown. Then I stepped onto solid ground and walked a few feet to a bus. A KORCOM called for me to step up and I felt my way to a hard seat.

"Lieutenant Harris?" an Oriental voice called.

"Here," I answered.

The voice ordered me to my feet and pushed me off the bus. I had no idea what was coming next.

They led me back across the plank and below deck to the communications shack.

"Open door!" the KORCOM commanded.

I pushed the buttons in proper sequence which would have opened the door had the main combination lock been released. I turned to the KORCOM and said, "I can't."

"Why don't you have key?" he asked in obvious irritation.

I knew he meant combination. "I don't know it," I said truthfully. The combination had been recently changed and I hadn't committed it to memory.

"We must shoot you, then."

13

I've never been the impulsive type. I did not raise my voice. "Go ahead, but I still can't open the door."

They pushed me around, then yanked the blindfold back over my eyes. Wham! I saw a flash of white and felt searing pain. The KORCOM officer had snapped his finger in my right eye. Amazingly, the contact lens had stayed in place.

They led me back on deck and across the plank and back into a bus. I suppose they blew the door open later.

The bus moved forward over a rough unpaved road. Suddenly I felt a rough hand pull my bound wrists forward to rest on the seat in front. The hand pushed my head down between my arms. Because of the discomfort I lifted my head slightly. Two or three savage chops on the back of my neck put my head back where it was.

A few minutes later I felt the bus slowing. I heard crowd noises up ahead—angry Oriental voices yelling. The bus stopped and I heard the yells and howls closing in. It was just as well that I couldn't see. The captain's blindfold slipped and he saw them shaking their fists and spitting at us. Guards had to knock some of them to the ground to clear a path for us to move off the bus.

We climbed some stairs and walked into a narrow place. A whistle blew up ahead. As a student of railroad lore I knew it was a locomotive steam whistle. From the echo of my footsteps, I judged we were in a railroad car. A hand pushed me down into a leather upholstered seat.

The train didn't move for a few minutes. Later I learned that the first bus they had put me on had stopped at a building (possibly a police station) and some of the men were taken off and beaten.

The train jerked forward. I heard occasional pounding

sounds in front and in back of me and figured some of my shipmates were being punched around. After awhile, voices drifted back through the car. I recognized the nasal twang of Captain Bucher. I caught the drift of a wild tale about how we had been observing sun spots.

Someone pushed a hunk of bread into my hands. It tasted soft and sweet. I took a dipper of warm water.

Farther along, they moved us around for some reason. Once I was asked my name, rank, and age.

I dozed off and on. Far into the night, a KORCOM came and jerked up my blindfold. A flashbulb burst in the semi-darkened car. Before he put the blindfold back, my eyes adjusted enough to see that some of the light bulbs were burned out in the ceiling of the dingy brown coach. I recognized shipmates in front of me and across the aisle—all blindfolded and with hands tied.

At times the train slowed, indicating we were climbing grades. We passed through several tunnels. The muffled click of the wheels told me this. The train stopped a few times at what I guessed to be remote country places. The thought ran through my mind, "If they're going to kill us, they're taking us a long way to do it."

Just before dawn, Wednesday, the train pulled into a big station. The KORCOMS untied our hands and said we could remove the blindfolds.

We crowded onto a concrete platform beside the tracks. Movie lights glared in our faces. They ordered us to put up our hands, then to put them down. One of these propaganda pictures later appeared on the cover of *Newsweek*.

They put us aboard two Russian-built buses which carried us into the square of a large town. The thought

15

hit me that as an intelligence officer I should remember all I could about this place.

We passed through the square just before dawn. I learned later it bore Premier Kim Il Sung's name as did everything else in the country. As I peered through the cracks in the heavy layer of frost on the bus windows, I surmised this must be the capital, Pyongyang.

The cold blue fluorescent lights were still on in shop windows. Workers beginning to line up to board parked buses seemed not to notice us. Otherwise, the square was empty under the mercury vapor lights. Sterility was the word that hit me. Stark and bright. The loneliness of an empty, well-lighted parking lot.

We crossed a bridge over a large river (the Daedong River, I learned later) and chugged through nondescript neighborhoods. Yellow street lights were still on.

After a few minutes of climbing over bumpy roads the old buses jolted to a halt before a four-story cement building. The KORCOMS motioned for us to get out and pass between two lines of guards. When I was about halfway down the line, one guard abruptly stepped out and slugged me hard in the mouth. Blood trickled down my chin.

We entered the building through a warped door and were directed toward the central stairs. I noticed that the mortar had been slopped around the joints in the cement block wall. Poor workmanship by American standards.

Part way down the hall of the second floor I was shoved into a room with three enlisted men. A KORCOM officer came in behind me and pointed towards a cloth hanging between the double windows. He was calling our attention to a piece of paper stuck to the window frame with an official rubber seal. The KORCOM sliced his hand horizontally across his throat. We got the idea. Then the KOR-COM dropped his arm toward the bed. He wanted us to lie down.

After the officer left, we looked around the room. There were four crude bed bases, each having a thin pad for a mattress and a blanket. The wood-slat floors were discolored and warped, with big spaces in between. The yellow plaster walls were flaky and faded. There were four wooden chairs around a table. A hot water radiator scarcely dispelled the chill.

I removed my contacts and put one in each khaki shirt pocket. Hospital Corpsman Herman Baldridge, an eighteen-year navy veteran who had a Japanese wife and two children in Japan, whispered a report. "Duane Hodges is dead. Before they boarded us, the KORCOMS shot off his leg and ripped open his stomach. Steve Woelk is badly hurt and two or three others were hit."

We stretched out on the pads and lay quietly. Through the walls we caught the sounds of blows and groans. A bare 15-watt light bulb hanging from a ceiling chain burned in the gloom.

I whispered, "Lord, take care of us," then dozed off from exhaustion.

I awoke when a dowdy, unattractive woman entered carrying a pitcher of warm water, some soup, and bread on a flat plate. She put the stuff down and left.

"What a way to lose weight," I said dryly. "But we'd better eat. Next time they might not bring us so much."

The soup tasted like dishwater. I tried not to think of the turkey dinner we had enjoyed the day before.

I wondered how the other guys were faring, especially the captain.

The CO had first been put in a room by himself, then

17

taken to a long assembly room that ran the length of the building where an interpreter waited with several KORCOM officers. We would later call this interpreter Wheezy because of his attempts to cover up his translation blocks by coughing. The senior officer, a colonel who smiled like a horse baring his teeth, we would nickname Super-C.

Super-C seemed anxious, even frantic. The captain felt he was worried about the possibility of U.S. retaliation. So he played on this concern by telling them he had radioed his position just before capture and the U.S. would quickly be demanding our release.

They soon sent the skipper back to his room where he refused to eat. A little later in the day they brought him back to the interrogation room and confronted him with his service record they had taken from the ship. Super-C noted that the captain had attended the Navy's Combat Information Center School at Glenview, Illinois, in 1953. Wasn't CIC the same as CIA?

"No," the skipper replied.

A guard booted him in the back and again he denied being a CIA agent. They kicked him some more and sent him back to his room.

About mid-morning the door to my room burst open. "Lieutenant Harris, come," an English-speaking KORCOM commanded.

He led me down the hall to join the other *Pueblo* officers in the big room. At one end, tables were arranged in a horseshoe and at the center sat a smiling general. The interpreter, whom we later nicknamed Max (for the movie actor Maximillian Schell), sat beside the general. Super-C sat a few feet away.

We six *Pueblo* officers sat according to rank within the horseshoe facing the general. The skipper was first, Lieutenant Ed Murphy, the executive officer, next, then me, followed by Lieutenant (j.g.) Carl "Skip" Schumacher, Ensign Timothy Harris (no relation to me), and Chief Warrant Officer Gene Lacy. Skip had talked about attending theological seminary when he got out of the Navy.

The general, through Max, addressed the captain. "Your White House is aware of your capture within our territorial waters. What were you trying to do?"

The skipper, a tall rugged twenty-four-year Navy veteran, had worked his way up from the ranks to a command after graduating from the Catholic Boys Town High School in Nebraska. I knew him as an excellent commander and a good friend whose interests ranged from Shakespeare to Oriental religions.

The man whose hair would turn gray during the next eleven months stood up. "The *Pueblo* is an oceanographic ship, sir. We were taking samples of the water."

The general scowled and made some nasty remarks. "Why does the U.S. have 50,000 troops occupying South Korea?" he wanted to know. The captain answered that to his best knowledge they were there at the request of the president of South Korea.

The general demanded to know why the ship had "intruded deep into the territorial waters of the Democratic People's Republic of Korea and committed hostile acts there." The captain stood up again and said we were 15.8 miles from shore and had fired no weapons.

The general went down the line and asked our names and jobs aboard the *Pueblo,* and the purpose for the voyage. On the latter point, we backed up the captain. I identified myself as the ship's research officer.

The general's frown deepened as Max gave him our

answers. When we finished, he shouted, "You are not prisoners of war with rights under the Geneva Convention. You are espionage agents. How do you want to be shot, one at a time, or all together at sundown?"

The captain jumped to his feet. "Shoot me, sir, and release the crew and the ship."

"No, never!" the general shouted back. "You will all be shot at sundown."

"You captured my ship in international waters where we had every right to be," the skipper protested. "You have committed an act of war against the United States."

The general flushed with anger. "The guards will escort you to your rooms. You will be shot as spies at sundown."

My roommates had one question after the guards had closed the door: "What are they going to do to us?"

I gulped the words. "They plan to shoot us at sundown."

The three crewmen stared at me in shock. Sweat moistened their faces. One looked toward the covered window. I glanced at my watch. We had maybe five hours.

No one could think of any small talk to break the tenseness. We just sat, busy with our own thoughts.

I wondered if I would feel pain. Would I die first or would I feel the pain of the bullet going through my head or heart? How soon would I be with the Lord? This thought lifted my sagging spirits and I felt great joy about the certainty of being with the Lord in a short time.

Then I thought of Esther, my beautiful blonde, hazel-eyed *Vuokko*. Her parents were Finnish. Her father then pastored a church in Montreal. Her Finnish name, *Vu-*

okko, meant "windflower," the first flower of spring in her native land. She had been born on March twenty-first.

Esther's brother, Gus, a major in the Army Dental Corps, had introduced me to her in the narthex of Fourth Presbyterian Church in the Washington suburb of Bethesda, Maryland. I had met Gus at an Officers' Christian Union meeting some months before.

Tall and statuesque with a delicate soft voice, she looked stunning. I felt like saying, "Why hasn't your brother introduced you to me before." I discovered she was a secretary for a trade association, had an apartment downtown, and didn't have a car. Would she let me drive her home? I thought her eyes twinkled. It became convenient for me to take her home again, and again, and again. The life of a bachelor started looking singularly unexciting.

But Esther wasn't in such a hurry to fall in love. When her mother predicted she would marry me, she laughed and said, "That's silly."

I soon changed that attitude. About a year after Gus introduced us we became engaged, and thirty-five days after that we were married. Gus arranged for the ceremony to be held in the chapel on the grounds of Walter Reed Army Hospital. Their father came to preside and to sing the Lord's Prayer.

Because I was in intelligence work, I could say very little about my job. Esther knew I had an interest in electronics, had been studying Russian, and would shortly be assigned to a ship that was being outfitted in Bremerton, Washington.

After the three happiest months of my life, I left her

21

in the capital and went to Bremerton. That first month's separation cost $170 in phone calls. Being a practical New Englander, I hopped a Navy plane headed east and brought her back to Bremerton. Shortly before the *Pueblo* sailed south for a scheduled stop in San Diego in preparation for leaving for Japan, Esther's mother became critically ill with diabetes and had to have a leg amputated. Esther went to be with her in Canada.

I had handled all our financial affairs. I had already shipped our car to Yokosuka, Japan, the home port of the *Pueblo,* anticipating that Esther would join me there. Our furniture and belongings were in storage in Washington. There were some bills that needed to be paid, including an airline installment charge for the trip Esther and I had made to see my mother three months before.

I thought of my widowed mother in Massachusetts. So vivacious and independent, yet so concerned about her only son. I was more like my father who had died the year before I finished Harvard—the nuts and bolts, practical, casual type. Mom, a public school music teacher, was artistic, gay, and interested in everything. After Dad died she had built a house on Boston Rock, one of the highest points in the Boston metropolitan area and overlooking the city. There she had her collection of antiques, stone and metal elves and fairies, pictures of my boyhood, and the music room where she taught piano and organ. I worried about how Mom would take the news of my execution.

"Lord, You'll have to take care of Esther and Mom," I prayed. "I leave them in Your hands."

What else does a fellow think about on his announced day of execution? I thought that here I was a Christian,

22

confident of being with Christ, yet here were three men doomed with me whose eternal future might depend upon what I would tell them.

I looked around and saw that one was fidgeting uneasily. I cleared my throat. I've never been the pushy type in a group.

"Uh, I guess you fellows are thinking that we don't have much of a future. But for a Christian this can be the greatest moment of all."

The three looked at me and said nothing.

"I, uh, haven't always had this confidence which I have now. If it wasn't for the grief that it would bring to my loved ones, I could actually look forward to being with Christ."

They remained silent.

"You know, I used to think of Christianity as just going to church, living a decent life, not harming anyone. I even helped the chaplain on board the ship, kept the hymn books under my bunk, that sort of thing. Then, when we got in port, he invited me over to his house for dinner and confronted me with my need for forgiveness and a personal relationship with Christ.

"They took my Bible away back on the ship, but the chaplain—his name was Stan Beach—gave me this verse, one of the few I remember."

And this is the record, that God hath given to us eternal life, and this life is in His Son. He that hath the Son hath life; and he that hath not the Son of God hath not life (I John 5:11, 12).

23

"He told me how Christ had died for my sins and how He would accept me if I would repent and ask forgiveness.

"I've never been the kind to make quick decisions. I went back to the ship and pondered what I should do. It seemed so simple—just to trust in Christ. I mulled over the Scriptures Chaplain Beach had showed me. Finally I decided I would believe and follow Christ. I drove over to the chaplain's house and found him working in the attic. He stopped his work and prayed with me, then showed me more Bible verses that promised forgiveness and new life to those who would only believe that Christ is sufficient."

I paused and looked at the men. They were listening, but had yet made no response.

"I imagine you men belong to a church."

Baldridge spoke up. "I'm a Baptist." Gunner's Mate Ken Wadley and Fireman Tom Massie said they were Baptists, too.

"That's fine," I said. "But I would urge you to be certain that you have Christ. You can, uh, tell I'm a little nervous and it's not just because they say we'll be shot. I, uh, haven't been too faithful in telling others about Christ. You can do this in your own way. You can pray silently and ask Him to forgive your sins and give you eternal life."

I stopped, not wishing to press the matter, and lay back on my bunk and closed my eyes. From outside I could hear the pounding and nailing of boards. I visualized a platform on which we would be lined up and shot.

Then I turned over and went to sleep.

While visiting her seriously ill mother in Montreal, Esther awoke one January morning and saw me standing in my dress blues with a troubled look. She reached for me and the figure dissolved. She sensed that I must be in trouble.

The Sunday before our capture, she arrived back in Washington. Tuesday her father called to say her mother had suffered a stroke. She and Gus, her dentist brother, made plans to fly to Canada. Wednesday, she and her sister-in-law Fannie had just returned from shopping when the Navy called to report the Pueblo's *capture. For a few moments they sat in shock, then both began crying.*

Mother called from Boston. (The Navy had also notified her.) Esther stopped crying and began trying to assure Mother that the Lord was with me and had a purpose in what had happened.

The story made front page news around the world. Several senators angrily denounced the seizure. Senator Wallace F. Bennett of Utah said the U.S. should send "an armada steaming into Wonsan harbor, throw a tow rope around the Pueblo *and get her out of there." Senator Frank Church of Idaho, a dove on Viet Nam, called the capture "an act of war." Secretary of State Dean Rusk described the situation as "a matter of utmost gravity" and added, "I strongly advise North Korea to cool it." Negotiating sessions began at Panmunjom in the demilitarized zone between North and South Korea. The sides could agree only that subsequent sessions should be held in secret.*

2

█▚▞▚▞▚▞▚▞▚▞▚▞▚▞▚▞▚▞▚▞▚▞▚▞▚▞▚▞█

Comfort in Hell

When I awoke the light on the sheet-covered window was dimming. "Must be about sunset," I mused to the guys.

"Yeah," one replied laconically. "I guess they'll be coming for us any time."

The patch of light disappeared. Another equally unattractive woman came and fed us. No one else appeared.

We slept fitfully through the long night.

When I awoke the next morning, I felt sure a miracle had taken place. "Thank you, Lord," I said over and over to myself. "Please continue to take care of us." I remembered Jesus' promise to His disciples:

> I am with you always, even unto the end of the world (Matthew 28:20).

I felt we were as close to the end of the world as anyone could get.

Later in the morning a KORCOM English-speaking officer entered and a guard remained by the door.

The officer spoke English, but not very clearly. The guys later called him King Kong. I called him Mush Mouth. He ordered me outside and escorted me to a room with the guard dutifully clomping along behind. This room was like the one I was occupying, except there were only two chairs.

King Kong sat about six feet away holding a pencil and a little blue notebook—the kind I had used at Harvard for exams. He flipped a butt into a tray and lighted another cigarette.

He asked my name, rank, and political party. "Lieutenant Stephen R. Harris, United States Navy," I said crisply. "I am not a member of any political party." He looked puzzled. "We don't have party membership as you have here. Sometimes I vote Republican; sometimes Democratic. It depends on the candidate."

The KORCOM curled his lip. "I think you vote for whoever your imperialist rulers want."

"No, sir," I said. "I vote for the person I think is the best candidate. We have a choice. Even before that we may have primary elections in which the candidate of a particular party is nominated by the people."

We argued about political parties in the U.S. He clearly didn't understand our electoral processes and couldn't perceive of genuinely free elections.

He lit another cigarette and handed me a pencil and paper. "Give us a list of all the things on the ship."

I put down such items as six brooms, three dust pans, one ice-cream machine, two engines, one steering wheel. He gave the list a cursory glance, and looked puzzled

27

again. "Now tell the truth about what your ship was doing?"

"Sir, we were an oceanographic ship," I responded. "We were measuring the temperature of the ocean and sunspots." This was the truth. We did have two men on board with degrees in oceanography. Dunnie Tuck had a Master's Degree. We called him Friar. Harry Iredale III had a Bachelor's Degree from Penn State. Both were civilians.

King Kong flew into a rage. "You are spies! Spies! You will be severely punished."

He barked at the guard to take me back to my room.

"When's the new execution date?" one of the guys asked when the guard had left.

I shook my head. "I don't know what they want with us, except maybe to make propaganda mileage."

A woman brought the dishwater soup and bread at noon along with some foul-smelling turnips. After eating, we just sat back and waited for whatever might happen. We could hear the guards pacing up and down the hall. One had a squeak in his shoe.

The room didn't come with private bath. One of us wanting to go to the bathroom knocked on the door and when the guard came, said, *"Benjo,"* the Japanese word for toilet. This was close to the Korean word *byenso*. The gray toilet paper was stiff and rough and issued to us in rectangular sheets the size of a newspaper page. It was unavailable in the place of use and had to be carried in.

After supper (more of the same slop), the KORCOMS took us to a supply room for new clothing. Following instructions, I rolled up my clothes, wrote my name on a piece of paper, and stuffed the paper in the bundle. I

28

left my contacts in my shirt pockets and never saw them again.

This suggested that we might be kept around for awhile. We never knew for sure why they didn't carry through their initial execution threat. Maybe it was just a bluff. Or maybe they had learned that units of the U.S. Seventh Fleet, which included the carrier *Enterprise,* had started steaming in the direction of North Korea.

Max grabbed my ID card and Geneva Convention card from my hand. He looked at the Geneva card which spelled out the international rules for handling prisoners of war and laughed. The rules require that prisoners be treated humanely and protected against acts of violence or intimidation.

We each got a pair of shorts, long johns, a matching long-sleeved undershirt with two buttons at the throat, a pair of sweat pants, and a blue quilted uniform which we called a Charlie Brown. We got identical caps with ear muffs, canvas shoes with rubber soles, toothpaste and toothbrush, a bar of soap, and towel. The soap was part lye.

I wasn't surprised at the absence of variety. The guards and officers all wore the same drab olive uniforms with only the insignia and patches showing their rank. Their hair was always trimmed short, with sideburns halfway down their ears. The only individuality permitted was bright-colored undershirts and socks.

Thursday, King Kong came to my room and told me to collect my toilet articles and come along to Room 17. This room was down the hall and like the other, except there was only one bed, a small table, and a chair. The same type of rubber seal was taped over the window frame. "You will be given special treatment here," he said in his mushy English. "You will sit in the chair and think about your crimes against the Korean people."

Kong and the guard left me with my thoughts and a growing pain in the neck. I estimated we were only a hundred miles from South Korea and freedom. So near and yet so far.

Suddenly I heard a door slam—shouts, pounding, and moans from one of the rooms adjoining mine. When I heard a KORCOM yelling, "Bucher! Bucher!" I knew they were working on the captain. A few minutes later my door burst open. A guard looked in to see if I was in the ordered position, then closed the door. He kept looking in at different times during that long night. The pounding and moans continued at intervals from the skipper's room. I prayed hard that the Lord would help him.

At five A.M. a guard came after me.

The guard took me to the small interrogation room where Wheezy and Super-C sat waiting. Super-C wore a gray overcoat with lapels, and four big stars studded his flat shoulder boards. Not recognizing his rank, I thought he must be one of the biggest generals in the country.

Super-C held up my service record from a pile of material stolen from the ship. Through Wheezy, he began hurling questions. I soon realized that they knew the *Pueblo* was an intelligence collection ship. I felt I had no recourse but to confirm what they already knew.

"If you are sincere (*cough*) and repentant (*cough*) for your crimes," Wheezy recited for Super-C, "you may not be punished (*cough*). But you must (*cough*) make a full confession."

The interpreter handed me a thick pad of paper. "Go back (*cough*) to your room (*cough*) and write."

30

Back in my room I sat at the table with the pad before me and began writing. The chilling noises kept coming from the captain's room. Occasionally a guard looked in to see if I was writing. The day dragged on. A woman brought tasteless food. Time lost all meaning.

They came after me for another session of questioning. When Super-C got into technical matters, I sensed he was pretending to know more than he did. I also sensed it was terribly painful for the KORCOMS to lose face and admit lack of knowledge on any point.

When, for example, he asked me to explain a piece of coding equipment, I replied with a straight face, "It's based on a simple binary code with 120 bits per second." After adding some more jargon, I said, "Of course, you understand all this." Unwilling to lose face even in the presence of a prisoner, he went on to the next question.

The interpreter read over what I had written for Super-C. "Go back and write some more," Super-C said. "You must confess that your ship was in the waters of the Democratic People's Republic of North Korea."

I protested that this was not true. "Sir, we were almost four miles beyond your limits," I said meekly.

Super-C's face hardened. He shouted to the interpreter who conveyed his anger to me. "You will confess all or we will kill your men one by one. Now go and write."

Back in my room I sat before the paper and tried to think of literary dodges. I started to doze off, then jerked my head up when I heard a guard in the corridor. He passed my room and I heaved a sigh of relief. I wanted to sleep, but I couldn't turn out the light. The switch was on the outside.

Time crawled on. I figured the other men, especially

31

the officers, were getting beatings, too. I wondered how they were faring. I prayed for them more than I ever had before. I prayed the hardest for the captain. From the groans coming through the wall, I knew he was really getting inhuman treatment.

I prayed for strength not to hate the KORCOMS. Scripture helped me.

Fortunately, the chaplain friend who had showed me the way to Christ had recommended that I enroll in the Navigators' program of Scripture memory. I remembered looking up the Navs in the Boston yellow pages. A strong manly voice had answered. Bob Stevens said, "We're having an annual get-together this evening. Why don't you come?" He gave me an address and I showed up.

This was my first experience in real Christian fellowship. Several servicemen gave testimonies, then Bob gave a straight-from-the-shoulder talk about the necessity of spiritual growth. He stressed Scripture memorization. Afterward, I told him I would be stationed in Washington and did the Navs have a representative there. He gave me Jim White's name and phone number. I called Jim in Washington and we got acquainted. He enrolled me in the Nav program and I started working on the first packet of Scripture verse cards.

Now sitting in my room alone, trying to stay alert for the slightest noise at the door, I remembered Romans 3:23:

For all have sinned and come short of the glory of God.

I began feeling pity for the KORCOMS. "They're slaves of a Satanic ideology and a brutal system," I told myself. "They're doing what they're taught to do by the system." I reflected on the crucifixion of Christ. I prayed, "Lord, help me to love the KORCOMS as You love them."

I'm sure that if I had been in the captain's shoes then, it would have been much harder for me to pray that way. They gave him extra special treatment, as he testified later.

After several bouts of beating, they made me kneel on the floor. I knelt down, facing the wall, and an officer with a pistol drew back the slide and stood behind me . . . . Super-C said, "You have two minutes to sign the confession or be shot." I was somewhat relieved at the prospect of being shot without being tortured. At this point I thought it would be a blessing. I knew through human torture it is possible to get somebody to say anything, whether they mean it or not.

I spent two minutes on the floor and repeated over and over "I love you Rose. I love you Rose." At the end of two minutes, they asked me again if I was ready to sign. I said I would not sign. Then Super-C told the officer at my side to move, apparently so that when I was shot, and the bullet passed through my head, it would not hit the officer standing in front of me. Then the colonel said, "Kill the SOB." The gun clicked. Then the interpreter said, "Well, it was a misfire. You will have another two minutes. You were lucky the last time."

I had fully expected to be shot, but when the slide was drawn back, presumably to insert another bullet, and I did not hear any bullet hit the floor, I knew it was a game they were playing with me, and they weren't going to kill me.

The two minutes went by and I refused to confess. Then the colonel said I wasn't worth a bullet, and I would be beaten to death. . . . They beat me to the floor, and I lost consciousness after a few minutes.

Then I was carried out to my room and thrown on the bed. . . . I asked permission to go to the bathroom and they marched me to the head. All I could urinate was blood.

At ten o'clock that night, Chipmunk . . . and Super-C came with drawn pistols and said they would show me what happens to spies . . . . I was led down into a semi-basement.

A South Korean was there with a strap around his chest, strapped to the wall. They explained to me that he was a South Korean spy. He was alive but had been through a terrible ordeal. He had a compound fracture of the upper right arm. The bone was sticking out. He was stripped to the waist. He had completely bitten through his lower lip, and it was hanging down from the side of his mouth. His right eye had been put out. His head was hanging down. . . . Black matter had run out of his eye and down his right cheek. . . .

Then I was taken back to the interrogation room. . . . They asked me if I knew I was responsible for the lives of my crew and I answered *yes,* . . . and told them they had murdered one of my men. . . . I received a blow that sent me across the room for that statement.

I felt it was urgent for him [Super-C] to get some

sort of confession in order to . . . justify the piracy they had committed. . . . He said, "We will now begin to shoot your crew one at a time in your presence until you sign, and if you do not sign you know we have the means to persuade you."

I was not prepared to see my crew shot. They said they would start with the youngest man first and they would shoot them in order. They had already sent for Bland [Fireman Second Class Howard E. Bland, 21, and a close friend of Duane Hodges]. I was convinced they would do it . . . . They were animals. . . . They were desperate to get a confession and would shoot my men. I told them I would sign their confession, and I did sign it. Then I was taken back to my room and brought a huge tray of food—eggs and other goodies. I did not touch it. . . . I attempted to drown myself in a bucket of water . . . but I was unable to accomplish that.

This was the way the captain told it at the Navy inquiry. All I knew during these first terrible days was that they were beating and torturing him. I assumed they were working on the other officers and probably the enlisted men, too.

But they were determined to break the captain down first and they got to him by threatening to kill his men. Otherwise, I think he would have let them beat him to death. He's that kind of a guy.

The first I knew the co had made a false confession was when they accidentally turned up a tape recorder for a few seconds. I heard his voice clearly saying we were guilty of espionage and invading the territorial waters of North Korea. That's when I began to think that

35

resisting any more wasn't worth getting killed or causing some of the enlisted men to get tortured or killed.

Sure, I knew the Code of Conduct. Part Five says:

When questioned, should I become a prisoner of war, I am bound to give only name, rank, service number and date of birth. I will evade answering further questions to the utmost of my ability. I will make no oral or written statements disloyal to my country and its allies or harmful to their cause.

But Part Four of the Code also says,

I will keep faith with my fellow prisoners. I will give no information or take part in any action which might be harmful to my comrades.

There is little purpose in trying to justify what we did. Some will always say we were traitors. Some will say we were heroes. Neither designation applies in my opinion. We were just ordinary American servicemen who happened to be seized by Communist pirates. We were just trying to do what we sincerely thought was right in this life-or-death situation.

There are a couple of points I will make here. First, we could not possibly keep all the Code. If Captain Bucher and I, and the others who were ordered to write confessions, had refused, the KORCOMS would have started killing members of the crew. Certainly we felt they would. By provoking them to take this action we would have violated Part Four of the Code.

So I finally forced myself to write and sign their fake "confession" and read into a tape recorder. Then they demanded I copy the "confession" in my own handwriting several times. I learned later that the captain had been forced to do the same while photographers snapped pictures.

There is not space enough here to relate all the tortures which other *Pueblo* officers and crewmen had to endure during our first few days in hell. They made "Skip" Schumacher, the operations officer, squat and kicked him in the back and chest while guards stood on both sides with cocked machine guns held inches from his head. They beat Gene Lacy, the engineering officer, severely, then made him sit naked on a steaming radiator. Executive Officer Ed Murphy lost consciousness six times during a beating session. Sometimes the guards pushed a table leg with square corners behind a prisoner's knees so that in squatting he soon lost all feeling. Other times they bound the prisoner's upraised hands with wire or forced him to hold a chair above his head, squatting with the stick behind his knees. When the chair fell, they kicked him savagely. Sometimes they stomped on the backs of legs and ankles and made the prisoner run on his knees on the rough floor until his legs were bloody and raw.

The beatings and tortures were coldly programmed and calculated to break us into total submission. They did nothing from passion or impulse. Guards would come to my room, for example, with instructions to administer ten kicks on the ankles and shins. In one questioning session the officers might smile and show a hint of cordiality. In the next they might be grim and sadistic.

On the morning of February 8, Major Floors came to my room with a razor. We gave him that name later because it was his job to see that we mopped our floors each morning.

"Today is the twentieth anniversary of the glorious Korean People's Army," he announced grandly. "Since you have confessed and repented, we will allow you to share in our celebration."

When he saw that I didn't know how to use the straight razor, he sharpened it on his wide brown belt and did the job himself. Then a woman brought in cake, bread, some chicken, dried octopus, and a glass of ginseng wine. A three-day-old hamburger would have tasted better. But I didn't want to offend them. I was holding out hope that we might soon be released.

After the "Army Day" meal, a woman brought candy, cookies, and an egg. A man carrying a movie light and camera trailed in behind and set up for pictures. Jack Warner, we nicknamed him. Whenever he came around we knew something was up.

But there was little joy in my lonely room. I still had not been permitted to talk to a single member of the crew since our capture over two weeks before. The loneliness and the uncertainty of not knowing the welfare of the rest of the crew was worse than the beatings. The days that immediately followed merged one into another. I was permitted to sleep now, but the daily pumping for information and the beatings continued. I prayed constantly, "Lord, help me not to say anything that will hurt my country." I took care never to tell them anything of importance that they didn't already know.

I started each dreary day by running a damp dirty rag which I had rinsed in a rusty bucket of dirty water over the floor. A woman brought in breakfast—more of the same slop, then I was left alone with my thoughts and memories and the suspense of not knowing when they would come for me again.

While I sat and waited, I prayed for my loved ones, my country, my shipmates whom I hoped were still alive, that we would be released soon, and that I would not hate the KORCOMS. I dredged up all the Scripture verses I could remember. There were two that were of special comfort.

Thou wilt keep him in perfect peace, whose mind is stayed on thee: Because he trusteth in thee (Isaiah 26:3).

And,

Casting all your care upon him; for he careth for you. (I Peter 5:7).

I had heard that the Lord is always there just when you need Him most. And, boy, I needed Him the most!

One morning I used a piece of leftover confession paper to write down a Scripture verse when I felt sure the guards would not intrude.

I can do all things through Christ which strengtheneth me (Philippians 4:13).

This was the beginning of the *Pueblo Bible*.

The Navy assigned two officers to help Esther. They broke through red tape and helped her get power of attorney to receive my check. She didn't want to take another job because she didn't know how long I would be held captive. One weekend she visited her sick mother

39

in Montreal who reminded her, "Remember that I once predicted you and Steve will have a son. I still believe that." Esther reluctantly left her mother and returned to Washington to be with her brother Gus in case my situation should suddenly change. Gus kept her informed of diplomatic developments.

On Boston Rock, Mother got word that her brother, a communications consultant for the U.S. Agency for International Development, was caught in a Viet Cong suicide attack during the Communist Tet offensive. This and not knowing about me put a double burden on her. (News came later that my uncle had survived unhurt.)

One evening in late January, Mother arrived home in her little green car to find her house on the Rock had been ransacked. Dishes had been shattered, cabinets left open, and the beds and floors littered with papers and costume jewelry. The back door was open. But nothing seemed to be missing. The culprit(s) was never caught.

The telephone startled her. "Eleanor! Steve is on the radio making some kind of confession!" a neighbor exclaimed. Mother twisted the dial and found the station carrying the recording. It "sounded like" me.

The Navy helped Esther keep away from reporters. But Mother made them all feel welcome. After the broadcast, one quoted her as saying: "I am a patriot. Five of my brothers have flown for my country. I have the utmost faith in the integrity and power of this country to do what is necessary to bring my son back."

But President Johnson said in reporting on the failure of negotiations at Panmunjom and the United Nations that he "was not hopeful of getting the men back soon."

3

█▄█

We Meet the Press

After I signed the "confession" and it was accepted, an English-speaking KORCOM came to my room and read off the "Rules of Life" from a paper.

1. The daily schedule will be strictly observed.
2. You will always display courtesy to the duty personnel when they enter your room to deal with you.
3. You must not talk loudly or sing in your room.
4. You must not sit or lie on the floor or bed except on Sundays and during prescribed hours but should sit on the chair.
5. You must wear your clothes at all times except while washing your face and in bed.
6. You must take care of the room, furniture and all expendables issued to you.
7. You will keep your room and corridors clean at all times.

8. You must keep in good order while engaging in collective activities in the mess hall and elsewhere.
9. You will entertain yourself only with the culture provided.
10. If you have something to do, ask permission from the guards, who will escort you to the appropriate place.

He stopped and looked to see if I was listening.

"You will be punished severely and unconditionally if you commit one of these offenses:

1. In case you make false statements or refuse questioning or hint to others to do so.
2. In case you attempt to signal other rooms by this or that means.
3. In case you make unauthorized writing.
4. In case you show disrespect to any of the duty personnel.
5. In case you make any other offense.

"Keep these and you will be treated well," he said. Then he turned on his heels and left.

Super-C called me in again. "How fast did your ship go?"
"Not fast enough, sir," I replied without thinking.
Wham! The guard hit me.
He switched to Polaris submarines. "How deep can they go?" he asked.

I pretended to think for a few seconds, then replied, "About 3,000 meters [9,000 feet], sir." He seemed to believe this ridiculous answer.

The KORCOMS kept the crew apart from the officers. They even prohibited the enlisted men from talking to us when we met in the latrines. The guards searched them for messages on toilet paper when they came out.

One morning two of the crew, Lee Hayes and Charles Ayling who were next door to each other, got a Morse code conversation going by tapping on the radiator pipes. When Hayes heard another tapping, he thought someone had broken into the conversation. He scratched the pipes to tell Ayling to stop and waited for the guards to burst in. They didn't. Later the crew was warned that sending messages was a crime punishable by death.

A few days after the KORCOMS' Army Anniversary, a guard took Hayes to clean the captain's room. The guard stepped out, giving them the chance to talk a little. The captain told Hayes that he'd had no choice but to sign a confession, or see the crew shot one by one. Hayes told the skipper where some of the crew were in the building.

The second time Hayes was taken to the captain's room, he managed to slip a note into the skipper's pocket when the KORCOM duty officer turned away for a few seconds. The third time the KORCOM was all eyes. Suddenly the captain began drumming on the table with a pencil. Hayes got part of it in Morse code, SEND ME ALL THE MESSAGES . . .

The duty officer became suspicious. "Stop!" he shouted. "Message? Message?" he asked Hayes.

Hayes replied, "No. He's just nervous."

Either the KORCOM didn't understand or didn't believe

Hayes. He snatched the pencil and got so mad Hayes thought he was going to shoot the skipper. Later, Hayes figured out the rest of the message, . . . PUT THEM UNDER MY PILLOW. But he was afraid to try another note.

The KORCOMS thought the oceanographers were linked up with the CIA. They called in Friar Tuck.

"Who gave you your orders?" Super-C demanded to know.

Friar smiled thinly. "My secretary, sir."

When the interpreter repeated this answer, Super-C frowned.

"That's right, sir," Friar assured him. "She handed them to me just as I walked out of my office."

The three wounded crewmen suffered in agony and filth in a room next to Super-C's big office. The ship's baker, Dale Rigby, was the fourth man in the room.

The dark-haired Mormon youth from Utah knew only Boy Scout first aid. He helped his roommates clean their infected wounds and helped them to the head. Charles Crandell had pieces of shrapnel in one leg. Bob Chicca had a bullet wound in his leg. Steve Woelk from Kansas was in worse shape from a body wound, delirious with pain, and unable to move.

Each time a guard stuck his head in, Rigby begged, "Please get a doctor." The only response he got was a command to accompany a guard to an interrogation room across the hall. When Rigby refused to give more than his name, rank and serial number, the KORCOM officer screamed and put the stick behind the baker's knees. He made him squat and hold the chair over his head.

The baker held out for forty-five minutes before dropping the chair.

The guard stripped Rigby naked and kicked him repeatedly with a heavy boot. He beat a hole in his back with the table leg. He pressed a gun barrel against his head and clicked the trigger on an empty chamber.

Four hours later the KORCOM who had been shouting questions at Rigby started getting answers. It seeped through the baker's throbbing head that they had his service record and he could tell them nothing they didn't already know. For two more hours he gave them information about the meals and food supplies of the *Pueblo*. Then the guard took him back to his foul-smelling room.

Finally on the third night of captivity two guards carried Woelk on his blood-soaked stretcher to an improvised operating room. Under the light of a bare bulb a doctor performed major surgery—without anesthesia.

The infection returned and Woelk's pain got worse. The stench in the room became so foul that one man opened the door and vomited. Rigby finally convinced the North Koreans that Woelk might die. On the tenth day they carried him to a jeep and drove him through the zero degree night to a hospital.

The KORCOMS beat and tortured other enlisted men in varying degrees until they volunteered personnel information which our captors already had. Frank Ginther got one of the worst beatings. When he had been beaten savagely and made to squat over the stick and hold the chair in the air, he groaned, "God, help me!" The questioner grabbed a broad belt from the table and cracked the buckle across Ginther's temple. Ginther instinctively started to slam the chair over the head of his assailant, but held up at the last second. A KORCOM officer yelled in English, "Kill him! Kill him!" He got the belt again and a ruler, and so many kicks that he lapsed into semi-consciousness.

When his senses returned, they demanded that he admit the *Pueblo* was in their territorial waters. "And in Russian waters, too," one of the officers added. Poor Ginther couldn't see how the *Pueblo* could be in two places at the same time, but he agreed to fill out a questionnaire. Like the rest of us, he planned to make it so obviously false that it would not stand up before an impartial international court.

The KORCOMS immediately began publishing our "confessions" in their propaganda sheets. They were patently false to anyone with the most basic knowledge.

The captain added two extra digits to his serial number and confessed that the U.S. Central Intelligence Agency had promised "a lot of dollars" for successful performance of our mission. The CIA was never involved. We said we had fired on the KORCOM patrol boats while trying to escape. Our radio communication before capture indicated that we had not. And the captain asked to be "forgiven leniently," adding, "the crime committed by me and my men is entirely indelible."

I suggested some strange wording in a recorded radio broadcast for the crew. After "confessing" our intrusion in their waters, I cited the definition of rape from the U.S. Uniform Code of Military Justice: "Any penetration, however slight, is sufficient to complete the offense." Anyone checking this statement would have noticed that the manual continued, "Rape is a most detestable crime . . . but it must be remembered that it is an accusation easy to be made, hard to prove, but harder to be defended by the party accused, though innocent."

Skip Schumacher wrote that he was "deeply moved by the humanitarian treatment accorded its guilty persons by the government of the Democratic People's Republic of Korea. I am grateful for this opportunity of confession offered to such a criminal as I."

A few evenings later they began taking us six at a time on a bus to a communal bathhouse about a half mile away where we splashed around in a huge Japanese tub. Outside the bathhouse we could see the mercury vapor lights on the bridge over the Daedong River. We heard children chanting close by and felt they were students at a military school.

At the start of our fourth week in captivity, we officers and Friar Tuck, one of the civilian oceanographers, were suddenly brought to the big interrogation room where we had received the death sentence. Major Robot (he acted like one) was waiting, a big smile wrapped across his ugly face. "We're going to have a press conference," he told us grandly.

While they were passing out questions, Skip Schumacher leaned over to me and whispered, "I thought you were dead."

Robot told us to begin phrasing our answers. The questions were a rehash of what they had demanded in our "confessions." We saw no point in being stubborn. They would only beat and torture us again. Considering what had actually happened, our answers were ridiculous. For example:

Q. How is the health of the crew, Captain?

He was supposed to say that the Democratic People's

Republic of Korea is "very progressive and has a gentlemanly and understanding people."

Then there were questions relating to our "criminal acts" in which they dragged in Prime Minister Sato of Japan. We had to reply to Sato's claim that the *Pueblo* was captured on the high seas. Robot obviously wanted to show how Japan was helping U.S. "aggression" in Asia.

The skipper was to say, "That's nonsense. Prime Minister Sato and his officials were not on board our ship. If they had been, they would have been captured together with us and detained, wouldn't they?"

I was instructed to "volunteer" this gem of wisdom: "Obviously the prime minister of a country where the espionage ship was based did not wish to admit that such a ship has committed a crime."

And Skip Schumacher was handed this little delight to offer to the "patriotic" press: "The unfounded statements made by Prime Minister Sato remind me of an American saying that the faithful dog will not bite the hand that feeds him."

At the appointed time, about twenty Korean reporters trotted in wearing fake smiles and pretending to act very professional with their notebooks, tape recorders, and cameras. Jack Warner was Johnny-on-the-spot to help set up movie cameras.

That day I gained a healthy appreciation for American freedom of the press. We may gripe about prying reporters and slanted stories, but our system is a million times better than the flow of information under Communism. Truth to Communists is what best serves the party line. Facts are of no importance to them unless they happen to suit ideological purposes.

Before the questioning, the KORCOM officers passed around a carbonated cider drink. Robot was the moderator. Wheezy, Major Flat Face (his mug looked like it was painted on a board) and Silver Lips (he had a soft delicate voice) were the interpreters who handled the canned questions and answers.

The reporters asked us the questions on the list. We gave the answers they wanted. They could have just mimeographed this stuff and sent it to printers and announcers. But they apparently wanted us on film in a posed interchange with the reporters for the greatest propaganda value.

At the end of the press conference, one of the reporters suggested that a letter of apology should be drafted and signed by all the crew. Robot pretended to think this was a great idea; he or Super-C had no doubt planted the proposal. Looking very pleased with himself, Robot instructed Captain Bucher to appoint a drafting committee. The CO went along—I think because he knew this would be an opportunity to let families back home know that all except Duane Hodges were alive—and named me, Skip Schumacher, Friar Tuck, and several enlisted men.

We weren't allowed to work privately. Silver Lips hung around and appeared not to be interested, but we knew he was listening to everything that was said.

Silver Lips took our first draft back to Super-C who said it lacked emotional appeal. So we added:

Eighty-two crew members of the U.S.S. *Pueblo* have all their parents, wives, and children at home.

They are sorrowed because of us and are anxiously waiting for our return.

Those of us who are young have long futures and cherish great hope in human life.

Our families and relatives have already undergone great sufferings. They are entrusting everything in us whose future is unknown.

We, the 82 men of the *Pueblo,* make an earnest appeal to the Government of the Democratic People's Republic of Korea in the name of ourselves and our families.

Please take mercy on us and our kin. Please give us a chance for regeneration and forgive us generously and allow us to go home so as to bring new hope to them.

Silver Lips read it over and nodded his approval. "Good, I will show it to the colonel."

Super-C thought this would do and asked for a man with good penmanship to prepare two copies. Elton Wood, a whiz in electronics and one of my men, got the job. He laboriously copied the long joint apology to the KORCOM government and a letter to President Johnson asking that the U.S. government also apologize.

Super-C decked out the big interrogation room for the signing ceremonies. He displayed the *Pueblo*'s doctored log and other impressive-looking documents. When the officers marched in, Jack Warner and his movie crew were there ready to grind away with their West German Arriflex cameras and Japanese photo lights and film.

Silver Lips told us to sign first and then take our seats in the usual order of command. Then they paraded the crew in and ordered them to sign. The captain passed word for us to count the crew and look each man over closely to determine his condition. Some of the men limped painfully, but it was hard to tell how badly they had been beaten. We figured the KORCOMS had handled them as they had us so that mistreatment would not show up on movie film.

At the CO's suggestion every man signed except Steven Woelk. The KORCOMS said he was still recuperating in a hospital. At this time, all of the crew learned for the first time that Duane Hodges was dead.

After they got the "joint apology," the KORCOMS lightened up. They let us come out in the hall and do push-ups and jumping jacks for exercise. One pitch black night they marched us about 100 yards to a small stadium for an outdoor workout. I could tell that the city was partially blacked out. Apparently they were worried about some kind of U.S. retaliation.

The fourth week we officers were allowed to get together after supper and play cards or Ping-Pong. We talked together about our possibilities for release. One of the KORCOMS had spread a rumor that negotiations were beginning at Punmunjom.

Back in my room I wrote down a few more verses. Psalm 119:11 was one:

Thy Word have I hid in mine heart, that I might not sin against thee.

Another that offered precious comfort was Lamentations 3:22, 23:

51

It is of the Lord's mercies that we are not con-
sumed, because his compassions fail not. They are
new every morning: great is thy faithfulness.

With the sheet still nailed between the double windows
and the forbidding seal attached, I had nowhere to look
except to God. Every morning after breakfast, I prayed
for my loved ones, for the crew, for our captors. "Lord,"
I said with determination, "Your power is greater than
Satan's and the whole Communist system. Help me to
love and not to hate, to hope and not to despair."

Then suddenly a duty officer appeared on the afternoon of March 5, our forty-first day of captivity, and
ordered me to roll up the mattress and pack up my belongings. I grabbed a few propaganda magazines and
some picture postcards which they had dropped in the
room, pencil and pen, and my precious Scripture verses
which had not been discovered. I cleaned the room for
the last time.

They herded us outside and jammed us like sardines
into two Pyongyang city buses that had sheets hung over
the windows.

I heard the interpreter Chipmunk say, "Sit with your
hands in your pockets."

"But there isn't room," someone protested.

Chipmunk retorted, "You must overcome."

The buses pulled away. Could we dare to believe that
we were going to be released?

*By this time Esther had returned to Washington and
was living with her brother Gus. She and Mom stayed in
close touch by telephone between Washington and Bos-*

ton. *Esther attended the Fourth Presbyterian Church with Gus and Fannie and was encouraged by the prayers of Pastor Richard Halverson and church friends. With her mother seriously ill in Canada and not knowing whether she would ever see me again, Esther had a tough time. But she never lost faith that the Lord was going to take care of me.*

Mom developed a close friendship with the widowed mother of Communications Technician Ralph McClintock who lived in the southern Boston suburb of Milton. Hundreds of letters came to the two widows and the parents of other Pueblo *crewmen. In her duplicated reply to letters, Mother wrote:*

> *I realize in spite of my fears, I have much to be thankful for since Steve has been officially reported "alive." My country appears to be doing its utmost to secure their release through peaceful means. Believe me, forceful means would be a fatal mistake, and many now realize this.*

Negotiations for our release began during secret meetings between U.S. Rear Admiral John V. Smith and North Korean Major General Pak Chung-Kuk. But Administration officials in Washington were balking at apologizing since they did not believe the Pueblo *had violated North Korea's territorial waters.*

4

Nineteen Eighty-Four Is Here

I clung to the hope that we might be on our way to freedom, yet I feared they might be taking us to a place for execution. Our government had not apologized as the KORCOMS had demanded. Or if it had, they hadn't told us.

We were really in the dark about the outside world. Once they had assured me my mother and sister were in good health. I don't have a sister. They had also read us a statement from Secretary of State Dean Rusk. But this was all. The U.S. and Russia could have blown each other up in a nuclear war and we wouldn't have known it.

We bounced about half an hour over bumpy roads—about seven or eight miles, I estimated. Then the buses stopped and we were directed into a new three-story, U-shaped cement block building.

On both sides of the entrance I saw paintings of "victories" in the Korean War: a wrecked U.S. plane, a tank destroyed, and Premier Kim Il Sung congratulating his soldiers. The foyer had marble floors. Potted plants filled an alcove. I thought at first we were inside a courthouse. Later, when I saw obstacle courses and hurdles on the grounds, a rifle range, and barracks across the courtyard, I felt this was the headquarters building for an infantry training school.

Super-C, through Silver Lips, gave a little welcome speech. "Your captain has been concerned about your lack of recreation. Here you will have opportunity to play basketball, volleyball, walk around, and enjoy movies." He flashed his horse smile. "We hope your stay will be pleasant and that you will come to appreciate the glorious Fatherland which our brilliant, iron-willed Premier Kim Il Sung has won from the imperialist colonialist Japanese aggressors."

The guards took us to our rooms on the second and third floors. The enlisted men had larger rooms than in the first prison, but here they were quartered eight to a room. We officers were given individual but smaller rooms.

My new room on the second deck was well lighted. The bulb was encased in a globe and the switch was *inside* the room. The "Rules of Life" in English were posted on the door. There was a bed, chair, night stand with compartment, and a small round table with drawer. A three-paned, uncurtained casement window overlooked the dirt courtyard. The floorboards were warped and separated just as in the first prison.

When the guard left I looked down and saw a couple of Russian-built staff jeeps, two black West German Opel sedans, and one green Korean truck. Later I concluded that North Korea is the only country in the world that builds used trucks!

After supper they took us into a big room they called the "club" room and Jack Warner started, *The Girl from Mt. Kumgang* [*Diamond Mountain*]. The feature film first showed the "imperialist" Japanese stomping an old man's violin to pieces. Then came the "victorious liberation" led by the "iron-willed, glorious" Premier Kim Il Sung. Under the new socialist regime, the old man's daughter, "The Girl from Diamond Mountain," found a way to study music and became gifted on the *kayageum,* a North Korean harp-like stringed instrument.

I saw green rice paddies over an embankment and beyond the bluish mountains. The opening verses of Psalm 121 flashed into mind:

I will lift up mine eyes unto the hills from whence cometh my help. My help cometh from the Lord which made heaven and earth.

That day Colonel Specs came around smiling. "Arrange the room as you wish," he said. And as if he were offering me a free weekend in Hawaii, he added, "You may have your choice of any of the potted plants in the alcove."

I went out and picked out a small evergreen. I sat it on my table and moved the table to where it would get maximum sunshine. Each morning I watered it and turned it so that each side got a share of sunlight. The little plant grew and greened into a beautiful shrub. It was my one delight in the drab room.

They put us on a regular regimen. An electric bell jarred us awake at six; when the days grew longer it sounded at five. After room cleaning (using a dirty rag), we had breakfast at seven. The officers ate separately from the enlisted men. Next came "self-education," when we were supposed to read propaganda in our rooms. At one, we had lunch with background music—such socialist tunes as "The Road to the Factory," "Near the Seaside From Where a Blast Furnace Can Be Seen," and a march which we called "Hymn to Kim." After lunch, we exercised and played ball for an hour. This was followed in hot weather by an hour's nap. More "self-education" came before supper; then, when the meal was done, we officers could socialize and play inside games until ten. Twice weekly they let us bathe with water heated in a boiler house attached to the main building.

We couldn't see how anything could be worse than the slop we had eaten in the old place. But the food here was a gourmet's nightmare, probably because we had moved in between planting seasons.

An out-of-this-world breakfast menu included turnips, uniformly sliced and floating in a sauce resembling used crank-case oil. The bread was like stratified cinder block. The butter was like rancid vaseline and moldy. Sometimes we had rotten fish which we called sewer trout and adhesive rice. We used the rice to keep the "Rules of Life" stuck to our door. On very special occasions we each got an apple.

The only difference between breakfast and the other two meals was that lunch came at one and supper at seven. We found the diet an excellent help in bringing our weight down.

Twice weekly we had to endure four-hour indoctrination meetings. After a lecture and some discussion, the political officers whom we called "Room Daddies," gave us oral exams on the propaganda we were supposed to have been studying after breakfast in our rooms. We soon caught on that North Korea hadn't yet abolished corporal punishment in the school room!

Friday nights there were films—always political—with discussion and questions coming during the following week. Saturdays we cleaned up, and Sundays we rested. Later we discovered that except for work, our schedule pretty well matched the rest of the country. Everybody in North Korea gets up at six in winter and five in summer. Everybody eats at one, exercises afterward, then takes a short nap in the summer before returning to work. Everybody cleans up on Saturday, including field-grade Army officers. Everybody rests on Sunday and engages in group activities. Everybody listens to propaganda. We could hear the speakers blaring away in nearby villages. The Orwellian Society of 1984 is here!

The familiar bunch of KORCOM officers came with us to the new place, but we had a new set of guards. The officers lived on the first floor and the guards bunked in barracks across the courtyard.

We found their military rank structure similar to ours, except the North Korean Army has three lieutenant and three colonel ranks. I later learned that there is a huge gap between KORCOM officers' and enlisted men's monthly pay. A private gets 1.4 won ($.60). A sergeant receives 7 won ($2.80). At the next step, a junior lieutenant is paid 50 won ($20) and a senior colonel takes in 150 won

($60).* The officers probably get special benefits, but so far as I could tell our guards (enlisted men) were virtually slaves. They never left the premises except for trips with us. Like other U.S. servicemen, I've done my share of griping. But after seeing North Korea's system, I'll think ten times before sounding off in the future.

The KORCOM officers and guards never opened their personal lives to us. They claimed their families were killed during the Korean War.

They never gave us their real names. We had to stand up when an officer or guard entered the room, address them politely, and keep our heads bowed. We had to "sir" the officers and during later purges had to bow when meeting them in the hall.

We had to call them something among ourselves. Only Americans would come up with such nicknames.

Super-C, the senior colonel with the horse smile, was the big boss. He and Major Artful Dodger were Room Daddies for the *Pueblo* officers. Art got that name because he was always trying to fast talk answers to our questions about the propaganda. Major Possum (the worst liar in the bunch), Colonel Specs (he wore thick spectacles), and Major Robot were Room Daddies for the *Pueblo* crewmen.

A dozen or so English-speaking duty officers seemed to be omnipresent. Silent Sam had the poorest command of English. One day he admitted he had been listening to jazz on the Voice of America. He thought it immoral and wondered why Americans sang about love so much.

Snake was a crafty character who must have had spe-

* *Area Handbook for North Korea,* U.S. Government Printing Office, 1969, p. 410.

cial training from Satan himself. Bloke had evidently known British influence and was a halfway decent chap. Chipmunk, the guy who told us we had to squeeze together and "overcome" on the bus, looked as if he had cheeks full of nuts. Fetch was kind of a clumsy clod but about the nicest of any of our captors. He ended every sentence with "Huh?" Solutions, another duty officer, always told us, "When an officer comes in, you must give a *solution.*" Lieutenant Fuzz was young and inexperienced. Hatchet Face looked like a movie Indian on the warpath.

Silver Lips and Wheezy were interpreters whom I've already mentioned. Captain Nice (more cordial than most) and Captain Queer (an effeminate character) could handle English almost as well as Silver Lips and Wheezy. Bush-Around-the-Beat was always getting his words out of order. He would say to a guy who seemed to be evading a question, "Don't bush around the beat."

Deputy Dawg, a Colonel, fudged the *Pueblo's* navigation charts and data for press conferences. We named him for the cartoon character and the party achievement badge he always sported. The captain called another third-grade colonel, Colonel Skeezix, because he looked like the character in Gasoline Alley. Missile looked like a character in a James Thurber cartoon. He was always asking questions about U.S. missiles. We also called him All Right because when he meant yes, he always said, "All right." And I mustn't forget Oddjob. If you've ever seen the James Bond movie *Goldfinger,* you've seen this fat fellow. Buster Bulb, a junior lieutenant, seemed to have nothing else to do but hold a portable battery-run movie spotlight for Jack Warner.

The guards had names, too. Loud Mouth was exceeded in meanness and loudness only by an overzealous young corporal we named Trigger Tongue. We called another The Fly because he was constantly going from room to room, pointing at the swarms of flies and croaking, *"Kill! Kill!"* the only English word he knew. A rubber fly swatter (which the Koreans called a fly flapper) was standard equipment in every room during the summer months. The stick still had bark on it. We dubbed the fly the National Bird of North Korea. The KORCOMS blamed them on U.S. biological warfare. Some guys called The Fly "Dopey." He was always grinning, even when pounding on a guy. He walked stooped over—from the weight of his gun, I guess—and he did look a little like Dopey in the Walt Disney movie *Snow White and the Seven Dwarfs.*

Other guards were Frog-Face, Dum-Dum, Little Caesar, Blockhead, and The Bear. Flo (for Florence Nightingale) and Little Iodine were two nurses assigned to the new building.

I'm glad The Bear wasn't on my floor. Ginther and his seven roommates in Room 8 on the third floor called this sadist Halfbreed because his height and complexion suggested some Caucasian ancestry. They also called him Gooney Bird because for some reason he made them think of the birds that live on Midway Island.

The Bear was a good six feet and the tallest of all the guards. With his big fists and Paul Bunyan feet, he didn't really need the submachine gun he carried to enforce his authority. The guys in Room 8 said he seemed to be in seventh heaven when administering a beating.

No one on the third floor was ever safe from him. He

peeked through keyholes to catch a man nodding or staring at the wall when he was supposed to be absorbing the propaganda garbage. He administered punishment with a heavy hand or brutal boot.

The Bear was on duty when Norm Spear's belt broke while he was returning from the head. Spear grabbed his pants to keep them from falling. He had lost so much weight the belt was necessary to hold them up. The Bear saw him looking embarrassed and thought he had broken the rules. The big guard followed Spear to his room and chopped him on the head and grabbed his shirt. Poor Spear hung onto his pants for dear life while the other guys looked on not knowing whether to laugh or cry.

Finally, Ginther said, "Let him see your broken belt." Spear extended it and The Bear lunged at him like a wounded grizzly.

The Bear seemed to have a fixation on the eight guys in Room 8 on the third deck. He was always picking on the guy sitting in the chair opposite the door, so they took turns sitting in that chair to divide up the punishment.

A few days after we were housed in the new prison, Super-C magnanimously said we could write personal letters home and ask our loved ones to work on our government for an apology. He said this was a great humanitarian gesture toward "criminals" such as we. Actually it was nothing more than the old Communist ploy to persuade innocent people to help them get what they wanted.

Except for individual expressions of affection and personal greetings, there was very little difference in any of our letters. Most of us used the garbage which our "kind" captors dished out. Take this example from my letter to Mom and Esther:

It is no news by now that *Pueblo* was captured in the act of collecting intelligence in the territorial waters of the Democratic People's Republic of Korea. Since no state of war exists between the Democratic People's Republic of Korea and the United States, we are not prisoners of war, but espionage criminals who committed a crime against a foreign state. The penalty for espionage in this country is death, but our lives have been spared because we sincerely and frankly confessed the crime. However, we will not be released unless the government of the United States takes the following action: (1) Confess to the D.P.R.K. that U.S.S. *Pueblo* did conduct espionage activities in the territorial waters of the D.P.R.K. (2) Apologize sincerely to the D.P.R.K. for such action. (3) Assure the D.P.R.K. that such an act will never be repeated.

If these conditions are not met, then we will be executed for the act. Therefore, you must help me and eighty-one others of us here. You must contact our congressmen and senators and plead for proper action by our government.

. . . We are not in a prison or prison camp, but in a comfortable, clean, well-heated building. We are served three nourishing meals a day and have been provided warm clothing. We are in no way abused or harassed, but are treated humanely. But we are here and want very much to come home. Our hearts are torn with grief and we recognize that our loved ones are experiencing even greater sorrow.

Esther, you should be receiving my navy pay as well as my mail. . . . The beneficiaries on all my life insurance policies are correct and there is ample money for both of you if the worst happens. But don't think about that! Act in our behalf and pray. Esther, have faith in Aiti's [Esther's mother] vision that we will have a son and continue faithfully doing God's work. You will be highly rewarded.

I love and miss you both so much that even as a grown man I have broken into tears many times. I hope that I will be able to hear from you very soon.

With all my love,
STEPHEN

There was no point in telling the truth about the *Pueblo* and our inhumane treatment. The KORCOMS would have started a fresh round of beatings and would not have let up until we agreed to write the lies they wanted.

After we finished our letters, the KORCOMS demanded that some of us address personal, handwritten letters to senators, congressmen, the Secretary of State, and other U.S. government officials. They wanted the same requests made that we had put in our personal letters. Super-C ordered us to make two copies of our personal letters so our loved ones would get at least one. The "imperialist war-mongering President Johnson and the CIA will certainly intercept two of the letters," he assured us with a straight face. So I addressed my three letters to Mom because I was not sure where Esther would be staying.

The letters were approved, sent in some roundabout way to New York, and mailed from there with U.S. postage. We saw most of them a few weeks later reprinted in a North Korean propaganda newspaper printed in English.

Altogether, it was a sad way to let our loved ones know that we were still alive.

Esther remained in Washington. Mother called her as soon as the letters began arriving and mailed one on to her.

Mother sent letters to every U.S. senator and many other government leaders. Her letter to the senators read:

As the distraught mother of a fine young officer captured aboard the U.S.S. Pueblo, I have waited in vain for nearly 12 weeks for some word of progress by our government. Pueblo's 82 men are threatened with execution, as stated in letters home to parents and wives, unless our President apologizes and meets certain conditions. What is keeping him? What have you done to save these men?

While our Navy advisers at local levels right on up to Secretary of the Navy have tried to comfort us anxious parents, we want progress, not comfort. "Doing everything possible" seems to boil down to only one avenue of hope: i.e., negotiations at Panmunjom (which must be "carried on in secret" to be effective). While we parents appreciate the need for secrecy, after 13 such meetings, where are we?

What is our sons' captors' price for 82 lives? What ransom has been offered? There is only one thing they are asking—an apology. These eighty-two highly-trained young Navy men love their country well. During these long anxious weeks of incarceration, how many times have they asked the agonizing questions: Has my country forgotten me? Are they about to let me die through sheer negligence of my live-or-die request?

Last night on the newscast by Huntley-Brinkley, documents were shown of the Pueblo's records purportedly proving the ship was in North Korean territorial waters. Whether or not this eventually proves to be the truth, this entire nation would understand why our President is apologizing—if he so chooses.

I continue to have implicit faith in the power of my great country to resolve this dilemma with honor and dignity. In the case of the Pueblo, however, we are dealing with an "outlaw regime" [quotation from Rear Admiral John V. Smith]. Even outlaws can lose their patience.

An apology is about as "peaceful" a solution as one could find. Please get busy before it's too late!

Sincerely and gratefully,

ELEANOR VAN BUSKIRK HARRIS.

Mother received replies from many senators, including one from Robert Kennedy just before his assassination. She also heard from the Billy Graham Evangelistic Association:

We will be remembering your son as well as the other men captured on the Pueblo in our prayers. When the opportune time comes Mr. Graham will

66

give a good word in behalf of these men, to those in authority. Claim with us John 15:7, Jeremiah 33:3, and Matthew 18:20.

Meanwhile, the U.S. and North Korean negotiators meeting secretly at Panmunjom continued at loggerheads with one another. Rear Admiral Smith called the Pueblo's seizure, "War provocation of the most serious magnitude." Admiral Smith's counterpart, General Pak Chung-kuk, retorted that the Pueblo's "intrusion in North Korean waters was part of a scheme by the imperialist United States to start another Korean war."

In the U.S. some Pueblo relatives told reporters that they suspected the letters had been written "under supervision." And a private group called "The Remember the Pueblo Committee" helped keep our plight before the American public. REMEMBER THE PUEBLO bumper stickers began appearing from coast to coast.

5

School Daze

Life dragged on in the "socialist paradise." Monday
through Friday I could see the peasants trekking to the
fields in the morning and returning in the afternoon.
From my window they looked like a column of big ants,
all dressed alike, all walking at the same pace. Saturdays and Sundays and on special holidays they did not
go out.

I felt a special pang on March 21, Esther's birthday.
I wondered what she was doing and if she and Mother
had received my letter. None of us had yet been permitted to receive letters from home.

Sunday, March 31, was my thirtieth birthday. After
watering my plant, worshiping alone, and reciting my
verses, I fell to thinking about where I had been on past
birthdays.

The year before I had just arrived in Bremerton,
Washington, to oversee the installation of the electronic

equipment on the *Pueblo*. Captain Pete Bucher was already there. It was to be his first command and to be my first stint as an officer in charge of an independent detachment of men. The old supply ship had been in mothballs for twelve years before the Navy began readying her for a new mission. For the first time she got a name—from the city of Pueblo, Colorado. (I wonder what the North Koreans have done with her since the capture.)

Five years before I had been the communications officer on the destroyer *Forrest Sherman*. Life is full of coincidences. Still it had seemed strange to be on a ship named for the former Chief of Naval Operations who came from my home town, Melrose, Massachusetts. The *Forrest Sherman* was sleek and fast, carried five-inch guns and torpedos, and was one of the best ASW (Anti-Submarine Warfare) ships in the Atlantic fleet. My previous ship, the *Grand Canyon,* had been a 14,000-ton destroyer tender and sometimes sat in port for weeks while maintenance personnel did repair work on another ship. During the three years I served on these ships, I saw many of the fascinating cities of the Biblical world. I climbed the Parthenon overlooking Athens and stood on the hill from which the Apostle Paul preached to the philosophers. I rode a tour bus to Philippi along the road Paul was supposed to have traveled. I saw the ruins of an early Christian church built across from the traditional site of the jail where the apostle was imprisoned. And I looked at stone steps at Berea from which Paul is said to have preached. A few miles away I walked through the town of Naousa, where, during the Greek civil war, the Communists killed all the males. Little did

I realize then that one day I would be a prisoner of the Communists.

These places held for me then only passing historical interest. I thought of Jesus as only a good fellow who had battled the religious establishment of an ancient era and lost. Paul was an obscure preacher I had heard about a few times in Sunday school. I was the chaplain's assistant on the *Forrest Sherman* but about all that required was clearing the tables in the mess hall for the worship services, and keeping the hymn books under my bunk. His sermons hardly got through to me. I do recall one where he stressed, *You must have an anchor.*

Ten years before, where was I? The memories came racing back . . . Harvard . . . a lowly sophomore majoring in English literature . . . a visit to the chapel once every couple of months or so . . . the Congregational Church on occasions, mainly because of the girls in the youth group. Neither religion nor politics was a live issue for me at the 322-year-old Ivy League school. My roommates—Jim Roberts, a tall Texan, and Jack Briley, a quiet fellow from Illinois—and I gave God only a few passing nods in bull sessions. Jack later accepted Christ while stationed in Germany, at a Navigator's conference—about a month before I had accepted Christ. He sent me a tape with his testimony of Christian experience. I sent a tape back, saying, "The same thing happened to me."

Dad had been graduated from Harvard at the start of the Depression. He wanted to be a lawyer, but later fell into teaching because of the security it offered. He taught history and government in several suburban Boston high schools. Summers, he taught sailing in a boy's camp on Cape Cod. It seems odd, but I never learned how to sail, even though I enjoyed breezing across Buzzard's Bay with Dad.

I hadn't been impressed with the evidence that Dad's lineage ran back to the Thomas Harris who came to Jamestown in 1614, or that Mother's family tree went back to John Alden. Nor did I get a patriotic heartbeat over my great-great-great-great-great grandfather and two other ancestors fighting in the Revolutionary War. I now have the desk which belonged to his son who was lost at sea in 1797.

I spent my first elementary-school years in Concord. That the shots "heard around the world" on April 19, 1775, were fired only a mile-and-a-half from our front door didn't move me to raise the flag each morning. That I lived in a little frame house that formed a triangle with the Emerson and Hawthorne houses didn't send me running to the library. I was surrounded by so much history that I failed to see the significance of any of it.

But on March 31, 1968, my thirtieth birthday, I longed to kiss the ground of free America. For me, freedom and my American heritage never became precious until I was held captive in an alien land, not knowing if I would ever see my homeland again.

Dad and Mother both taught school, but their combined salaries then didn't equal what a beginning teacher receives today in Massachusetts. I was born in Melrose near Boston. We moved to Acton (a village west of Boston) and from there to Concord in 1943. I can remember well only one grandparent, my maternal grandmother whom I dearly loved. Mother had five brothers, including twins. Dad had only one sister. I saw Mother's twin brothers Willard and Gilbert board the train to join the Army Air Corps in which one brother was already serving. Their family motto was *Amor Patriae Excitat:* "Love of country motivates."

I, an only child, am more like Dad than Mother. I have his sloping forehead and dark hair, but the prominent nose of my mother. I have his penchant for keeping everything in place and in good repair. I still ride the bike my parents gave me when I was fourteen. And I have his tenacity to finish a hard job. Once, when I was about four, Mother tied me on a rope with about twenty knots to keep me in the yard. I sat down and painstakingly untied every one.

Mother is artistic and has a beautiful soprano voice. She met Dad when singing at a social event in a hotel where Dad was doing a radio show while working his way through Harvard.

Dad loved mechanics. He learned to drive at twelve and taught his own father how to drive, but he couldn't afford his own car until he was in law school. I began tinkering with electronics at eleven when my folks gave me a radio kit for Christmas in 1949. This spiked a desire to learn all I could about the subject. Just about every penny I could scrape up went for electrical gadgets and books. For the sixth grade science fair I devised an electronic map. I listed the state capitals on the bottom, beside small metal contacts, and put matching contacts in each state on the map. When I touched the capital that matched the state with a metal pointer a bell would ring.

I never learned Morse code while in public school. I

hated math, though I did manage to graduate in the top 10 percent of a high-school class of 240. I enjoyed biographies of great Americans and Thornton Burgess animal stories. I could hardly wait each weekday afternoon to hear "Jack Armstrong," "Superman," "Sky King," "The Green Hornet," and that sort of stuff.

Sunday school was a bore. Church was just as bad, although I enjoyed singing in the choir for a while and helping Dad take up the offering. We usually went to the Congregational Church, when we did go, which was a compromise between Dad's Baptist heritage and Mother's Episcopal upbringing.

Being accepted by Harvard didn't seem at the time to be a great achievement, but I quickly discovered that the student body was far above average. From the honor roll in high school, I dropped to a C average in Harvard. The courses were so tough I decided to move on campus during my freshman year.

I worked at Harvard's FM radio station. Several times each week I walked down into Dudley Gulch, the alley connecting Holyoke and Dunster Streets, and into the little glass chambers where semiprofessionals spun records and directed student productions. I enjoyed announcing and "running the board" and toyed with the idea of making radio my career.

I settled on English as a major for no other reason than that I had acquired the most credits in that field. Dad encouraged me to take naval ROTC. It would pay a small stipend my junior and senior years and I could take my stint in the service as an officer. I think Dad secretly wanted me to be the naval officer he had wanted to be. A heart condition had kept him from accepting a commission.

Dad died the morning of the day (April 24, 1959) Fidel Castro spoke in Harvard Stadium. The speech was on the car radio while I was driving to the funeral home in my roommate's car.

Dad's death was the biggest blow of my life to date. I knew how badly he had wanted to see me graduate. We had been closer than most fathers and sons and had spent a lot of time together in bull sessions during my college years. There was no generation gap between us. Only once have I gone sailing since his death.

My graduation the next year was especially hard on Mom. The New Year's Eve following Dad's death would have been their twenty-fifth wedding anniversary if he had been around to celebrate. His absence at the exercises was very conspicuous to both of us.

When I was sworn in as an ensign, I didn't hear bells ringing or see flags flying in my mind. I was just another middle-of-the-road young American, perhaps a bit more patriotic than some, but definitely not the type who got goose pimples reading about service heroes of the past.

But the Cuban missile crisis in 1962 shook some of the cobwebs loose. As the communications officer on a ship in the Sixth Fleet, I sweated it out during a suspenseful, sleepless alert.

Now as one of eighty-two hostages inside fanatical North Korea, I was eyeball to eyeball with the Communist system at its worst.

By April I was resigned to a long stay. I felt it might be a long time before the U.S. "apologized" to a little tinhorn Communist nation. I also felt that time meant little to the North Koreans who wanted to "remold" us to the Communist way of thinking.

One day back at the old place, Max had dropped a propaganda pamphlet on my table. He knew that having nothing else to read I would inevitably look at it. On their Army Anniversary, they had given some of us books of the translated speeches of "our beloved leader of 40,000,000 Korean people, Premier Kim Il Sung, peerless patriot, national hero, iron-willed genius commander and one of the outstanding leaders of the world Communist movement."

I brought my book with me to the new place, and at their insistence read it through two or three times. It was duller than what American politicians write. Kim was calling for the workers to help build the country's self-reliance (something they called *juche*) by meeting higher crop quotas, building more tractors and trucks, remaining vigilant against the "lackeys and running dogs of the U.S. imperialist aggressors who oppress our brothers in the south."

I wondered why they wanted to build more tractors and trucks since the ones they had didn't seem to work well. Their method of starting a cold vehicle was to build a fire under it! Some of the guys actually saw a farmer burn up his tractor, one cold morning, by this method on a nearby rice paddy. It was hard to keep from laughing at KORCOM soldiers struggling to start a truck in the courtyard. One morning I saw three of them on the green truck in the courtyard. One fiddled with the carburetor, a second turned a crank, and a third was doing something mysterious inside the cab. They finally had to tow it away with another green truck that sounded as if it were about to expire.

Living in this second prison was like being adrift in a polluted lake. Day after day they tried to "correct our thinking." We had to begrudgingly admire their ruthless dedication.

They put ideology into everything with the "glorious Premier Kim Il Sung" always at the center. Late one afternoon Colonel Specs observed to some of us, "The sun is setting on our beautiful land which goes forward under the leadership of our ever-victorious, iron-willed, genius Commander Kim Il Sung."

Colonel Artful Dodger gave us a cram course in modern Korean history as it had been "reinterpreted" Communist style. "Our beloved Premier," he said with a smug smile, "started patriotic anti-Japanese guerrilla activities in 1932 and fought gloriously until our independence was won in 1945." Art failed to mention that the United States had played the dominant role in defeating Japan and helping Korea become an independent nation. He gave only a passing nod to the Soviets for their "comradely aid" in defeating Japan. He didn't say that Russia declared war on Japan only five days before the Japanese forces in Korea surrendered and afterward occupied the northern part of the country. He didn't say that Russia refused to permit United Nation's supervised elections in the north for the purpose of unification. Nor did he say that Kim Il Sung disguised himself in a Russian major's uniform, clawed his way to the chairmanship of the Communist Party, and imprisoned the northern nationalist leader Cho Man Sik who has not been heard from since.

"Your U.S. imperialist aggressor army is now occupying the southern half of our country," Art snarled. "Those in the U.S. ruling circles have sacrificed over a million of your soldiers in the Patriotic War of Liberation, the only war your country has lost. They keep 50,000 soldiers there now to keep our enslaved brothers from sharing the benefits we enjoy here in the northern half of the Republic." There was never a whisper from the Dodger about the million refugees who fled the "socialist paradise" before the war.

Besides the twice-weekly four-hour classes under the Dodger or Super-C and Friday night political films, an unscheduled "education" period could come any time.

A guard would suddenly open my door and motion me out into the hall. I'd line up with the other officers in order of seniority and we'd march down to Room 6 and stand at attention. Shortly, Super-C or the Dodger would stride in and sit down at the big desk near the interpreter. Only then could we sit down.

Super-C invariably began by asking, "How is your life these days?" The captain would stand up and say the usual lie, "Fine, sir." Then he'd give a brief report on the crew. With these preliminaries done, we might be asked to tell what we had learned from study materials given out earlier. Or following a lecture or a "Korean feature film," we had to give back answers showing our "sincerity." We discovered right off that "sincere" meant giving the right answers and not causing trouble.

The plot of a typical Communist celluloid melodrama usually hung around a poor factory worker or farmer who came up with some innovation that glorified Premier Kim. Another one showed a tractor driver always getting stuck in a rice paddy. His solution was to put a boat underneath the front half of the tractor to keep it out of the mud. It was miraculous how he was able to steer it with the front wheels in the boat. Another centered on a "brave patriot" soldier who single-handedly defeated a company of hideous-looking American soldiers with the actors' faces made up in a Frankenstein style. If we didn't give back the answers they wanted, we got long lectures from Super-C on "insincerity" lasting into the small hours. We saw no alternative but to play along. "This film shows how Worker Li glorified your great Premier by increasing production of cotton cloth," I would say in a typical "sincere" response. "It inspires us to work for the common good of all." Or, "The railway engine driver was lazy and didn't set a proper example for the Korean people."

Silver Lips would translate the answer and if Super-C liked it he would smile and say, "A fine, sincere answer. You understand the deep meaning of this film, Research Officer."

But if he didn't like the answer, he would yell and Silver Lips would translate, "You are provocating!" Then he would deliver a harangue that kept us standing for the better part of the next hour.

The Captain had one standard answer when asked why he had given an insincere answer. Standing stiff as a telephone pole but with his head bowed in a mock gesture of shame, the captain would say, "Abject stupidity, sir. Abject stupidity." Every time he gave that answer, we cracked up inside. But we didn't dare laugh. Once the seat of my chair collapsed under me while I was answering a question. I sat there with my knees in my mouth and half a straight face while finishing my answer.

Again, laughing would have caused them to lose face and brought punishment.

Sometimes they anticipated our thoughts. After a film of a soccer game in which England beat North Korea, the interpreter explained, "The referee was a cunning Israeli or we would have won."

Some of their ideas about the U.S. were hilarious. Super-C solemnly assured us that Benjamin Harrison had a razor strop made from the skins of Indians he had annihilated. He believed us when we said that members of the U.S. National Guard took their tanks home at night. Colonel Specs declared that Walter Reuther and other U.S. labor leaders whipped factory workers on the assembly lines. Specs grudgingly admitted that U.S. technology was ahead of North Korea. "But that's because we were enslaved by the imperialist Japanese for so long and our country was devastated by the U.S. imperialist army and the South Korean puppet army of traitor Syngman Rhee," he said. "We'll catch up with you."

"We have nothing against the people of the United States," Super-C said repeatedly. "Our enemies are the imperialist rulers of Washington and the decadent Wall Street warmongers." Just to let us know he knew who these mean people were, he would reel off a list of capitalists, some of whom had been dead for over twenty years.

And yet we saw movies where a Korean boy was asked, "What do you want to do when you grow up?" And he would answer, "To honor our glorious Comrade Kim Il Sung by killing 100 Americans."

They always ended a get-together by repeating what the United States must do to secure our release: Confess that the *Pueblo* performed espionage activities in their territorial waters, apologize sincerely, assure their government it would never happen again.

Their propaganda was pitifully ineffective. They couldn't get to first base with us, although they thought they were making progress. We were just trying to stay alive. They could make us mouth their party line back to them, but they couldn't make us take the garbage seriously.

About the twentieth of April the guards rounded us up for a special meeting. We filed into the big movie room, which the KORCOMS called the club, uncertain as to what was to happen. After a few minutes, Super-C and Silver Lips arrived with a sheaf of papers. Super-C frowned and said, "I regret to tell you that your government has not seen fit to apologize. So we must keep you here."

Then Silver Lips added a news report. "There is much trouble in your country," he said in lip-licking satisfaction. "The Negro civil rights leader Dr. Martin Luther King has been murdered in Memphis, Tennessee. His death was arranged by that warmonger who sits in your White House, Lyndon Johnson." The interpreter went on to give details about the shooting of Dr. King in Memphis. There was enough accuracy to indicate some basis of truth in the report.

Silver Lips then read a report which he claimed came from a U.S. wire service telling of bloody riots by Negroes in Chicago and Washington. After mentioning riots on several college campuses, he declared, "The people are rising up against your imperialistic rulers. They will soon take power.

"There is news from Russia also," he continued. "The

Soviets have made another achievement in space exploration. They have successfully brought together two unmanned satellites." He looked at us coldly and added, "The Soviets have shot your God out of the sky."

Esther and Mother secured an appointment to see Dean Rusk. The Secretary of State talked to them an hour, impressed them as being sympathetic, but told them no more than they already knew. When the interview was over, Mother placed my picture on his desk and said, "You are our last earthly hope. Promise me you will keep my son's picture there as a reminder until the Pueblo crew is released."

The secret negotiations continued to drag on in Panmunjom. The U.S. negotiator was willing to acknowledge that the Pueblo was on an intelligence mission, but not that it was actually engaged in espionage. That would have exposed the crew to spy charges, the penalty for which was death.

6

"The Gates of Hell Shall Not Prevail..."

Before the *Pueblo*'s capture I had been reading *Markings,* the diary of the late Dag Hammarskjold. The book, a gift from Esther, had been left on the ship.

The mystical, devout Secretary-General of the United Nations sought a close walk with God amid the loneliness of his high office.

He wrote:

In the faith which is "God's marriage to the soul," you are one in God, and
    God is wholly in you,
    just as, for you, He is wholly in all you meet.
    With this faith, in prayer you descend into your-
       self to meet the Other,
    in the steadfastness and light of this union,
    see that all things stand, like yourself, alone be-
       fore God.
    You are liberated from things, but you encounter

in them an experience which has the purity
and clarity of revelation.
In the faith which is "God's marriage to the soul,"
everything, therefore, has a meaning.
So live, then, that you may use what has been
put into your hand. . . .*

Our Communist captors could not understand the faith
of the *Pueblo*'s crew. They seemed puzzled by our references to prayer and faith in our letters home. While insisting that we follow their party line in making our false
confessions, they let the references to God and religion
stand as we wrote them. They held no reverence for God.
I think they wanted to give the impression that we enjoyed freedom of religion.

"We are no longer slaves to superstition. We are
atheists," Super-C told us in a discussion. "Of course our
Constitution, Article 14, stipulates that 'citizens enjoy
the freedom of religious beliefs and of religious service.' "
What I wanted to say, but didn't dare, was that religious
services were not allowed for the *Pueblo* crew.

God and religion came up on occasion in both formal
and informal discussions with the KORCOMS.

Sometimes this was prompted by movies. One showed
a "missionary" branding "thief" on the forehead of a
Korean boy because he had stolen an apple. Another
pictured a priest siccing his dog on a small child. Once,
Super-C solemnly assured us that some spies pose as missionaries and carry secret messages in their Bibles. He

* *Dag Hammarskjold: Markings,* Translated from the Swedish by
Leif Sjöberg and W. H. Auden, Alfred A. Knopf, New York, 1964,
p. 165.

83

added, "We don't oppose true missionaries, of course."

Super-C and his cohorts kept bringing up the idea that the Russians had explored space and couldn't find God. Colonel Specs once smugly declared, "We dug holes all over this country and never found hell."

They ridiculed the supernatural events of the Bible. "You believe Christ was born of a virgin," the Dodger snorted. "That's scientifically impossible. How could you believe such a myth?"

Once Specs jumped on Ramon Rosales about belief in God. "The Russian cosmonauts didn't see God. I've never seen God. How can I believe in what I can't see. Where have you ever seen God? What does He look like? Is He short and fat, or thin and tall? Do you have his picture?"

"Yes, we've seen God," Rosales shot back. "We've seen Him in the flowers He's made. We heard Him in the singing of the birds He created."

Ginther was in on this conversation and added, "The Bible teaches us not to steal or kill, and to love our enemies. God helps us follow the Bible teachings."

But Specs only laughed.

Some of us wanted to have at least a special Easter service on April 7. (I learned later that Easter fell this year on April 14.) "Political holidays are forbidden for you," Specs said. Poor Specs couldn't conceive of a holiday not related to politics.

We tried to explain the meaning of Easter. "You have special days when you remember great events of the past," I told him. "At Easter we remember the resurrection of Jesus Christ from the dead."

84

Specs pounded a table. "Ridiculous! Silly! No man ever died and came alive again."

Specs finally told us we could have our holiday, but a religious service was out of the question. "As captured spies you have no rights," he declared. They gave each of us an egg for the occasion.

We were permitted to talk among ourselves during recreation periods and during meals, though at mealtime we officers were separated from the enlisted men. I don't remember when or who made the suggestion that we write down all the Scripture verses and books of the Bible we could remember. Friar Tuck, Charles Crandell, and Skip Schumacher worked on the project with me. We remembered the twenty-third Psalm, portions of the Sermon on the Mount, John 3:16 and about twenty other passages. Most of my verses came from my Navigators' study just after I became a Christian. Back in 1964, when I started the memory course, I never thought I would ever be without access to a printed Bible!

We made a complete list of the New Testament books, but the Old Testament gave us problems. We couldn't remember some of the minor prophets and a few other short books.

We wrote the verses and lists of books on sheets of paper left over from the confessions. We never tried to make a book or pamphlet out of them, nor did we give the collection a special name. It was after our release that people began calling our efforts *The Pueblo Bible*.*

* Some of the verses which I remember are: Exodus 21:3–17; Psalms 23, 91, 119:11; Isaiah 26:3; Lamentations 3:22–23; Matthew 18:20; John 3:16; Romans 3:23–24, 6:23; I Corinthians 10:13; Philippians 4:13; Hebrews 12:5–7; I Peter 1:7–8; 5:7; I John 1:9; 5:11–12.

We kept our verses and book list in our pockets because they searched our rooms quite frequently. "Unauthorized writing" was a major offense.

Quartered eight to a room, the enlisted men had opportunity to share their faith and pray together in groups. Not until after our release did I learn about some of their experiences.

Ginther's group on the third floor often had prayer and spiritual discussions. The big eight-year navy veteran from Pottsville, Pennsylvania, used Bible passages which he wrote on scraps of paper and kept in his night stand. When one man confided that he didn't think God was hearing their prayers, Ginther countered, "Let's just keep asking God to help us. We've got to trust Him to get us out of here."

Bob Chicca and Angelo Strano, two devout Catholics were in one room with three ministers' sons, Rodney Duke, Donald McClarren, and Charles Crandell. They had some heated discussions over differences in beliefs. One led to a water fight.

My chief assistant on the ship, James Kell, had his rosary taken away before leaving the ship. He and four other Catholics in his room used grains of rice and their fingers to keep count of the prayers while three Protestants took turns at the keyhole watching for a guard.

None of us dared kneel when we prayed. We talked to God while sitting at a table and in our bunks. The guys in Charles Sterling's room talked every night with "COMWORLDFLT" (Navy lingo for the Commander of the World's Fleet). The KORCOMS had cut off all communication with our seniors in the chain of command

and from our government; they couldn't cut us off from God.

The KORCOMS didn't even approve of private grace before meals. They spotted Sterling, one of my men, bowing his head, and ordered him out of the mess hall and into the passageway. "What were you whispering?" one demanded.

Charles repeated the prayer he had learned from his minister-father: "Lord, we thank You for these blessings and all of us ask for Christ's sake, Amen."

They wanted to know what "blessing" meant.

"It means life, wife and children, the air, the sun, the food," Sterling replied.

"The food is a gift from the Korean people, not from your God who doesn't exist," one shot back.

They asked about the phrase "for Christ's sake." Sterling told them it meant getting God's forgiveness.

"You are laughingstock. You make fool of yourself," the accuser declared. "Stand at attention here until we give permission to leave."

He stood there until they dismissed him with the warning not to pray again in the future.

While we were allowed to have penknives (later taken away), another of my men, Donald Peppard, noticed an old ammunition box had been discarded at the edge of the ball field. When the game was finished, he maneuvered over and picked it up. Back in his room, he carved a tiny model of the *Pueblo* which he concealed in a match box. He also carved a small cross and used it as an aid in his nightly prayers.

But the guards searched his room and found the cross. One snapped it and kicked the two pieces angrily across the floor as if it were a living enemy. Another kicked and cursed Peppard. It seemed every KORCOM guard knew at least one American curse word. "Don't do that again," Peppard was told.

But loss of his cross didn't keep Peppard from praying.

Guys talked about God in ways they never had before. For example: Herman Baldridge, one of the three enlisted men put in a room with me when we were first captured, confided on the ball field that he had found prayer "made things better." One of the guys standing nearby said, "I know it helps." Later Baldridge said, "I wasn't especially religious before being captured. But when I realized things were bad, I turned to God in prayer. My wife's Japanese and a Buddhist back in Japan. I never tried much to help her understand Christianity. But when we get together again, I'm going to do all I can to help her become a Christian."

Wayne Anderson, a drawling, dark-haired boy from Waycross, Georgia, wrote his Southern Baptist pastor that it was the knowledge of God that kept him alive and sane.

"Many, many times in that awful prison, I sat with my eyes closed and imagined myself sitting in our church," he wrote. "I could hear your sermons and the congregation singing the hymns I loved so very much. No amount of Communist propaganda and lies could take these thoughts away from me."

I couldn't assess the depth of every man's commitment, but this much was evident: instead of becoming less religious because of Communist indoctrination, the *Pueblo* crew became more religious. Here was an average group of Americans with varying religious backgrounds (Protestant, Catholic, and two Jews) who became acutely aware that a vital relationship with God was more important than anything else when the sea got rough.

Our experience revealed that every man has, as the mathematician Pascal said, "a God-shaped vacuum within his heart." When stripped of diversions, we realized this vacuum and reached out for God.

I saw this illustrated even in the lives of the North Korean officers and guards who were assigned to us. They had rejected the old beliefs of Buddhism and Confucianism and had installed Communism in their place. I was astounded at the shocking parallel between North Korean Communism and Christianity.

Their antithesis to Christianity was Communist ideology; to the Gospel, the party line; to elders and deacons of a local church, the Central Committee of the Party; to Christ, Premier Kim Il Sung.

Kim Il Sung has been all but deified by the North Koreans. They never mentioned his name without prefixing a list of adjectives: "glorious, iron-willed, ever-victorious," and so on. We were given hymns to Kim written in the Korean language. Workers in film plots toiled to honor the glorious premier. Pictures and statues of him are everywhere.

A final astounding antithesis is between the Virgin Mary, as she is venerated by Roman Catholics, and the premier's mother, Kang Ban Sock. We saw movies of Korean people walking solemnly to her grave. The men walked with hats in hand, carried flowers, and stood by the grave with heads bowed. We got the impression that it was an experience of worship. The significance of this is that under Communism the Koreans have been discouraged from the ancient tradition of venerating ancestors. There are substantiated reports that lineage records have been burned by the government. Kim's mother is an exception; his father is apparently not venerated, because we heard his name mentioned far less often than his mother's. Nor did they talk about Kim having a wife and children.

The Bible teaches that love of fellow man goes along with love for God. I saw no evidence of affection between any of our captors. Once I saw two KORCOM sergeants scuffling over a paper flower. How could there be affection when party discipline demanded strict obedience and informing on those who showed "bourgeoise tendencies."

But among the *Pueblo* crew our affection increased for each other. Except for the twenty-nine men in my detachment and the ship's officers, I hardly knew the rest of the crew before capture. By nature I'm not a good mixer nor the life-of-the-party type. But while we were held captive, I'm sure I asked every man about his family and other interests back home. We shared our mutual woes and dreams.

Back in Boston, Mother set aside one room in her house as a special prayer chamber. She kept writing letters to high officials demanding action be taken to get us released. One news commentator called her efforts "a masterpiece of diplomacy."

Esther remained in Washington and kept in close touch with her seriously-ill mother in Canada and my mother in Boston. Esther wished she had a child as many of the other Pueblo *wives did. Still she found comfort in Romans 8:28:*

> *And we know that all things work together for good to them who love God, to them who are called according to his purpose.*

After three months and fifteen private meetings at Panmunjom, the U.S. negotiator still reported "no progress" on securing our release.

7

The Shadow of the Almighty

After Dr. Martin Luther King's assassination, the North Koreans took some of the *Pueblo* crew to a long building adjoining the guards' barracks. They gave them beer and cookies and a propaganda pitch about the Communist way of life. But they got nowhere. North Korea and its slave system held no attraction for them or other *Pueblo* personnel.

Naturally they kept us up-to-date on their version of the Viet Nam war. They had the "brave patriots and champions of the enslaved South Vietnamese" winning every battle against "the American imperialists and their Saigon lackeys, the Thieu-Ky clique." The casualty figures they gave were ridiculous. We divided the American and South Vietnamese losses by ten and came up with a reasonable figure. We had a guide to go by: their claim that "the U.S. imperialists and their traitorous lackeys and running dogs [South Korea] suffered 1,093,839 casualties and lost 5,729 planes and 164 warships in the Korean War. Actually, no U.S. ships were lost at all.

They never told us about the Russian invasion of Czechoslovakia. They said very little about Russia and even less about China. They talked a lot about "our revolutionary comrades in Cuba and North Viet Nam," and "struggling revolutionaries" in several Latin American and African nations.

In May they started distributing copies of the *Pyongyang Times,* a weekly "newspaper" printed in English which was unique in that it contained virtually no news. We had to read and report on this stuff, too.

The *Times* printed the party-line version of the *Pueblo* capture and our "confessions" and "apologies." We saw our pictures, both individual and in groups, and letters we had written home. "They not only read your mail," one of the guys griped, "they publish it in their yellow sheet."

The *Times* featured long slanted stories about the "struggle to liberate our enslaved brothers in the south." The newspaper lambasted the presence of American troops in South Korea and accused President Johnson of planning another Korean War. For example, the *Times* ran this story under the headline:

SCHEME OF U.S. IMPERIALISTS FOR
NEW WAR IN KOREA

As was seen in our previous issue, the American imperialist aggressors suffered a crushing defeat in the Korean War they started eighteen years ago and began to go downhill. But they, far from drawing a lesson from the defeat, are running wild to start another war in Korea.

As Comrade Kim Il Sung, the respected and beloved leader of the 40 million Korean people [total

93

population of both North and South Korea] pointed out, "The U.S. imperialists' maneuverings for the provocation of a new war in Korea have already reached a grave stage.

The propaganda clearly showed the rabid hatred which they kept whipped up against the U.S. Under a picture of a North Korean soldier poised with extended bayonet, the *Times* ran this story about the training of a military unit.

The servicemen of the unit make it a rule to profoundly study every word of the leader's teaching and discuss how to carry it out to the end and put it into practice.

Soldier Li Jong Nam whose father was mercilessly killed by U.S. imperialist beasts in Shinchon during the Fatherland Liberation War always sums up his daily work in accordance with the teaching of Comrade Kim Il Sung: "To be a good shot, you should conduct much sighting practice with a bitter enmity against the enemy and when you aim at a mark you must think that you stand opposed to the enemy and make untiring efforts to implement his destruction."

Thus Li Jong Nam has become versed in various arms and military techniques in a brief span of time, and become a crack shot and trained himself into a one-matches-a-hundred revolutionary soldier.

This is what he said:

"I see clearly on the mark the disgusting faces of the Yankee devils who killed cruelly my father. The bullet of a man of the Korean People's Army who sees before his eyes the inveterate foes of the Korean people should never miss the target!"

This feeling is shared by all servicemen.

Impregnable is our defense line as it is guarded by the one-matches-a-hundred revolutionary soldiers who are firmly armed with the revolutionary ideas of the respected and beloved Leader Comrade Kim Il Sung, infinitely faithful to him with whole heart, filled with a determination to defend with their lives the Party Central Committee headed by him and fully prepared to knock down at a sway any enemies.

This kind of drivel was fed to us day after day. Only faith in God, memories of loved ones and home, recreation, and our sense of humor kept us from going nuts. My beautiful plant helped, too.

The two most looked-forward-to times of day in our drab prison life were afternoon recreation when we could play together and night when we could escape in our dreams.

After a lunch composed of the same old rotten menu with an occasional change (sewer trout instead of hogs' hair soup, for example), we lined up to march out on the playing field. On my floor men got behind Charles Law and third floor guys stood behind Francis Ginther. We counted off in English, then one of the two floor leaders announced the total to our supervisors in Korean.

The KORCOMS first said we had to march Korean style, swinging our arms with fists closed and cocking our heads sideways as we turned. We almost drove them crazy. When the duty officer yelled, "Right-a-foot, forward," we led with our left. When he shouted, "Left-a-face, march," we turned right. When he called, "About-a-face," we went forward. The KORCOM cursed and raged and tried to get us in order while we milled around pretending to be confused. They finally decided to let us march as Americans do.

The ball field included a basketball court and two volleyball courts. The KORCOMS tried to arrange us in teams according to rooms. This way, it was easier for them to keep track of us. They frowned on our choosing up sides.

They preferred that we play volleyball, but for a while they let us play touch football. One of the guys very cleverly took an old broken volleyball and a needle and shaped it into a pretty good football. But when they saw what he had done, they took it away and said we must play with a soccer ball. They couldn't stand innovation or improvement.

So we used their "round" ball until they discovered we were talking about other things in the huddles besides plays. After that, it was volleyball with twenty on a side or nothing. One afternoon, King Kong got so mad he almost threw up. "You men *will* enjoy yourselves," he declared sternly.

On the ballfield we could talk discreetly to one another. Ralph McClintock and I discovered we both liked to eat at the well-known Durgin Park Restaurant in Boston. Just talking about their inch-and-a-half roast beef, live boiled Maine lobster, and strawberry shortcake served in a soup bowl made the saliva rise in my mouth and supper taste worse that night. "But at least I'm getting thinner," I told Ralph. "I just hope my belt doesn't break as poor Spear's did."

Whenever possible, we passed notes and Bible verses written on the "confession" paper. We encouraged one another by confiding how prayer helped. We discussed the merits of one car against another. When Specs heard us talking about cars, he scoffed and said, "Lyndon Johnson owns all the cars in America." We speculated on what our favorite baseball teams were doing and which teams would win pennants and the World Series this year. Ralph and I told Skip Schumacher and other Cardinal fans that the Red Sox would get revenge in the 1968 Series. Above all, we recalled our dreams which remained vivid to us for weeks at a time.

The KORCOMS gave us more news reports from time to time. Skip Schumacher showed us the toilet paper blueprint of a $56,000 dream house he was going to build when he got home. But the captain deflated his plans by telling him what the taxes would be!

After supper we played chess, cards, and Ping-Pong. Charles Ayling devised a way of playing Monopoly, using the chess boards. Players moved chessmen and match sticks around the outer edge of the chess board. It was quite complicated, but interesting. The KORCOMS never caught on to our "capitalistic fun."

In the evenings before going to bed, we'd pick a word with the object of seeing how many different words we could make from the letters in it. The next morning, when we were supposed to be in our rooms doing our homework, we'd work on this project. I was often the judge for this game because of my aptitude in catching misspelled words. The ever-suspicious KORCOMS came to believe we were working on some kind of secret code.

"Unauthorized writing" was a strict no-no.

But Peppard sewed a piece of cleaning cloth in his sleeve to make a pocket and kept a hidden diary there.

Skip Schumacher wrote a poem called "The Captain's Lament" which ended with the couplet:

> Instead of victory,
> Sorrow is our lot,
> Trapped by the pirates
> Of the runny snot.

Tim Harris, the *Pueblo*'s supply officer, worked out math problems on toilet paper and passed them among the crew when we were playing ball. I've already mentioned that several of us wrote down Scripture verses, books of the Bible, and hymns which we passed around.

Showing disrespect to the KORCOM duty personnel was a "Rule of Life" frequently violated. But to discourage the guards from looting while he was out of his room, Ramon Rosales loaded his cigarettes with match heads. The guys in one room went further and left an apple marinated in urine. The guard who swiped it didn't show up for three days!

The KORCOMS never did appreciate our humor. Sometimes, it was impossible not to laugh at them. One day King Kong and Charles Law got into an argument over what Americans could do. Finally, Kong said confidently, "You Americans can't imitate birds and animals the way we Koreans can. Why I can even imitate the wind. Would you like to hear me?"

Law looked around at his seven roommates. "Yes, we would," he told the duty officer.

Little "Stevie" with Mother and Dad in 1939. *Below*: Esther's parents, the Reverend and Mrs. William E. Uotinen, are beside her at our wedding, and Mom stands next to me.

North Korean propaganda picture of the *Pueblo's* officers taken while we were in captivity. Left to right: Ensign Timothy Harris, Lt. (j.g.) F. Carl "Skip" Schumacher, Commander Pete Bucher, Lt. Edward R. Murphy, me, and Chief Warrant Officer Gene Lacy. *Below*: The (KORCOMS) prepare to hand over the body of Duane Hodges. (Official photograph, U.S. Navy)

The captain takes the walk to freedom. (Official photograph, U.S. Navy) *Below*: Steve Woelk, the man who had major surgery without anesthesia, is checked off by the naval officer who greeted us on the freedom side of the Panmunjom bridge. (Official photograph, U.S. Navy)

Rushel Blansett (left) and Bob Chicca (smiling) enjoy their first American meal in eleven months. I can still smell that coffee! (Official photograph, U.S. Navy) *Right*: Ralph Reed at the Christmas Eve service in Seoul. Every member of the crew attended on the day following our release. (Official photograph, U.S. Navy)

Welcome home! I'm the skinny guy in the center and the lady is my mother. (Official photograph, U.S. Navy) *Below*: Christmas dinner following our release. To the left of Mom is Ralph McClintock and his mother. Red Cross nurses stand behind me and Esther. (Official photograph, U.S. Navy)

Getting a trim from barber Sam Mays at the Balboa Naval Hospital in San Diego, the day after Christmas. (Official photograph, U.S. Navy) *Below*: John Wayne hands me a plaque at a special reception honoring the *Pueblo* crew. (Official photograph, U.S. Navy)

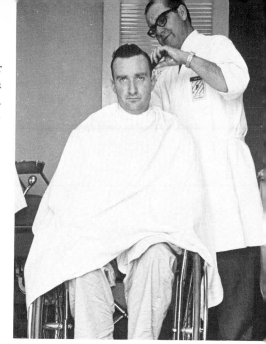

Commander George Powell, my legal assistant (right), and I leave the Court of Inquiry with Commander Bucher. (Official photograph, U.S. Navy) *Below*: The 82 surviving members of the *Pueblo* crew. I am on Captain Bucher's immediate left. (Official photograph, U.S. Navy)

Speaking in the "Chapel of the Presidents,' National Presbyterian Church, Washington. (Photograph by Nicholas Penovic) *Below*: Esther and I with Christina and Colby, our twins. (Photograph by Nicholas Penovic)

Kong screwed up his face and moaned, "Wind, winnnnnnnd, wiinnnnnnnnnddddddd."

Harry Iredale (one of the two oceanographers aboard) bit his lip to keep from laughing. This broke the others up and Kong turned as red as the N.K. flag. He left the room and didn't return for days.

There were more incidents that rankled the KORCOMS. The enlisted men in one room laughed at an unusually short guard. Some guys clanked their teapots to call for more drinking water. Word was passed among the N.K.'s that we had become "insincere" and "uncooperative."

They started applying pressure. A duty officer spotted Chief Kell chewing his food as he was coming out of the mess hall and hit him in the face. The rest of us got kicked and cuffed around for various offenses, both real and imagined. They ordered us to walk around with our heads bowed and to sit in our rooms with coats on. To demonstrate the discomfort on these hot days of early summer, the captain dumped water all over himself and said it was perspiration.

One sad morning they came and took away the one joy of my room—my beautiful evergreen. They replaced it with a frowzy bush that looked like the last twig of summer. They probably put the good one in some KOR-COM officer's office. I never saw it again.

Life ran in cycles. We would build up a pile of offenses. They would start putting on the pressure. We would confess our naughtiness and promise to be "sincere" and "cooperative." They would slacken up, but keep pouring on the propaganda. Then the cycle would start all over again.

My worst offense was "making unauthorized writings."

They found the Scripture verses and a testimony I had written out to pass around. Loud Mouth and another duty officer kicked and cuffed me around until I promised not to do it again. But they couldn't confiscate my memories of God's Word or of experiences back home.

The most pleasant memories of my life returned to me in my dreams. Many nights I sailed with my Dad across Vineyard Sound or along the coast of Maine. Once I was a child again and identifying birds in the woods around Concord. Several nights I enjoyed family reunions at Christmas. More frequently, I dreamed of being with my beloved Esther.

But the harsh morning always came with the shattering ring of an electric bell and I had to grab the bucket and rag and get my room cleaned before the call came to line up for breakfast.

In May, the heat became oppressive as we entered our fourth month of captivity. The KORCOMS called us in by groups and announced that a work program was planned. Any hopes we had of getting released soon dropped twenty fathoms when we heard that.

"What can you men do? What are your skills?" Super-C asked through Wheezy.

Friar Tuck said he could drive tanks. The captain said he was an expert navigator. I said my abilities lay in electronics. Several guys said they could do carpentry and mechanical work, but the only work we ever did was cleaning up the grounds. We picked up broken glass, pulled weeds, and cut the lawn North Korean style. Using penknives (which they later took away) all eighty-two of us crawled across the lawn like an army of leaf-cutting ants. This has to be the world's worst way to cut a lawn.

"The reason the KORCOMS don't have lawn mowers is that they haven't perfected the goat yet," I cracked one day when the guards were out of earshot.

Naturally we thought and talked about trying to escape. The compound was not fenced but was surrounded by an embankment. However, guards were posted all around and next to the steel gate across the entrance road. They were there both to keep us in and to keep peasants out. A couple of times they fired at curious people approaching from a rice paddy on the far side of the embankment.

We saw a few decrepit biplanes of the "invincible Korean People's Army" flying low and we assumed a small airport was nearby. Just below the crest of the hill, we could see the smoke from a train that passed at half-hour intervals. We heard locomotive whistles and felt we were near a station. One engine had a sick whistle that sounded as if it were taking its last breath. Because the sick engine never left the area, I felt we were near a freight yard.

The captain appointed Skip Schumacher, Tim Harris, and Gene Lacy to be an escape committee among the officers. They got hold of a propaganda book with a map of North Korea. Assuming that we were in Pyongyang, the capital, they figured we were about eighty miles north of the Demilitarized Zone between North and South Korea, eighty miles from the east coast where we were captured, and only thirty miles from the west coast.

They thought an escape party reaching the east coast might be able to find a boat and get picked up by a friendly ship. Policarpo Garcia of Filipino ancestry looked the most like a Korean. The escape committee considered asking him to try it alone or lead a group out the windows on a rainy, foggy night after the last bed check, with hopes of reaching the nearest mountains before the sun came up and before the morning check.

I thought we should wait several months before trying to get away. I argued that the country was well organized. We were Caucasians and would be instantly recognizable. Even Garcia couldn't pass as a North Korean, and he didn't know the language. We had no way of traveling except on foot. Also there seemed a good chance that the KORCOMS might keep their promise and let us go if our government presented an acceptable apology for the "intrusions" that had not taken place. And some of us clung to the hope that terms of an armistice agreement between the United Nations and North Korea required all prisoners to be returned within a year.

So while we talked among ourselves about escaping, no attempt was ever made. Later we learned that escape in any direction would have been practically impossible. There were checkpoints at every access road, intersection, and village.

In June they treated us fairly well. They told us about Senator Robert Kennedy's assassination. The killer, they said, was hired by President Johnson, who also, they claimed, had engineered the killing of John F. Kennedy.

July was good because a storm blew down the big propaganda billboard at one end of the playing field. It had shown several bayonets, each marked with the flag of a Communist country, being pointed at a hideous caricature of Lyndon Johnson who was wearing an olive army helmet stenciled with the letters U.S. What a relief to get rid of that aggravation!

On July 16 they gave us extensive physical examinations, but the biggest morale boost came that day in letters from home. Both Esther and Mom said they were trusting God that we would be released soon. Mom said she had written all our U.S. senators, asking them to work harder for our release. Her letters charmed Super-C who said everybody should get their families to redouble efforts to extract an apology from the U.S.

Mom sent a picture of herself. When I showed it to the KORCOM officers and mentioned her age, they looked amazed and exclaimed several times about her youthful appearance. Mom is still a good looking gal, of course, but their reactions also suggested something about how women fare under Communism.

One man got a sad letter. Angelo Strano learned that his brother James had been killed in Viet Nam the same day we were captured. Ed Murphy, the *Pueblo*'s executive officer and navigator, heard about the birth of his second child. His wife chose not to mention that his mother had died four days after the *Pueblo*'s capture. But he had heard one of the KORCOMS say inadvertently that she was dead. Ed was a devout Christian Scientist and found consolation through his faith.

Ralph McClintock's mother quoted the entire Ninety-first Psalm in her letter. He shared this tremendous comfort with the rest of us. The first three verses were of special consolation.

He that dwelleth in the secret place of the most
High shall abide under the shadow of the Almighty.
I will say of the Lord, He is my refuge and my fortress: my God; in Him will I trust. Surely he shall

deliver thee from the snare of the fowler, and from the noisome pestilence.

Janice Ginther wrote her husband, "Nobody can break me down, for I have the Holy Spirit living within me." She enclosed some Bible verses which Francis shared around. A duty officer discovered a copy of the verses on Lee Hayes and asked what they were.

"Just some sentences that give me comfort," Hayes replied.

"Did you write them?"

Hayes thought briefly and decided not to implicate Ginther. "I did," he said slowly. He preferred to risk a beating rather than to jeopardize mail from home.

The KORCOMS told us we could write more letters home. "The Lord never fails to give continuing comfort," I told Esther. "My faith never wavers; it's only stronger than it has ever been. I am certain I shall return."

Naturally we had to mention our "kind" and "humane" treatment and to request our loved ones to keep doing all they could to get the U.S. Government to apologize.

I wrote my letter straight. But several guys tried some monkey business. Ralph McClintock longed for some of his mother's wonderful apple pie (not his favorite dessert) and to swim again in Cape Cod (he never had).

Some of the dots over the "i's" in the propaganda sections of Lee Hayes' letter were actually dashes. They spelled in Morse code, "This is a lie." Don Peppard preceded the propaganda in his letter by asking his father to say hello to an old friend, Garba Gefollows (*garbage follows*). Earl Kisler sent his best to Uncle Ben, Aunt Jemima, and Jack Spratt. He said he was eating so well

104

he soon would look like a chubby neighbor of his family's —who actually weighed seventy pounds. Tim Harris asked his wife to greet Tom Swift for him. Captain Bucher wrote his wife Rose that their family friend, Andy Farkas (her old nickname for him), was a good man and could be trusted to follow orders. Seaman Stu Russell told his fiancee Sharon (their wedding date had been postponed) he planned to repaint his car when he got home because the present color made him sick. It was red. Earl Kisler told his family he "hadn't met such nice people (the KORCOMS) since our high-school class visited St. Elizabeth's" (a mental institution in Washington, D.C.).

Fruitless diplomatic efforts continued. Some U.S. officials proposed that the Pueblo *crew be turned over to a neutral nation and an impartial investigation be made of the alleged intrusion. If the investigation confirmed that the ship had intruded, then the U.S. would express regrets. Senator Stephen M. Young of Ohio said that $100 million in ransom would be paid to get the crew back, but the State Department denied that any deal was under way.*

Esther felt more lonely than ever when her parents left for Finland, even though her mother was still partially paralyzed from the stroke. It was the last time she was to see her mother alive. Esther decided to leave Washington, D.C., to be near her brother Vic, a nuclear physicist in the State of Washington. While changing planes, she mailed a letter to me from Chicago's O'Hare Airport which she signed "Flower."

Mother kept up her whirlwind efforts to persuade gov-

105

ernment officials to do "everything necessary" for our release. In a second letter to all 100 U.S. Senators, she suggested that they pass a bill stopping all trade with Communist nations until the Pueblo crew was released.

Rose Bucher talked with Secretary of State Dean Rusk in July, then announced to the press that she opposed military action to free the ship and crew. In July, she and several other Pueblo wives rode in the Fourth of July parade in San Diego.

Earlier in San Diego, fourteen-year-old Marcee Rethwish had organized a huge Pueblo prayer meeting in Balboa Park on the 100th day of our captivity. The meeting was attended by 1,500 people.

8

█░█

Hope Rising—Hope Falling

As the hot summer wore on, the monotonous, distasteful diet began showing results. That ancient disease of sailors, scurvy, began appearing. Dysentery and diarrhea plagued us. Lee Hayes came down with infectious hepatitis. Ramon Rosales fell ill with viral meningitis and couldn't get out of bed. Dale Rigby broke out in a rash with running sores that covered 90 per cent of his body. Charles Law's eyesight bothered him.

Pete Bucher begged that his men receive treatment.

The Korean doctor we called Quack gave Rigby some kind of mud pack that only irritated the rash. Quack replaced the eyeglasses for men who had lost them in beatings. He did little else.

Flies swarmed inside and out. Each of us was assigned to kill fifty of the pests each day and guards went around shouting, "Kill! Kill!"

Nights were the best. The temperature cooled. We

could dream of happier days. But the morning bell always roused us from bed.

One day Super-C suggested that we should ask influential people and news media in the U.S. to work on our government for an apology.

We knew his "suggestion" was a command. To ignore it would bring charges of "insincerity" and "arrogance," punished by beatings.

"List some names," the KORCOM said.

Captain Bucher started off with Tom Dooley.

"Who's he?" Super-C asked.

"An important minister in the South," the skipper said without cracking a smile.

Super-C nodded gravely.

"Jimmy Hoffa," someone said. "He's a big labor leader."

Super-C nodded again.

Billie Sol Estes was also thrown in with other names. Then the captain volunteered Elwood P. Suggins. Tim Harris, the supply officer, just about broke up.

Super-C eyes narrowed.

"He's laughing," Pete explained, "because Suggins is a preacher from Florida who drowned three people trying to baptize them."

I suggested, "The Reverend Dr. Hugh Hefner," adding, "he has a ministry that reaches large numbers of people." Super-C half smiled, but by this time the other officers were gasping to keep from breaking up. Obviously he didn't know how to take this. He might have been afraid he would lose face, so he said nothing and dismissed the meeting.

Super-C then told us to write our political leaders and newspaper and magazine editors, asking them to put pressure on our government for an apology. He asked that we submit a second joint apology to the North Korean government signed by every man of the crew. This apology was to mention seventeen "intrusions" (upped from the old claim of six) plus the same old garbage contained in the fake statement we had given shortly after capture.

The captain said, "Let's go along as we have been doing." I went ahead and signed with the rest of the officers. But some of the enlisted men balked at letters to the news media back home.

The Bear clubbed Ronald Berens under the eye and gave him a lasting scar. Berens then signed a letter.

Earl Kisler told Highpockets and Robot where to go and wondered out loud why the United States had not retaliated and "wiped" North Korea "off the face of the earth." The KORCOMS said he would indeed write a letter to *Newsweek* magazine. Kisler still said no.

Highpockets and Robot took him to a separate room. Highpockets asked him again if he would write the letter and again Kisler said no.

Robot whacked the husky crewman from St. Louis repeatedly across the face, neck, and shoulders with a stick. Then he beat him with a rubber-soled sandal while Highpockets screamed, "We're going to kill you." Kisler lost consciousness several times. Once he came to on the floor while they were kicking him in the chest.

Highpockets read a statement charging that Kisler had been "insincere" all along and would have to stand trial. Would he write the letter now. "No," Kisler said defiantly.

His bloody face almost unrecognizable, they ordered him back to his room. One crew member observed later that his bloody head was "the size of a pumpkin."

Later in the day Highpockets sent for Kisler. Believing they would beat him to death if he didn't go along, Kisler wrote the letter. But he still refused to sign.

Early in August Super-C told the *Pueblo* officers, "Think of ways to resolve your fate." At the next meeting he dropped the idea of a news conference. We knew what he wanted to hear. "Good idea, sir," the Skipper said in mock respect.

So we had to clean the grounds, cut the grass, and carry chairs to the long building by the rifle range. As we were returning to our quarters, I asked Skip Schumacher if he knew what was in a small out-building. Skip grinned. "It's full of used slogans—old signs and banners. I can't read them. But they look like political slogans."

We figured they used them for parades when people showed "spontaneous" and "unanimous" support for the "iron-willed, genius" premier.

Super-C brought the whole crew together to rehearse the conference. The captain stood up and said with a fake smile, "Yes, sir, Colonel, we'll push on with speed and hope for good luck through the Hawaiian good-luck sign." Then he made a gesture with his forefinger which the KORCOMS didn't understand. But the *Pueblo* crew did.

They selected the six officers and nineteen of the enlisted men for this conference and put the rest in the club room back in the main building. Here they could watch on television sets provided just for this occasion. The captain had already slipped word that they should not

110

laugh at anything they saw because KORCOMS would be observing them.

The North Korean reporters were welcomed by Major Robot and the press conference began. They asked the canned questions and we gave back the canned party line which the KORCOMS wanted. The captain and several of the guys flashed the "Hawaiian good-luck sign." I wasn't one of them.

The North Korean correspondents asked the questions which they had submitted in advance. We gave back the drivel we had been told to deliver.

For example, a guy asked Stu Russell about the food. His answer: "The meals we receive here are both adequate in quantity and quality. . . . We receive three hot [at least they were that] meals a day. Besides the abundant main staples of bread, red meat [ha!], rice [North Korean glue], and fish [sewer trout], we receive other necessary foods to make each meal different [ha!], healthful [ha!], and add meal variety."

Steve Woelk described his medical treatment as "far more than our greatest expectations." (Well, that *could* be said about operating without anesthesia!) "Eventually I was healed enough to return to the crew. I have never been so tickled in all my life when I came back and met the officers at the top of the stairs waiting for me and later meeting the rest of the crew." (This, too, was staged by the N.K.'s and they had taken photographs.)

Naturally, several of us had to run through the request that our government apologize. But we figured the whole affair was fakey enough—if they printed the canned answers we gave them—to show that we were speaking under duress.

A few days later the KORCOMS told us the Republican and Democratic nominees for U.S. President. Some of the guys said, "Who's Spiro Agnew?" I told them he was the governor of Maryland.

About the first of September, Super-C announced we would have an "international" press conference to coincide with the twentieth anniversary of the founding of "our glorious Democratic People's Republic of Korea." He said that Communist reporters from all over the world and in Pyongyang for the big celebrations would attend.

After Sunday breakfast (the same old junk) on September 8, twenty of us paraded in to face about eighty Communist reporters from thirty-four countries—or so the N.K.'s claimed. Later when the correspondents were listed in the *Pyongyang Times,* I noticed that China was not represented. The list did include newsmen from Russia, Hungary, Poland, Japan, and various Asian, Arab, and black African countries, and a mystery man (we called him "Scoop") who claimed to represent the *New York Guardian.* He was the first "American" we had seen since leaving Japan.

As before, the first questions were about the *Pueblo,* its alleged intrusions (for this conference Robot, the moderator, had prepared a new chart on which he had the new number of claimed intrusions) and its mission. (If the *Pueblo* had moved between these locations at the times indicated, she would have had to travel at an impossible speed.) And as before, we gave out nothing the KORCOMS didn't already know.

They finally got around to questions about our "treatment," and we gave back the usual fairy tales. Mike Barrett got one true statement in when he said, "The diseases of grief and sadness are quite prevalent among the crew and cannot be cured until we are reunited with our families and loved ones."

And Ralph McClintock, when asked what was his most ardent desire, said that he wanted to go home, too. "If permitted to do so," he promised, "I will never again commit such a naughty crime as espionage against such a peace-loving people as these." Some of the foreign correspondents forgot their demeanor and tittered.

The last question was directed to the captain from some Egyptian and Iraqi reporters: "What do you think of the policy of United States aggression against the United Arab Republic and the other countries?"

The Skipper replied that he wasn't "well aware of the U.A.R. or world affairs in general and was therefore not qualified to comment."

Robot then noted that the conference had been going for almost five hours and it was time for our lunch. He thought the correspondents might like to see how we lived.

Suddenly the mystery man got up and asked to make a statement. We had never heard of him nor of the paper they said he represented.

He said: "I'm convinced that the *Pueblo* crew has been treated humanely after hearing the declarations of the crew. It is quite evident from the testimony of the officers and men that they were violating Korean territorial waters. I think the proof is irrefutable. And I would like to say that I agree with them that the U.S. Government, our government, shirks moral responsibility for this. I'd like to tell the members of the crew as the only American correspondent here that I will do my best to convey their ideas, their aspirations to the people of the United States through our newspaper in New York."

The rest of the day was worse than open house at college. The reporters watched us eat (naturally the food was better that day), paraded through our rooms, and mingled with us on the ballfield while photographers buzzed around snapping pictures of life in the "socialist paradise." At least one roomful of crewmen displayed the "Hawaiian good-luck sign" when photographed.

The captain thought of trying to slip a note to the mystery man, the "American" reporter, telling him the conference was staged. He had the opportunity when he came to his room, but the captain decided not to take the risk. Later, we learned that this man *was* an American— based in Havana. He would undoubtedly have passed the note on to the North Koreans.

Right after this press conference Super-C had us prepare and sign a "joint petition" to the "heroic" Korean people for our release. When he got that, he strutted like a boy who had finally qualified to become an Eagle Scout.

He disappeared for two or three days and returned a general—"Glorious General," we called him. We knew he had received the promotion for "success" with us. But what the Glorious General didn't realize was that after eight months we were more convinced than ever that the "socialist paradise" was man's best route to misery. Nor did he realize that we had been faking answers and playing games with our captors.

The food got better. They stopped beating us. Several of us began praying that we would get home for Christmas. James Kell led the Catholics in his room in a novena that this hope would be realized.

Early in October, the Glorious General said he wanted to take us on some cultural trips. We hadn't been off the grounds since arriving in March.

We boarded a couple of buses and started out with a military escort. Like a conquering hero the Glorious General led the way in his personal jeep. The bus was not curtained as it had been when we were brought to the building that had been our prison for eight months.

We passed through rice paddies and other land, then entered a residential section of drab, gray, concrete block houses on the eastern side of Pyongyang. The few people we saw were dressed in peasants' work clothes. Except for having longer hair, some of the women in their bulky clothing looked just like the men. Other women wore the traditional Korean high-waisted dress. We saw a few cars, some of which were American jalopies of Korean War vintage. Nobody on the street seemed to pay any attention to us.

The trip to downtown Pyongyang took about twenty minutes. The drivers parked west of Kim Il Sung Square and in front of the "Grand Theater of Pyongyang." We were escorted off the buses and through a crowd of curious people that had gathered. Uniformed guards stood on both sides of us as if they were there to protect us from a riot.

We walked inside and took a block of reserved seats in the front rows of the front balcony. Guards took seats around us and the pageant, "Glorious Is Our Fatherland," began.

A giant choir (they claimed 2,000 people) was massed below the stage. The choir began singing, supported by an orchestra, and the curtain rolled back to show Korean

115

prisoners being bossed around by Japanese lords. The next scene showed fighting in the woods between the prisoners and their captors. One guy pretended to be the "glorious" Kim Il Sung who led the Koreans to victory.

Then came independence under the leadership of Kim and prosperity through Communism. The Russian invasion of Korea in the closing days of World War II was not mentioned, nor were Russian occupation troops shown. The United States did not get the spotlight until the pageant depicted the landing of American soldiers for the Korean War. To depict this, ugly looking soldiers wearing helmets marked MP danced across the stage. Children carrying guns sprang from behind a curtain and danced toward the MP's. They apparently wanted viewers to relate these soldiers with the American MP's who patrol the dividing line between North and South Korea.

The next scene showed how life had improved in North Korea after the war: new power plants, fruitful harvests, mining, industry, and production of consumer goods. The final scene looked to the future and the "liberation" of their "enslaved brothers and sisters in the South."

When we got back to the prison, the beaming N.K.'s wanted to know how we liked the show. We said it was great and gave them the other answers they wanted. There was no point in telling them how we really felt.

I never thought politics and acrobatics could be mixed until our second cultural jaunt. They took us to another theater where the acrobats did a show in a center ring. As at the downtown theater, we sat as a group with soldiers surrounding us.

This show started with trapeze acts and other straight acrobatic stunts. Suddenly a clown appeared representing

Chung Hee Pak, the President of South Korea, and began beating a drum on which was painted a large dollar ($) sign. Just as he started to collapse, an American general jumped in the ring with a tire pump, hooked the hose to his clothes, and began pumping like mad. I guess they wanted to show that South Korea was dependent on the United States.

About a week later they took us out to hear the Korean Peoples' Army Chorus and Ensemble. The coed orchestra and choir hit very few sour notes. They were quite good, but, here also, they interjected politics. There was a skit showing ugly, leering Americans taking a hill, then the brave Koreans retaking it with one noble lad giving his life for the glorious Kim Il Sung and the Fatherland.

The next time they bussed us to the train station late one evening and put us on a Russian-built sleeper train. The beds were just hard benches with blankets thrown over them. They warned us not to open the curtains and invite attack from the peasants outside.

But the captain peeked several times and saw armed guards at half mile or so intervals along the tracks. He got the idea this might be a trial run for the dreamed-about trip to the Demilitarized Zone and Panmunjom. I hadn't thought this was the real thing because there hadn't been a big propaganda send off before we left, and we hadn't been told to bring our personal belongings.

We got to Sunchon, our destination, about midnight and stayed on the train until morning. We breakfasted on sour turnips and a thick sludgy cereal, then boarded two buses for a short ride to the atrocity museum.

As we were entering the place, the captain feigned lockjaw. The twinkle in his eyes told us he was acting,

117

but we didn't dare laugh. The pained look he gave the KORCOMS when they tried to get him to comment about the exhibits was hilarious.

It was hard to see how any thinking person could be convinced by this "museum." I saw, for example, a rock in a glass display case. The interpreter said the rock was used by Americans to bludgeon to death a pregnant Korean woman. There wasn't even a picture to go with it. Another exhibit displayed a bunch of shoes on a sand pile, said to belong to innocent people burned to death by Americans. Another was a gasoline can which they claimed had been emptied by Americans burning down a village.

On the trip back that afternoon, I peeked several times and viewed the "socialist paradise" in action. I spotted checkpoints at intersections where soldiers were inspecting the credentials of travelers. I saw people toiling in rice paddies under the blazing sun, and workers bent over lathes and tables in factories near the tracks. When we stopped, I saw listless, bored travelers hurrying along the station platform to their cars. No one was smiling in this land of the living dead.

Back in the prison, I kept expecting every day that we would be put on a train for Panmunjom. The Glorious General told us that diplomatic negotiations were moving along nicely and that the American government was preparing an apology. I prayed harder than ever that God would help us get home by Christmas.

Suddenly the situation turned bleak. They started feeding us turnips and cream of petroleum soup again. Special privileges were taken away. They increased the number of guards at night on each floor from two to twelve. We had to start walking around with our heads bowed again.

The Glorious General called us into his office and pointed to an American publication showing the guys in Room 13 flaunting the sign. The caption read: "Once again the navy has made fools of the Pyongyang flacks."

A short time later the captain met Charles Law in the head and told him about the discovery. "Warn everybody you can that we may be in for a tough time. If anyone has to admit anything, he should tell what he has done and not squeal on his shipmates."

Esther was living in an apartment alone a few blocks from her brother in Washington State. She kept busy by reading, swimming, and taking gymnastic classes at a nearby YWCA. During September and October she kept expecting our release would come soon. But when the leaves began dropping and the November chill began, she became more depressed than ever.

Vic and his wife Kay invited her to accompany them to Seattle for Thanksgiving dinner with Kay's uncle and family. While there, a man told her, "If you have enough faith and pray, Steve will be released by Christmas." Esther prayed, but she wasn't sure if her faith was strong enough.

Mother's house on Boston Rock was broken into again. A more pleasant interruption came when an elderly man serenaded her over the phone with his harmonica! She kept up her music teaching assignments in public school and tutored private pupils. She wrote more letters and made more telephone calls to people of influence. One

Sunday in church she thought of a passage that seemed to describe my experience:

My son, despise not thou the chastening of the Lord, nor faint when thou art rebuked of him: for whom the Lord loveth he chasteneth, and scourgeth every son whom he receiveth. If ye endure chastening, God dealeth with you as with sons; for what son is he whom the father chasteneth not (Hebrews 12:5–7)?

Admiral John Smith at Panmunjom asked the North Korean negotiator, "If we acknowledge receipt of the Pueblo *crew, will you turn them loose?" On September 17, the* KORCOM *negotiator Pak Chung Kuk replied, "If you'll sign our document [the apology with assurance it would not happen again], we'll release the crew. But negotiations bogged down again and the N.K. general at Panmunjom denounced the Americans as "petty tricksters."*

===

9

We'll Be Home for Christmas

I earnestly hoped that this was the darkness before the dawn. But sometimes I doubted. All I could be sure of was that even in the valley of the shadow of death God would be with us.

Early in the morning of December 11, Wednesday, I heard the KORCOMS moving furniture around. Duty officers went from room to room telling us to stay in our chairs with heads bowed and fists clenched on our thighs. We couldn't even blow our noses without seeking respectful permission. One guard made a man ask permission each time he flicked ashes from his cigarette. That afternoon they began changing roommates among the enlisted men. They put twelve men in each of six rooms and four men in one room. They kept us six officers where we were.

Oddjob, the Glorious General's assistant for logistics, and Silver Lips jumped on Pete Bucher. "You are a CIA man," Silver Lips screamed. "You are to blame for everything."

121

That evening Possum and Captain Queer punched me around and told me I would have to confess everything. Fortunately, I had not made the finger gesture. I wrote reams of stuff, confessing such crimes as failing to put on my coat in the presence of duty officers, sending secret messages in word games, complaining about the food, and being "arrogant" and "insincere."

Skip Schumacher fed them seventy pages, mostly stuff from his senior year college thesis on the duplicity of human nature in interpersonal relationships.

But Charlie Law and the guys from Room 13 who were in the photograph on Super-C's desk got the worst treatment.

Robot handed Law's twenty-four-page confession back to him. "We know about this," he snarled. "We want to know the rest of your crimes."

Law sat down before Oddjob's desk and began making up stuff. He said he had told crew members to open the windows to waste heat, that he had urinated out the window, that he had thumbed his nose at the authorities behind their backs, and anything else that came to mind.

"Who the CIA agent," Oddjob demanded.

Law threw up his hands in pretended despair and said, "I am."

Oddjob argued back that the CIA agent was the captain (or Schumacher) and Law was only taking orders. Law kept insisting he was the agent.

At Oddjob's insistence, Law wrote down a "secret" code to prove his competency. He made up the words as he went along.

Suddenly Oddjob yelled for The Bear. The sadistic guard ran in with a two-by-two board about five feet long. He put down the board and punched Law hard enough to break his jaw. After a few more punches, The Bear picked up the board and whammed it across Law's shoulders. With Oddjob yelling and cursing, The Bear beat Law until the board was broken in four pieces. Half conscious, but furiously angry, Law rose from the floor and declared that everything he had said was a lie. Then another guard came in with a four-by-four and hit him across the back, knocking him on his face.

They carried Law to the captain's room next door where Pete was kneeling with head bowed.

Silver Lips stood over him.

"You CIA man," Silver Lips screamed.

"Yes, yes," Pete replied.

"You give orders to Law?"

"Yes, yes."

Silver Lips glared at Law. "What orders he give you?"

Law gasped, "Pardon me," and two guards slammed him against the wall. They kept beating Law until he gave him an escape plan, one of eight "confessed" by the crew that week.

Finally they put Law back at his desk and demanded more confessions. He wrote all through the night and whenever he stopped a guard hit him. Next morning Oddjob came and said, "You are beginning to be sincere."

The beatings went on day and night. Because I was in a room all day every day by myself (exercise periods had been stopped), I wasn't fully aware of what they were doing. It was so bad that Fetch gritted his teeth while watching a beating administered by Oddjob and mumbled, "Brutal! Brutal." Law and Bob Hammond, whom the KORCOMS thought were the ringleaders of the troublemakers got the worst treatment. Hammond broke a mirror and tried to slash his wrists in an effort to get them to leave him alone. Then he threatened to punch back the next guy who touched him. For some reason they left him alone after that.

None of the KORCOMS ever seemed to have grasped the significance of my work on the *Pueblo*. This is the only explanation I can offer for not having received the worst treatment.

Only one man weakened and tried to implicate two shipmates. His roommates straightened him out—fast.

James Kell helped keep up the sagging spirits of the enlisted men. "I still believe God will get us home for Christmas," he said. "Keep praying."

December 19, Thursday, a week and a day after Hell Week started, we got fish, bread, cabbage salad, and chopped pork instead of the usual slimy stew for supper. The men who had taken the most punishment were put in one room where the Korean doctor, the nurse Flo, and the *Pueblo*'s corpsman, "Doc" Baldridge, worked on them. The KORCOMS wanted hot wax, raw eggs, hot pads, and a salve applied to lighten the eyes and reduce the swellings and bruisings. Still Law, Hammond, Pete Bucher and other guys who got the worst treatment looked pitiful when they came to the mess hall. Something was up. I began to believe again that we would get home for Christmas.

Two days later, Saturday, the Glorious General called us all into the big club room. Jack Warner and Buster Bulb were scurrying around getting cameras in position. The General acted like Santa Claus at an orphans' picnic.

"We believe you men are now sincere and repentant," he said with a broad smile.

We waited and dared to hope for the best.

"Your government has promised to kneel down and admit its crimes against the Democratic People's Republic of Korea," he continued.

We held our breath.

"We don't know whether this will happen during the Johnson administration or the Nixon administration."

The next morning, the General assembled all of us again and said definitely, "You will be going home soon." Silence hung in the air. We didn't dare yell—not yet.

"When your name is called, we suggest you stand up and speak your gratitude to the Korean people for their good treatment. You will also repeat the repentance of your wrongs."

The North Koreans were staying true to character.

Some of us stood and told them what they wanted to hear.

The Glorious General gave us some garbage about Communism being the wave of the future that would bring world peace. He asked us to remember the humane treatment we had received. Then he dismissed us to our rooms.

He hadn't said so specifically, but we felt that tomorrow would be the day.

Somebody began humming the tune of "I'll be Home for Christmas." There were cautious smiles all around.

Back in my room I had a praise service all by myself. The doxology, "Praise God From Whom All Blessings Flow," never seemed more appropriate.

The food was decent again that night. After dinner

Fetch came around to where some of the enlisted men were cleaning up.

"Guess you be leaving soon, huh?"

Charles Law grinned and nodded.

"Family be happy to see you, huh?"

Law was sure they would and added, "We'll miss you, Fetch."

"No, you just say that, huh?" Fetch said as he turned away.

Law felt that we might have been the only friends Fetch ever had.

That evening the KORCOMS took us across the icy ballfield to the building by the firing range for a press conference. Less than a dozen correspondents there awaited us, all North Korean, and all had been at previous press conferences. They merely asked a few questions regarding our feelings about going home. We gave the right answers.

They still hadn't told us when the moment of departure would be. December 22 would soon be gone. But we had the extra day ahead in the time difference between Korea and the U.S.

Later that night they started calling us individually from our rooms; some of the enlisted men became nervous when no one came back. For all they knew, the KORCOMS might be taking the crew out one at a time for execution. Being alone, I was only aware of a lot of footsteps in the corridor and doors opening and closing.

Finally they came for me. I was taken to the barber shop and issued new clothing; a gray cotton suit and white shirt, white-soled black sneakers.

126

They herded us together one final time. The General said, "I will bid you goodbye now. You will be catching the 11:31 train."

We shed no tears.

We rode to the train station on buses just as we had done on the trip to the atrocity museum. We boarded a sleeper train; it may have been the same one. When the train jerked forward I began counting the clicks of the wheels.

Except for Glorious General all our familiar "hosts" accompanied us. For awhile they paraded through the cars making conversation. We listened to more recitals of the "advantages" of Communism. We responded in the usual way.

I finally stretched out on the bench and pulled the heavy blanket over me. My legs felt numb and stiff from the effects of malnutrition. My calves ached painfully.

Specs sat down next to Chuck Ayling and asked if he knew his father had been to Moscow and East Berlin. Ayling was surprised to hear this. "Yes," Specs said, "and he asked to come to our country, but we wouldn't give permission."

About sunrise, December 23, the train pulled into the Kaesong station. They fed us, then we boarded buses which had windows covered with sheets and rode for about fifteen minutes.

The buses stopped. We couldn't see and hoped this was the end of the road. They spelled out the procedure. Except for the captain going first, we would walk across the border at twenty-foot intervals in inverse order of rank. This meant I would be next to last. There must be no running, talking, looking back or gesturing. Violators

127

would be shot. I grinned, thinking that there was no likelihood of this order being disobeyed.

There we sat for an interminable half hour.

Finally, they took the captain off the bus and led him to an ambulance where Duane Hodges' body lay in a plain wooden box. They pulled back the lid and removed the windings from the face while photographers stood by. The skipper nodded gravely while the lights flashed.

The big hand on the watch I had borrowed from Chuck Ayling crawled to 11:00 A.M. Suddenly Bloke and Captain Queer appeared and began a propaganda duet. I shrugged. Considering we had waited eleven months, what were a few more minutes!

At 11:30 they drove the ambulance across the "Bridge of No Return." Duane Hodges was free first.

A minute later the captain was waved forward. As he walked, a recording echoed behind him from a propaganda speaker.

"I am Commander Lloyd Bucher, Captain of the U.S.S. *Pueblo*. I was captured while carrying out espionage activities. . . ."

I was listening and watching as Oddjob called off the names of the crew. When a man's name was called, he shouted loudly, "Yes, sir," and began to walk.

Charlie Law started in the wrong direction. He may still have been dazed from the beatings. A guard swung him around and pushed him toward freedom.

Oddjob began calling the officers. Finally:

"Lieutenant Stephen R. Harris."

I stepped from the bus and started the walk I'll never forget. A light snow was falling in the cold breeze. I could see the half-dry river bed and the trickle of a stream with patches of snow along the banks.

The walk took no more than two minutes, yet it seemed I was traveling thousands of miles over the years of time. I was deaf to the propaganda blare behind me.

A navy lieutenant commander welcomed me to freedom with a handshake and a pat on the back. An MP handed me a gift kit from the Red Cross—candy, gum, toothpaste, toothbrush, and a razor—American things!

Ed Murphy came a few steps behind me. When he was across, our welcoming committee hurried us onto buses. They wanted to get away as quickly as possible.

While we were boarding, a guy called to Ginther. "You were right, Frank. God did bring us through. Say a prayer of thanks." All I could think of was, "God be praised! We'll be home for Christmas!"

How had our release been effected?

Just before we arrived on the Communist side of the bridge, the U.S. Negotiator, Major-General Gilbert H. Woodward, read a public statement declaring that it was still the U.S. position that the *Pueblo* had not engaged in illegal activity, and had not intruded into North Korea's territorial waters, and that the U.S. "could not apologize for actions which we did not believe took place.

"The document which I am going to sign," he continued, "was prepared by the North Koreans and is at variance with the above position, but my signature will not and cannot alter the facts. I will sign the document to free the crew and only to free the crew."

Then he signed the document the North Koreans wanted. It acknowledged the validity of our confessions, admitted illegal espionage and intrusion, offered an apology and promised it would not happen again.

The North Korean negotiator looked at the paper and

abruptly announced that General Woodward had violated previously agreed upon terms by making the announcement. "We will release the men thirty minutes later for this violation," he added.

It was the North Korean way of administering one last kick.

We got into buses and rode to a mess hall where the U.S. Army served us a simple meal of chicken soup, ham sandwiches with milk, coffee, and orange juice. I drank three cups of the coffee. It was the best meal I ever ate.

Then we boarded helicopters for the short flight to a field hospital just outside of Seoul. As I looked down at a new expressway, rows of new homes, and freshly plowed fields, I wished our captors could see how their "enslaved brothers" in the South were really faring.

A band was playing when we landed and a military police detachment waited to escort us into the hospital. I saw an old friend coming towards me—Lieutenant Commander Ross Olson. "Congratulations and welcome back. I'll see you inside the hospital," he said.

When we walked into the hospital a telegram was handed to the captain:

IT IS A SOURCE OF THE DEEPEST SATISFACTION TO ME AND TO ALL OF YOUR FELLOW COUNTRY-MEN THAT YOU HAVE RETURNED TO YOUR FAMILIES AND TO YOUR HOMELAND IN TIME FOR THIS HOLIDAY SEASON.

WE ARE ALL AWARE OF THE ORDEAL THROUGH WHICH YOU HAVE PASSED, AND WE THANK GOD IT HAS ENDED.

WE EXTEND OUR HEARTIEST WELCOME HOME

AND I WISH YOU AND YOUR LOVED ONES A JOYOUS
CHRISTMAS AND A HAPPY NEW YEAR.

LYNDON B. JOHNSON,
PRESIDENT

After I got rid of our prison garb and got comfortable, Ross Olson came to see me. I knew him from days in Washington, D.C., and the Officers' Christian Union.

"I forgot to tell you when you landed," Ross said. "You have been selected for promotion to Lieutenant Commander."

I grinned back. "The money will come in handy if my creditors haven't foreclosed on me yet."

Ross assured me the navy had taken care of my financial problems. He also told me that Esther and Mother had been notified and would meet me in San Diego.

My memory skipped back through the years. "You were at the first Officers' Christian Union meeting I attended," I said.

"Was I?" Ross said.

"Yes, and it was there I met Esther's brother, Gus— the Army dentist."

"And I suppose Gus introduced you to Esther?"

I nodded.

I found out later that Ross had missed part of Christmas with his family by coming to meet us.

After a steak dinner, I had trouble going to sleep. I was excited and anxious to start for home. My legs were hurting more than ever. They gave me two or three doses of seconal before I dropped off.

The next day was Christmas Eve in Korea, still only the twenty-third in the U.S. Despite our sorry physical shape—I had lost fifty pounds—all of us attended an ecumenical Christmas service at the hospital. Remembering the last service on the *Pueblo* when only two had appeared, I had to smile.

"And it came to pass in those days, . . ." I read the familiar Christmas story from Luke. How tremendous it all seemed. Just when the world seemed darkest the Saviour had been born. And just when our circumstances had seemed the bleakest, the news had come that we were going to be released.

Late that afternoon we boarded the choppers again for a short hop to the airfield where we transferred to two big C-141 Star Lifter jet transports.

We landed at Midway Island about two A.M. local time for refueling. The Navy Exchange opened up the cafeteria and said everything was on the house. We gulped down hamburgers with orange juice and saw our release headlined in the *Honolulu Advertiser*. The next biggest story was the Apollo 8 flight to the moon. Commander Bucher and Admiral John J. Hyland, Commander-in-Chief of the U.S. Pacific Fleet, sat at a table against the wall and talked about the release.

We flew into the rising sun a couple of hours after takeoff. My legs were still acting up. I stretched out on one of the bunks and tried to sleep. There was nothing to see through the two windows but the Pacific Ocean below. There was much to anticipate when we arrived.

Finally the announcement came to prepare for landing at Miramar Naval Air Station in San Diego. The lead jet hit the runway at 10:58 A.M., the plane I was on came in two minutes later.

The planes taxied up to within a few feet of the ropes holding back our families. Commander Bucher stepped out first and waved. "It's so great," he said as he limped off the plane. "You'll never know how great it is."

Governor Ronald Reagan was there and Senator Margaret Chase Smith of the Armed Services Committee. A band was playing "This Is My Country" as I was helped off the plane.

All of us were looking for our families. The captain saw his wife, Rose, standing with Mr. and Mrs. Jesse Hodges, the parents of the dead sailor. He hugged his wife and two sons. He gripped Mr. Hodges' hand and said, "I sure wish your son was walking with us today. He was a great American."

I saw Mother—where was Esther?—standing near another woman who turned out to be Ralph McClintock's mother. They had flown in together at navy expense. "Thank God, you're home! You're home," Mother sobbed. It was the first time she had cried during the whole experience. My cheeks were wet, too.

Ed Murphy saw his nine-month-old daughter for the first time. Bob Hammond, Bob Chicca, and five other guys saw their new babies also.

The band began playing the navy hymn, "Eternal Father Strong to Save."

Realizing my anxiety, Mother said, "Esther couldn't get reservations on a plane until this morning. Maybe she'll meet us at the hospital."

Navy MP's made a path for us through the crowd to waiting buses. We sat with our families and the buses rolled south through town.

Downtown, the people stood three and four deep on

the sidewalk waving American flags and signs saying, WELCOME HOME.

"What are all these people doing downtown?" I asked.

Mother smiled back. "You don't know why? Wave to them. You're a celebrity, now."

"But we're not heroes," I protested mildly.

"You are, too. Wave."

I don't think any of us had expected this kind of reception. Back in South Korea, just after our release had been announced, one crewman had wondered if we would have any medals coming. Another guy answered him, "Only guys who charge machine gun nests get medals."

The buses took us to the Balboa Naval Hospital complex in San Diego. We were escorted into the Enlisted Men's Club which had been prepared for our special use and placed off limits to the public and press. They gave us all special "P" passes.

Shortly after we arrived I saw Esther coming across the lobby. She was pale and thin but her green eyes sparkled. She looked like a dream to me. We fell into each other's arms. For a moment neither of us could think of anything to say. Words couldn't express our happiness. When we were able to talk, she explained that her plane had landed at the commercial airport about the same time mine had landed at the navy field.

We all enjoyed a big dinner; then Mother left Esther and me at the hospital and went to the El Cortez Hotel. Next morning, Christmas Day, they opened the Navy Exchange on top of a hill for the *Pueblo* crew to buy presents for their families. But I was in too much pain to climb the hill.

After Christmas dinner, the captain stood up and read

a message from the families of the Apollo 8 astronauts: YOUR REUNION HAS BROUGHT GREAT JOY INTO OUR HEARTS THIS CHRISTMAS DAY.

We sent a telegram back reading: ALTHOUGH WE TRIED TO MONOPOLIZE THE HEADLINES, YOU THREE WERE JUST TOO MUCH. WE GLADLY RELINQUISH THE LIME-LIGHT.

It seemed especially significant to me that the day we arrived home, the Apollo 8 crew read the Bible from the vicinity of the moon to a worldwide audience. The testimony of the spacemen coming on top of our safe arrival home made the reality of an all-powerful God seem even greater.

The people of San Diego have to be among the finest on earth. The Chamber of Commerce raised $40,000 to pay for hotel and food bills of the crew and their families. Restaurants away from the hotels refused to accept payment from us. One pizza place offered each man a free pizza each day for each of the 335 days we had spent in captivity. Everybody seemed to know who we were. Strangers would come up to Esther and say, "You belong to the *Pueblo* family."

How sweet it was until a husky commander came to see me. "I'm George Powell, a navy lawyer," he said. "In your position you are vulnerable for legal action. With your permission I'd like to serve as your attorney."

Legal action had never entered my mind. I asked what might be forthcoming. He explained that there would be a Court of Inquiry where I would be asked to give testimony.

The formal Court of Inquiry convened shortly after New Year's in nearby Coronado, California. Opening testimony from Rear Admiral George L. Cassell, former Assistant Chief of Staff for Pacific Fleet Operations, showed that a rescue mission had been ordered, then vetoed by "higher authority." Reporters presumed that he meant the White House and the story ran in *Time* that President Johnson had been afraid of starting another war.

Among the *Pueblo* crew, the most heat fell on Captain Bucher and me. The crew backed up the skipper's testimony that the ship could not have been defended, but there was testimony that raised some doubt about our efforts to destroy classified materials and equipment.

The proceedings of the Court of Inquiry are of public record and were reported and interpreted *ad nauseum* by the news media. I said in essence that we did the best we could to destroy the materials and equipment with what we had available to do the job and under the most impossible of conditions.

Time, Newsweek, the *Los Angeles Times,* and some other media intimated that there were bad feelings between the captain and me. Apparently they didn't have us under surveillance during our off hours! If so, they would have seen the Buchers and the Harrises going to dinner together. And they would have found Esther helping Rose Bucher answer about 500 letters, over 95 percent of which were favorable.

The *Los Angeles Times West* magazine ran the worst story. The writer called me "the most shadowy and mysterious figure in the whole fascinating *Pueblo* story. Of him, virtually nothing was known . . . [but] . . . there was a rumor that Harris was married to a sensationally lovely blonde." At least the last part of that was correct!

But I didn't appreciate his interpretation that the captain and I hadn't gotten along and that I had been derelict in my duty when the ship was captured.

Some of the members of the press may have jumped on me because I refused to tell them much else beyond my name and rank. It wasn't because I was afraid of incriminating myself, but that I didn't want to give away information that might give aid to the enemy.

I felt relieved when the inquiry ended—not that I had anything to hide, but I wanted to get out from under the glare of publicity and start living a normal life again. Esther and I bought a car and drove to Washington State to see her brother's family. Then we drove across the North Central states toward Boston and a visit with my mother. The country never looked so beautiful and so free. Again and again I thought of the "socialist paradise" I had left where soldiers checked travelers at every intersection.

We reached Boston on April 16, four days before a welcome-home party Mother had planned for us. The day after the party, the Melrose Board of Aldermen presented a resolution "commending" me for "courage and loyalty as a member of the U.S.S. *Pueblo* crew during its unjustified incarceration by the Republic of North Korea."

At 10:30 A.M., May, 1969, while preparing to leave for Washington and the new assignment I had requested, a phone call came from Admiral Francis J. Fitzpatrick, the Assistant Chief of Naval Operations for Communications and Cryptology. He read to me the entire statement of the Secretary of the Navy, John H. Chafee. In substance he said I had been both charged and forgiven.

The Court of Inquiry had recommended that Captain Bucher and I be tried by courtmartial and that other *Pueblo* officers be admonished and reprimanded. Secretary Chafee had rejected the court's recommendation. "They have suffered enough and further punishment would not be justified," he said, adding, "Every feasible effort is being made to correct any Navy deficiencies which may have contributed to *Pueblo*'s seizure. The Navy's leaders are determined that the lessons learned from this tragedy shall be translated into effective action."

The announcement was released to the press at eleven o'clock. The phone rang off the hook and within minutes Mother's driveway was clogged with news people. Over the eleven months of our imprisonment, Mother had gotten to know many of the local reporters and cameramen. She greeted them like old friends and served coffee and cake.

The TV people set up their cameras in the back yard and began grinding away. I read a little speech expressing appreciation that the charges had been dropped. Esther tried to stay out of sight as much as she could. But Mother tripped through the crowd like she was at a Fourth of July picnic.

Esther and I rented a house on a quiet street in the Washington suburb of Bethesda, Maryland, a few minutes' drive from my office and Fourth Presbyterian Church. Here we are grateful to God that we can again benefit from the dynamic ministry of Dr. Richard C. Halverson and the fellowship in the congregation.

Our most looked-forward-to event occurred as I was finishing this book. Esther gave birth to twins—a boy, Colby, and a girl, Christiana. My father had no brothers and I am an only child, so this means the family name will be carried on.

It was just three years before the birth of our twins that Esther's mother told us we would have a son. Now God has given us a daughter, too. My dear mother-in-law died before she could see her faith fulfilled.

Our life is normal now—if life with newborn twins can be called that! I go to the office in the morning and return in the evening as most men in the neighborhood do. One of mine and Esther's greatest joys comes in sharing devotions together. We've recently been reading from *The New English Bible* and a devotional book, *My Utmost for His Highest,* by Oswald Chambers.

The historical sites in Washington have taken on new meaning since our release. I recently went through the National Archives and meditated over the most precious documents of our heritage—the Bill of Rights, the Declaration of Independence, and other treasures. I visited the Archives back in 1955 as a high-school student, but the documents were only curiosities to me then.

I have walked through Arlington Cemetery and thought about the men buried underneath the acres of white crosses. I have visited George Washington's home at Mount Vernon and Thomas Jefferson's residence at Monticello. I have visited the Senate and House chambers in Washington and reflected upon the greatness of our system. I am convinced that our system, despite the imperfections of those elected and appointed officials who administer it, is the best ever devised by man.

People continue to ask me about the whereabouts of the *Pueblo* crew. I have kept up with the movements of a few.

Captain Bucher is in Monterey, California, assigned to the U.S. Navy Postgraduate School's Management Course. We stay in touch by letter and phone. He says, "I'm going to church more now."

Skip Schumacher is in the insurance business in St. Louis and is writing a book about his remembrances. Ed Murphy's out of the navy, and wrote a series of articles for *The Christian Science Monitor*.

Gene Lacy, Tim Harris, and Frank Ginther are also still in uniform. Tim is the supply officer for a new ship under construction at San Diego. Electrician's Mate First Class Gerald Hagenson is helping take care of the mothballed heavy cruiser U.S.S. *Baltimore* which the KORCOMS told us on several occasions had been sunk during the Korean War.

James Kell is stationed in Hawaii. P. P. Garcia, the Filipino whom the "escape committee" thought might become our emissary to freedom, is a navy storekeeper at the Pacific Missile Range near Point Mugu, California. Herman Baldridge is stationed in Sasebo, Japan.

Bob Chicca is studying at the University of California (Oceanside campus). Ralph McClintock is an engineer for WSBK-TV in Boston.

Lee Hayes is speaking full time around the country for civic and patriotic groups.

The *Pueblo*'s civilian oceanographers, Friar Tuck and Harry Iredale III, are still taking the ocean's temperature. Friar, whom we thought was a confirmed bachelor, recently got married. However, the first *Pueblo* bachelor to be married after our release was Stu Russell. I suppose he has repainted his car by now—but not red!

I've also heard that Charles Law and Earl Kisler (he sent regards to "Uncle Ben, Aunt Jemima and Jack Sprat") have fallen into the sea of matrimony. One crewman is reported to have committed suicide early in 1970. This leaves eighty-one of the original crew of eighty-three who still survive.

I doubt if we will ever have a reunion. I hope to see some of the fellows in heaven. We'll have some good stories to swap.

I've already mentioned that Skip Schumacher is preparing a book. Captain Bucher wrote one. There may be more first-person books by *Pueblo* crewmen.

Trevor Armbrister, the former Washington Bureau Chief for the *Saturday Evening Post,* has written *A Matter of Accountability,* the most comprehensive book on the *Pueblo* experience. I have read his manuscript and found him to be objective and quite fair to all concerned.

I have accepted as many speaking requests as possible. I've found that Americans are vitally interested in the *Pueblo*'s capture and the issues relating to Communism.

Surprisingly, I seldom dream about North Korea, but many old memories have come back while the publisher's editor and I were at work. Along with the memories has come a deeper appreciation of our American heritage.

IN GOD WE TRUST is more than a slogan on a coin to me now. I know that God has made our nation great. He is the Foundation of our heritage of freedom.

10

Facing the Issues

As a U.S. Naval officer I am far more fortunate than the North Korean officers who held the *Pueblo* crew captive for eleven months. They are slaves of the Communist system and may not have their own opinions outside of the party line. Because I am a United States citizen, I may freely declare my political and religious opinions without fear of redress. I am pledged only to withhold information which would be of value to those nations dedicated to our destruction.

These questions are among those frequently asked me since my return. In answering, I do not pose as an expert; it is obvious that I know a little more about one Communist country than most Americans, and as a naval officer I understand to some extent our military stance. The answers I give here are entirely my own. Neither the material that follows nor the narrative of the *Pueblo* experience are intended to be expressions of official positions taken by the U.S. Navy or Government.

Does military intelligence work bother your conscience?

Not the intelligence work in which I have specialized, including my activities on the *Pueblo*. This does not require me to be deceitful nor to take unfair advantage. Trying to outwit a hostile power does not involve relaxing personal integrity.

Intelligence gathering and the making and breaking of cryptograms (secret messages) has a long history. The prophet Daniel may have been the first cryptanalyst. He deciphered the handwriting on the wall at Belshazzar's feast. The ancient Spartans were probably the first senders of military cryptograms.

A Greek named Polybius devised a system of signaling or sending messages that was widely used for hundreds of years. You can apply his system to the English alphabet by arranging the letters in a square with *i* and *j* together, and numbering the rows and columns.

	1	2	3	4	5
1	a	b	c	d	e
2	f	g	h	ij	k
3	l	m	n	o	p
4	q	r	s	t	u
5	v	w	x	y	z

Each letter in a secret message can be concealed in two numbers, one of a row and one of a column. Thus *s* equals 43, *v* equals 51, and so on. My name *Harris* would be 23-11-42-42-24-43.

Codes used by modern nations are much more sophisticated than this and are prepared and decoded with the latest computerized systems.

Popes in the Middle Ages had code experts on their staffs; so did kings and other rulers. According to code expert David Kahn in his voluminous book *The Code Breakers* (Macmillan), the earliest New World cryptogram extant is a disguised message sent by Cortez from Mexico to Spain.

We are fortunate that our government didn't continue to follow the advice of former Secretary of State Henry Stimson who stopped U.S. code breaking in 1929 on the grounds that "gentlemen do not read each other's mail." The naive Mr. Stimson actually believed that all nations will act like gentlemen. Our cryptologists broke down the Japanese codes a few months before Pearl Harbor, and almost prevented the attack from being a surprise. Some knowledgeable people think that World War II was shortened a year by the work of our code experts. Certainly code breaking and codes saved thousands of American lives. One story has it that John F. Kennedy escaped capture in the Pacific because the Japanese failed to solve a simple cipher code.

The *Pueblo,* as I have already mentioned, was an intelligence collection ship. Russia has many similar ships that hang around just outside our territorial limits. We have not bothered them and the Soviets, to date, have left ours alone.

If the Communists were not militaristic and if they could be trusted, there would probably be no need for our intelligence collection ships and other means of gathering intelligence. But not to be informed is to invite surprise, and to be surprised in a war between nuclear powers is to be dead. The Communists know we are listening and watching and we know they are, too. It's sort of like two mistrustful neighbors who stay up day and night keeping an eye on each other.

The *Pueblo* did, in a larger sense, what ham radio operators do all the time—listen in on other messages. In international waters we were doing nothing illegal when the North Korean pirates attacked.

But there is one big difference in the motive for our intelligence work and that of the Communists. They do theirs for both offensive and defensive purposes. We do ours only to maintain an alert defense.

What's wrong with trying to know the plans of an enemy who has declared he will bury you?

As you see it, what are the basic differences between our system and Communism?

We believe in the divine origin and inherent value of each person. Communism sees the individual as only a slave of the state. To put it another way: we believe that the state (government) functions for the common good of each citizen. Communism holds that individuals exist for the good of the state.

We believe in God and in moral values that keep a society healthy. Communism denies God and puts the party line above truth, with violence and subversion the main instruments of a materialistic and militaristic society.

We believe in the right to hold private property and

freedom of choice. Communism makes the state the owner of all productive property and the controller of families and individuals.

We believe in democratic elections with people having the power to choose between candidates. Communism believes in a one-party government which uses secret police, informers, and other terror tactics to suppress opposition.

What differences did you see between South Korea and North Korea?

Except for the brief time between our release and leaving for San Diego, I've never been in South Korea. My knowledge comes from reading and talking to people who have been there for extended periods. Esther's brother, Gus, was stationed in Seoul. We have frequently discussed the problems of Korea.

North and South, the people share a common heritage. They began at the same point at the close of World War II. South Korea is now much more advanced than the Communist North. Its growing economy is an embarrassment to the Communists.

Over a million people have fled the "socialist paradise" in the North to share the "hell" of their "enslaved brothers" in the South. Just as it is in East Germany, the "freedom-loving" North Korean Communists must forcefully keep their people from straying over the line.

The number two man of the North Korean central newspaper agency, a leading Communist agent, fled to the south from Pyongyang not long before the *Pueblo*'s capture. His story was published in *Life* magazine. He was amazed at the economic development of South Korea.

146

When he saw suits on sale, he said, "You mean people can actually buy these?"

South Korea enjoys religious freedom. Hundreds of thousands of people have become Christians since World War II. *The North American Protestant Ministries Overseas Directory* shows 573 missionaries serving there now. The North Koreans would say these are "imperialist spies." While the KORCOMS told us that Americans were cruelly oppressing their brothers in the South, the truth is that Americans have provided for thousands of Korean war orphans and built many hospitals and other institutions of mercy.

One of the greatest friends of South Korea was an Oregon farmer named Harry Holt who visited the country after the Korean War and was appalled at the suffering of children. He adopted a dozen children himself and arranged for other Americans to sponsor financially hundreds more at an orphanage near Panmunjom. This compassionate Christian layman, who recently died, was from Creswell, Oregon, the home town of Duane Hodges, the crewman killed on the *Pueblo*.

Of course, the North Korean government never tells its people about the acts of compassion by Americans in South Korea. The Communist government keeps working for "unification" with the South; meaning a take-over on Communist terms. The presence of 50,000 U.S. troops there, requested by the South Koreans, is a constant frustration to the North's war aims.

Is Christianity now permitted in North Korea?

We were not permitted to hold religious services. We had to worship in secret. North Korea's constitution ostensibly allows freedom of religion, but we saw no evidence of public worship on our trips around Pyongyang and into the country. The pagodas we did see looked as if they had been turned into museums as has happened to many religious buildings in Russia.

Before World War II, Christian missionaries worked in North Korea. They aided national leaders in establishing schools and colleges and helped advance the rights of women within Christian families. After the Japanese took over, the missionaries began leaving. So far as is known there are now no missionaries in North Korea.

After the North Korean Communists consolidated their power with Russian help following World War II, the Christians had to go underground or flee to the South. Chulho Awe, a brilliant young mining engineer, is one who tried to stay and practice his faith. He tells in his book *Decision at Dawn* of how he was fired from his engineering job and imprisoned because he refused to join the Communist Party. He subsequently fled to the South. His pastor and other leading Christians were arrested, not because they opposed the government but because they were Christians.

Is Communism the wave of the future?

That's what the North Koreans tried to tell us. Conceivably, Communist leaders could succeed in the world conquest which Lenin predicted. But Communism carries within itself the seeds of its own destruction.

It breeds distrust between individuals and nations. There's more than an inkling of truth in the comment that one of the first two Communists on the moon will be a spy to keep tabs on the other fellow. Look at Russia

148

and China. Russia is responsible for the Communists coming to power in China and now the two countries have grave differences.

Communism discourages the initiative that freedom encourages. I expect the next generation in North Korea to be docile and dependent upon their masters. They will not have the incentive to create and achieve. Already there's trouble along this line in Russia, the most advanced Communist country.

Communism simply goes against the grain of human nature. Man, as God made him, was not meant to be a cog in a bureaucratic wheel, a glob of energy in the power plant of a superstate.

Do you subscribe to the domino theory in regard to aiding Asian nations in their fight against Communism?

Yes. I don't believe we made a mistake in going to the aid of South Viet Nam. It's a matter of where do you want to fight the Communists—Viet Nam, Thailand, the Philippines, Hawaii, or on the coast of California? Appeasement only serves to feed the Communist appetite for more territory.

None of the Pueblo *crewmen defected nor asked to stay in North Korea. But a number of Korean War prisoners did decide to stay with the Communists. What made the difference?*

It may not be fair to make a comparison because many more prisoners were taken during the Korean War. However, I think there is a point in noting that the Korean War prisoners were the objects of Chinese brainwashing which is much more sophisticated than what we experi-

149

enced in North Korea. We played a game with the North Koreans, giving them the answers they wanted, and making them believe that we were "cooperative." We stayed on top all the way.

What made it possible for the Pueblo *crew to resist the Korean effort to convert them to Communist beliefs?*

We knew what we had as Americans: faith, freedom, opportunity, and loved ones back home. The North Koreans couldn't come close to offering anything better. Saul Alinsky, the radical activist, has said, "I'm very critical of this country, but get me outside the country and all of a sudden I can't bring myself to say one nasty thing about the U.S. You can't renounce something unless you have something else."

The major factor, I think, was our religious faith which actually became stronger instead of weaker while there. Here were eighty-two ordinary Americans, only a few of whom could be called devout, who drew from religious experiences in the past. I cannot say that everyone became a full believer in the evangelical sense, but I can say that God became more important to every crew member. I myself experienced the closeness of God as never before.

Should the military Code of Honor be changed in view of the Pueblo *incident?*

In my opinion there must be a code of conduct—a standard of behavior—but the existing one should be expanded to cover situations like the *Pueblo* experience. Other people who are more informed than I agree. Retired Rear Admiral Daniel V. Gallery—an old salt of the highest order and critic of just about everybody involved in the *Pueblo* incident—said in his book *The Pueblo Incident* that the Code is a "relic of the days when wars were fought by knights in shining armor" and "We must impress on our men that the Geneva Convention means nothing to savages." Admiral Gallery would delete just the sentence from Article Five. It reads:

I will make no oral or written statements disloyal to my country and its allies, or harmful to their cause.

Then he continues: "At the same time, I would have the United States issue a proclamation to the world, through the United Nations, explaining what we were doing and why.

"This statement should say that our own treatment of prisoners will be governed by the Geneva Convention whether they are from civilized or Communist countries. It should then document the whole history of brainwashing from the Moscow purge trials and Mindszenty case [the Cardinal who "confessed" in Budapest] through the experiences of our POW's in the Korean War, and now the *Pueblo* case. It should state that our way of life, ideas of morality, and civilized behavior are so different from the Communists' that we cannot deal with them as if they were ordinary human beings."

Admiral Gallery further suggests that ". . . our men, when captured, would be allowed from now on to appear on radio or TV programs, say anything the enemy wanted them to say, and to sign any 'confessions' the enemy wanted." This, he thinks, would serve a twofold purpose:

"(1) to cut the ground out from under the propaganda value of such 'confessions' and (2) to save our men from pointless torture."

What are the dangers that face America?

Communism is the greatest external danger. The one great obstacle that lies between the Reds and world domination is the United States. So we are their number one target.

I've already said they would try to defeat us militarily if they thought this possible. But Lenin reportedly said, "We will not need to attack [the U.S.]; it will fall like an overripe fruit into our hands."

Our greatest enemy may be ourselves.

The North Koreans constantly reminded us that the U.S. is divided, that the people do not support the leaders. They did not understand principles of freedom that allow dissent. Much of what the Communists see as disunity is simply freedom at work, but many Americans have gone far beyond dissent. They choose the laws they will obey. A fanatical fringe is now actively trying to overthrow all institutions and create anarchy. Communism is too tame for these nihilists who see no meaning in anything.

A third danger is racial conflict. I do not have all the solutions, but I know that some need to be found. We must act more like brothers and less like enemies.

A fourth danger is rising crime and disrespect for law enforcement. The year of the *Pueblo*'s captivity, crime rose in the U.S. 17.5 per cent over the previous year. The criminals are getting younger and bolder. But adequate and fair law enforcement will not happen until we citizens demand it and set the example.

A fifth is materialism. No nation has ever had so much or lived so well as the United States. And still there are poor and suffering people among us. Most of us are well off by anybody's standards, yet we never seem to have enough. We keep striving for larger homes, more expensive cars, longer vacations and everything else that is supposed to make up the good life. Instead of using things and loving people, we reverse the order by loving things and using people.

A sixth danger is apathy, which is closely related to materialism. We take the most important things in life for granted. I took freedom and the privileges of American citizenship for granted until landing in a North Korean prison. There, I realized what I had lost.

A seventh danger—and I think the greatest of all—is also related to materialism: departure from God and the Bible. We never were entirely a Christian nation, but any student of history knows that our early leaders were God-fearing men. The pillars of our country stand upon our Judaeo-Christian heritage: the Ten Commandments, the Sermon on the Mount, and other eternal verities. The danger now is that we will place our trust in scientific achievements, material comforts—even in a powerful defense establishment. No nation can survive very long when it departs from the moral and spiritual standards which keep a society cemented together. Dr. George Wald, the Nobel Prize winning chemist, told an academic audience recently, "This may sound like sheer nonsense to you, but our only hope is to return to the teachings of Jesus." I, personally, am totally convinced that this is the only complete and correct answer to all the problems of mankind.

Are the so-called "peace" groups in the U.S. helping bring peace to the world?

I doubt it, although I don't question the sincerity of most of the people in these groups. The North Koreans and other Communist nations consider them their allies in working for a "peaceful" (meaning Communist-dominated) world. Our captors took pleasure in reminding us of their activities.

I personally resent the implication given by some of these groups that they are the only Americans working for peace. Who doesn't want peace? This is a rather hard-nosed way of looking at it, but I believe that American defenses have done more to keep the world from exploding than all the "peace marches" in the U.S. The Communists respect strength.

Also, I resent their declarations that the U.S. is the main obstacle to peace in the world. If by *peace* they mean a Communist take-over, then the U.S. is the main obstacle to that. But over and over the Communists have declared their intention to impose their ideology on everyone. The only difference of opinion among Communists lies in how this can be accomplished. I don't doubt for a moment that they would move toward a hot war, if they could be sure we wouldn't retaliate with nuclear arms.

There are well-informed people who say that Communists have infiltrated some of the "peace" movements. They note that some names, long identified with leftist causes, keep popping up. I wouldn't be surprised. The so-called opposition to American support for South Viet Nam in her fight to stay independent has helped Hanoi prolong the war.

154

I went downtown and observed the "peace marchers" when they came to Washington for the big Moratorium Day in the fall of 1969. I looked at these people, mostly young, as they marched through the falling rain. Their sincerity was evident; their dedication admirable. Yet I wondered if they knew what they were doing or if they knew the ideologies of some of the leaders behind the march.

Jesus said, "Blessed are the peacemakers . . ." (Matthew 5:9). I think He meant people who are proclaiming the Gospel of peace and helping people on a personal basis with problems that furnish the seedbed for warfare. You don't hear the peace groups praising the work of Christian missionaries in South Viet Nam, for example. They risk their life every day in helping the homeless, treating the sick, and encouraging poor refugees, some of whom have fled from the Communist "paradise" in North Viet Nam.

I guess what I want to say is that I could have more respect for people who cry peace, if they would go out and make peace.

What do you think of the student protest movement in the U.S.?

I suppose it's better than swallowing goldfish or jamming into telephone booths. Seriously, I think students are frustrated by all the problems they see around them and want to do something. This is healthy.

Many of their protests are legitimate and needed. It's about time we become concerned about polluting, littering, and wrecking the environment which God created for man to use wisely.

But sometimes students overgeneralize. The statement, "The United States is a racist society," is not verifiable like, "The Hudson River flows into the Atlantic Ocean." It is more correct to say, "Some Americans—or perhaps even many—are racists."

Some statements are in general untrue, such as, "America is an imperialistic nation." That's one of the favorite words in Communist propaganda. Funk and Wagnalls' *Standard Encyclopedic Dictionary* defines imperialism as, "The maintenance, or extension of an empire, comprising many nations and areas, all controlled by a central government." Look what we've done since the last World War. We've withdrawn our occupation troops, given aid to conquered nations, and helped make West Germany and Japan two of the strongest independent nations in the world. It is Communist Russia that acted in an imperialistic fashion—"expansionism" they called it. The Soviets made colonies out of the lands they conquered. It's an old Communist ploy to tag America with the term "imperialistic" that best describes their own system.

America now is the protesting students' best (perhaps even the last) protector. They would be shot or sent to the mines in North Korea for protesting against government policies. Thousands of Americans have died to protect the right of dissent. I hope that students will not try to demolish the system that gives them that right. Under Communism they will be free no more.

I hope further that students will not be the hypocrites they accuse the older generation of being—talking and not acting, crying for freedom while denying freedom to those of opposing views, insisting that a self-imposed elite minority should ride roughshod over the majority.

156

And I hope they will not fall for innocent-sounding slogans such as "Power to the People." That's another old Communist phrase by which they mean power to the self-appointed totalitarian rulers of the people.

Are students better educated now than their parents?
They have more information at hand. Through TV and well-written popular magazines they are more aware of world problems. They have, on the average, attended school longer than their parents. They have more say about their studies and academic environment. A generation ago a student in the dean's office meant the student was in trouble; today it may mean the dean is in hot water!

But they have had less experience in the nitty-gritty and the complexities of human experience. They can give glib answers, but they have not participated in the struggle for workable solutions. They have unexcelled privileges but have not been allowed to shoulder responsibilities.

Many stay in school too long without an on-the-job break to help them understand how the producing world lives. All study and no work experience over a long period of time can result in an unbalanced personality.

What do you think of the slogan: "America: Love it or Leave it."?
I see a point here. Senator Ralph Smith of Illinois has said he is ready to help pay the fare for William Kunstler, one of the Chicago conspiracy trial defense lawyers, to reach any part of the world where Kunstler believes there is a better system of justice.

But we need to ask what is involved in loving America. Some of the things I believe it does not involve are:

1. Standing idly by while the law is twisted by those who would exploit the uneducated and the poor.
2. Obeying only the laws which suit us.
3. Using the privileges while neglecting the responsibilities of citizenship.

Conversely, I think loving America does involve:

1. Respect for the flag and our heritage.
2. Protecting the freedom of every citizen.
3. Working for change within the system by voting, participating in the politics of one's party, and staying informed.

(Before the *Pueblo* experience, I paid little attention to political speeches; now I read carefully those that affect me.)

Many churches and religious organizations are now promoting political and social action programs. What do you think of this?

Not much. As good as their intentions may be, I think they're digressing from the central purpose of the church, which is to proclaim the life-changing Gospel and inspire Christians to be good witnesses for Christ. The Bible teaches that man must be born the second time—spiritually. Individuals changed by God's Spirit can best effect changes in society. Until the church relates the significance of Christ's crucifixion and resurrection to the individual, I think it will remain impotent and ineffectual.

I attended another church in Washington for a while after becoming a Christian, but I soon realized I wasn't getting "fed." The minister gave interesting talks, but he didn't proclaim and apply God's Word. I can go elsewhere to hear a lecture on sociology or politics.

Esther and I love Fourth Presbyterian because the pastor centers upon what God says in Scripture and not upon mere human opinion. The ministry of this wonderful church is extended not only through the pastoral staff but through the service and witness of our members all over the Washington area.

Of course Christians should be concerned about social problems. A study of history shows that Christians have been at the helm of movements for needed social changes —the abolition of slavery and the humanizing of mental institutions, to mention just two. But God wants the church to put primary emphasis on spiritual ministries with Christians showing their social concern as individuals and through worthy secular organizations.

The majority of world population is still non-Christian. How can we get the message out?

I've been thinking a lot lately about the potential of radio and television. Communists greatly out-distance us in propagandizing their beliefs. Why shouldn't we who have the truth that sets men free utilize the best means of communication ever devised? Perhaps I feel this way because of my experience in radio broadcasting at Harvard and my vocational interest in rapid electronic means of communications; but the facts are that millions of people are now being reached instantly with volumes of information both good and bad about every conceivable subject.

We Christians have the greatest message of history to tell. It is incumbent upon us to make maximum use of the most effective media available to us.

If one person should read this book and be challenged to trust in God through Jesus Christ, then all the dreary months I spent in the North Korean "socialist paradise" will have been worthwhile.

Those wishing information on Underground Evangelism's mission to the Persecuted Church in Communist lands are invited to write to: Underground Evangelism, P.O. Box 808, Los Angeles, CA 90053 or Underground Evangelism, P.O. Box 1296, Calgary, Alberta, Canada, T2P 2L2.